*legal*WORKS®

Drafting Wills
in Ontario:
A Lawyer's Practical Guide

Robyn Solnik LL.B., TEP
Mary-Alice Thompson M.Litt., LL.B., TEP

CCH CANADIAN LIMITED
90 Sheppard Avenue East, Suite 300
Toronto, ON M2N 6X1
Telephone: (416) 224-2248 Toll Free: 1-800-268-4522
Fax: (416) 224-2243 Toll Free: 1-800-461-4131
www.cch.ca

A WoltersKluwer Company

Published by CCH Canadian Limited

Edited by:
Jenni Allerton, B.A.

The CCH design is a registered trademark of CCH Incorporated.

National Library of Canada Cataloguing in Publication

Thompson, Mary-Alice
    Drafting wills in Ontario : a lawyer's practical guide / Mary-Alice Thompson, Robyn Solnik.

Includes bibliographical references and index.
ISBN 1-55367-206-2

    1. Wills — Ontario. I. Solnik, Robyn II. Title.

KEO287.T46 2003   346.71305'4   C2003-906834-X
KF755.T46 2003

Typeset by CCH Canadian Limited.
Printed in Canada.

DEDICATION

Dedicated to Doris Margaret Thompson 1921-2002

P R E F A C E

The authors have had experience, both as drafting solicitors in private practice and as representatives of a financial institution, reviewing wills drafted by others. Our work reviewing wills from lawyers around Ontario persuaded us that a number of common and potentially costly errors recur in the drafting of even very good lawyers. After reviewing a will, and requesting changes, we would frequently be challenged to explain why we required a change, or asked to provide a clause or clauses to address the problem. That dialogue was the genesis of this book.

We learned a tremendous amount from the practitioners we worked with. From reviewing many wills, we garnered a large collection of precedents, crafted to address the needs of one client, but adaptable to be used again in the will of another client with a similar situation.

Therefore, we thank the legion of lawyers whose drafting inspired this book. They are truly unsung heroes and heroines, for if they have done their job well, their clear thoughtful wills are read only by a small and grateful group: the client, who sees his intentions elegantly embodied in words; the executor, who takes up her task with all the powers she needs and clear direction; and the beneficiaries, whose gifts arrive minimally reduced by tax, without delay and not eroded by confusion and costs. These wills are never before the courts for scrutiny, never quoted in a reported case and never the subject of academic analysis, for that is the very end they seek to avoid.

We would like to thank, too, a number of practitioners who generously read portions of the manuscript and offered invaluable comments: Risa Awerbuck, Kathryn Boone, Mary Ann Higgs, Theresa Lee, Eileen McIntyre, William Moore, Yvonne Pelley, Vincent Ramsay, Kelly Rivard, Douglas

Slack, Ian Sullivan, and Laura Tyrrell. The book is much better than it might have been because of their suggestions. We owe particular thanks to Sidney Solnik, who not only read portions of the book, but inspired us when he first suggested the idea on which it is based. We are also grateful to Katherine Willis, who checked references for us, and prepared the Bibliography in Appendix C. Nevertheless, the book's errors and omissions are all our own. As with any piece of drafting, we have made this book as good as possible within the constraints of our time and abilities, but if you, Reader, find faults, we sincerely ask you to tell us. Mary-Alice's e-mail address is mathompson@on.aibn.com, and you can contact CCH's customer service hotline at 1-800-268-4522.

Finally, we owe thanks (to what extent only they will understand) to Paul, Dan, Aaron and Jamie, whose mother has finally finished her REALLY BIG book report!

TABLE OF CONTENTS

CHAPTER 1

INTRODUCTION

Drafting is an art form. By that we mean that it has no simple set of hard rules. Rather, it takes shape in a complex network of factors. It has rational and emotional content, and it requires skill. Therefore, it can be learned. And the learning is a continuum, where even the most skilled drafters fall short of perfection. The drafting of wills is a small village in the great democracy of writing.

There has been a great deal of attention paid recently to alternative dispute resolution. This book is a modest attempt to address the family divisions, often irreparable, that estate litigation creates, by prevention rather than cure. Good drafting and careful planning are the hygiene and lifestyle of this area of law, less glamorous but more effective than open court surgery. We offer our collection of precedents in this spirit, and in the hope that they will assist the busy practitioner in the important, if underrated, work she does.

1

Nevertheless, though we hope that the precedents and suggestions herein contained will assist even a sophisticated drafter, we make a disclaimer: our precedents are intended to be useful to you. They do not come with any guarantees, and the best precedents in the world are no substitute for the application of your own intelligence to the particulars before you — so use them, please, but use them wisely. Adapt them. Consider them. Share them with your colleagues. In the end, you and you alone are responsible for the wills you draft.

The precedents offered here are conservative, but take into account the most recent developments in the law. They are, as good usage should be, "the eldest of the present and the newest of the past".[1] We do not offer any aggressive estate planning techniques. We aim for a lucid expression of some of the most common requirements of clients.

1. What Is (and Is Not) Included

This is not a book about tax planning. There are many good sources for that topic, but we have begun with the assumption that the estate plan has been made, and you are now sitting down to put it on paper.

We would like to say a word about the intended audience for this book. We have in mind the general practitioner with a significant wills and estates practice. Nevertheless, we hope that the book is also general enough to provide assistance to a lawyer who is new to will drafting, or to one who is shifting the focus of his or her practice to this area, and we hope that even seasoned drafters will find a helpful tip or two. This should be both a basic handbook and a refresher; and, finally, it should be a source book for those who, while not "specialists", are nevertheless too serious to rely on boilerplate or a computer program.

This book is a kind of precedent file, in which we have included those precedents that we find most useful and those that we like to keep handy. We have included precedents that we use in our own drafting practice and regularly share with drafting lawyers around the province. What you will find are precedents that can be used to correct, with ease, the commonest errors in drafting.

---

[1] The phrase belongs to poet and playwright, Ben Jonson, remarkable for a clean and graceful urbane style.

2. Why Drafting Matters — The Liability If You Get It Wrong

Drafting does matter, now more than ever. The old rule asserted that the lawyer owed his duty to the will-maker only; a beneficiary was a third party excluded by the privity of the contract between the lawyer and the will-maker, and thus with no status to sue a negligent lawyer. In the words of Lord Goff in the House of Lords: "The only person who may have a valid claim has suffered no loss, and the only person who has suffered a loss has no claim".[2] This doctrine is long dead.[3] In the new world of drafting, errors can and do return to haunt the lawyer.[4]

---

[2] *White v. Jones*, [1995] 2 A.C. 207, [1995] 1 All E.R. 691, [1995] 2 W.L.R. 187 (H.L.).

[3] R. Trevor Todd, a B.C. lawyer, lists on his website (http://www.disinherited.com/attacking-will.htm#Anchor-22760), the following errors by solicitors that have been brought before the court:

1. Failure to take detailed notes
2. Failure to declare that the will was made in contemplation of marriage
3. Failure to advise that marriage revokes a will
4. Failure to include a residue clause
5. Failure to dispose of the entire residue of the estate
6. Incorrectly drawing a Codicil that improperly reflects on the will
7. Failure to include a specific bequest, such as a residence, contrary to the testator's instructions, resulting in the gift falling into the residue of the estate
8. Failure to properly conduct Land Title searches
9. Failure to sever joint ventures contrary to instructions and provisions of the will
10. Incorrectly naming charities
11. Failure to promptly carry out testator's instructions
12. Using words such as "issue"
13. Having a spouse of a beneficiary witness the will
14. Missing limitation dates such as the six-month date from Letters Probate in the *Wills Variation Act*
15. Failing to probe the testator's mind to determine sufficient mental capacity
16. Failure to interview the client in sufficient depth
17. Failure to ascertain the existence of suspicious circumstances
18. Failure to react properly to the existence of suspicious circumstances
19. Interviewing the testator in the presence of interested party or parties
20. Failing to obtain a mental status examination
21. Using a term in a will that is ambiguous requiring an interpretation
22. Taking instructions from a person other than the testator and failing to confirm instructions with the testator
23. Failure to provide a discretionary trust for mentally disabled children

[4] See Richard Jackman, "Solicitors' Liability for Negligence in Drafting and Execution of a Will"(1971), 54 Ottawa L. Rev. 242; Bonnie Leigh Rawlins, "Liability of a Lawyer for Negligence in the Drafting and Execution of a Will" (1982-84), 6 E. & T.Q. 117; Tony Weir, "*A Damnosa Heriditas*"? (1995), 111 L.Q. Rev. 357; James C. Brady, "Solicitor's Duty of Care in the Drafting of Wills" (1995), 46 N. Ireland Legal Q. 434; Helen Roberts, "Liability of Solicitors to Disappointed Beneficiaries" (1997), 71 Australian L. J. 674; Mark Lunney, "In Support of the Chancellor's Foot"(1998), 9 King's College L.J. 116; Paul Milne, "Solicitors' Obligations — Suggestions for an Estates Practice" (2001), 20 E.T.& P.J. 230; Martyn Frost and Penelope Reed, *With the Best Will in the World*, 2nd ed. (London: Marie Kraus, 2003).

In *Ross v. Caunters*,[5] the English Court of Appeal found a solicitor negligent for failing to ensure that a will was properly executed (the spouse of a beneficiary acted as witness). The House of Lords went on to hold, in *White v. Jones*,[6] that a solicitor who had not produced a draft will for review in two months was negligent and could be sued by the disappointed beneficiary. More recent cases have tightened that period to as little as seven days in emergent situations.[7] Although these cases arise because of problems in executing the will, or executing it properly, they are framed in such a way that they would address the beneficiary who lost out because of a drafting error. *White v. Jones* held that: "The solicitor, by accepting the instructions, has entered upon, and therefore assumed responsibility for, the task of procuring the execution of *a skilfully drawn will* [our emphasis], knowing that the beneficiary is wholly dependent upon his carefully carrying out his function". Indeed, the whole judgment in *White v. Jones* is infused with the assumption that it will apply not just to procuring the execution of the will, but to drafting it as well.

In *Earl v. Wilhelm*,[8] the *White v. Jones* principle was applied in Canada. Again the case did not involve bad drafting *per se*, but the lawyer, who was presumed to know the particulars of his client's affairs (that the farm was held by a corporation not the client), was held negligent for failing to take those particulars into account to ensure that each asset made its way to the intended beneficiary.

Finally, in *Hall v. Bennett*,[9] the solicitor's responsibility was extended to the very act of drafting a will, even when instructions are incomplete and the client may lack capacity. Although the finding against the solicitor was reversed on appeal, on the ground that there was no retainer to prepare a will, Charron J.A. went on to add in *obiter* that declining the retainer, if the client were capable, might be a breach of professional conduct. The "death-bed" drafter is thus faced with a Hobson's choice: decline to do the will and face professional discipline, or accept the retainer and risk the civil suit (if you fail to produce a water-tight will).

To help ensure that you never have to study *White v. Jones* or any of these cases with intense personal interest, here are some general principles to follow:

---

[5] [1980] Ch. 297, [1979] 3 All E.R. 580, [1979] 3 W.L.R. 605, (1979) 123 S.J. 605.

[6] *Supra*, note 2.

[7] *X (an infant) v. Woollcombe Yonge* [2001] W.L.T.R., 291 suggests that "on the spot" is appropriate in emergencies.

[8] *Earl v. Wilhelm* (2000), 31 E.T.R. (2d) 193 (Sask. C.A.), additional reasons at (2001), 34 E.T.R. (2d) 238, [2000] 9 W.W.R. 196, 199 Sask. R. 21 (C.A.).

[9] *Hall v. Bennett* (2001), 40 E.T.R. (2d) 65 (Ont. S.C.J.); reversed on appeal: *Hall v. Bennett Estate* 64 O.R.(3d) 191 (C.A.).

a. **Talk to your clients.** In a busy practice, it is necessary to delegate routine tasks to staff, but the taking of will instructions, the drafting of wills and the execution of a will should not be treated as routine matters. The Rules of Professional Conduct clearly require that the solicitor meet with the clients face-to-face at least once.[10] Most cases of solicitors' negligence arise because matters were not given the solicitor's personal attention.

b. **Charge a decent fee.** If you do not, you will be tempted to cut corners. If you are delegating to staff because you cannot afford the time to meet with clients and to draft carefully, then find a way to afford the time. The days when a solicitor could discount a will, because the liability was small and the estate would pay, are gone. Both assumptions are false. If you are still operating on these premises, change now!

c. **Have a process.** Cases in solicitor's negligence have arisen because a will was not signed expeditiously, because the will was sent out for signature (and improperly executed) or because the will was prepared in an emergency. These are not drafting issues, but issues of office procedure, and best addressed by having a clear process for dealing with wills. But it isn't enough to have a process; write it down, and make sure that all members of your staff know it and refer to it.[11]

d. **Draft defensively.** The single theme of courts of interpretation is that they seek to discover the will or intention of the will-maker. The obverse of this, for the drafter, is that you should seek to make that intention clear. This is an exception to the general rule that shorter is better. If there is a possibility of doubt, add another sentence beginning "For greater certainty, I intend ...".

3. How to Use Precedents (Ours and Anyone Else's)

A precedent is a place to start, not to finish. Use it with care and attention. Here are some simple rules for the use of precedents:

---

[10] See Rule 2. Law Society of Upper Canada, *Rules of Professional Conduct* (Toronto: Law Society of Upper Canada, 2000).

[11] See Paul Milne, "Solicitors' Obligations — Suggestions for an Estates Practice", *supra*, note 4. We have some forms and suggestions for the process of dealing with wills in Chapter Thirteen, "Practice Matters".

a. Use good precedents that are up to date. We wish we had a dollar for every will we have reviewed that includes authorization for the trustees to invest in mutual funds. The law was changed in 1998, and the *Trustee Act*[12] now explicitly states that mutual funds are authorized investments. There is no longer a legal list in Ontario, and yet many drafters continue to include an investment clause that refers to one. You must review and amend your precedents to change with the law.

b. Read the precedent right through. Many standard clauses included here are "omnibus" clauses, covering a number of situations and possibilities. They may not all apply to your client, and they may actually work against the scheme of the will you are drafting. Do not rely on the "title" to a clause, which is at best one person's way of remembering it. For example, if you did not read right through the clause entitled "Definition of Relationships", you might miss the fact that it excludes from inheriting the very grandchildren that your client has planned the will to benefit, or conversely, that it includes the stepchild that the will-maker has clearly indicated she does not want to benefit.

c. Customize them. All good drafting has three sources: precedent clauses, the information from a client intake sheet,[13] and your own knowledge of the law. While there is definitely a place for standard clauses which supply those useful tools that almost all executors will need, you should at least review which clauses you are using, and the dispositive clauses should be drafted for each particular client's needs.

d. Don't change it unless you understand it. Many drafting errors arise because classic precedents have been altered without a full understanding of the effect of the change. For example, clauses that directed that the share of a minor was to be held until she reached the age of majority were inserted to prevent the payment of funds into court. Since a minor was not legally competent, the funds could simply be held by the trustee until the child reached majority. When the legal age was changed to eighteen in Ontario, however, some practitioners simply changed the clause to authorize the trustees to hold funds until the child reached the age of twenty-one. While this met the will-maker's intentions, it ignored the impact of the rule in

---

[12] *Trustee Act*, R.S.O. 1990, c.T.23, as amended.

[13] See the intake sheet in Chapter Thirteen, "Practice Matters".

Saunders v. Vautier.[14] If the will lacked a gift-over of the child's shares, the child could collapse the trust on reaching eighteen, and thus frustrate the intention of the will-maker.

e. **If in doubt, leave it out!** If you include a clause without really knowing why, it is as likely to be redundant or antipathetic to the overall plan as it is likely to be necessary or helpful. Solicitors love precedents — they are somehow comforting, familiar and easy to paste into the current will. But remember that the client may not read all those administrative provisions, and may not understand them if she does. Weigh the probability that any particular power will be needed against the risk of producing a will that the will-maker has not understood and approved. Longer is not usually better.

4. The "Architecture" of a Will

A well-drafted will is like a story, complete with a beginning, a middle and an end. It starts with the cast of characters, the most important being the will-maker and the executor. It then goes on to address the "action" — what is to happen with the worldly goods of the will-maker. The will-maker speaks to the world at large, and says: "This is my will. I have some contracts that I want to deal with outside of my estate. This person will be my executor. He should give some of my things in the form they are in right away, and then turn the rest into cash, pay my debts and other expenses, and dispose of the remaining cash to these people, on these terms. By the way, here are some tools my executor can use in carrying out these tasks, and some restrictions, and a few pointers about family matters".

A standard will follows exactly this logical order. It begins with the introductory clauses, then appoints an executor, directs him or her to make certain gifts (usually personal property) in kind, then directs the conversion of assets to cash, and the payment of debts, taxes and testamentary expenses.

The order of the will matters, in part, because it is traditional, and it allows anyone who is familiar with wills to know where to look for certain instructions. Drafted in the standard order, a will also provides a step-by-step guide to the executor on how to settle the estate.

Moreover, the order of the will may determine how assets are actually distributed, especially if the estate is insufficient. Debts will be paid first, then specific legacies, then general legacies and finally residual legacies. The rule

---

[14] See the Chapter Ten "Trusts" for a discussion of the rule in *Saunders v. Vautier* (1841), 1 Cr. & Ph. 240, 41 E.R. 482.

of abatement is that the residual gifts will abate first, then any general legacies will abate ratably.[15]

Most wills need a place to put what we refer to as "quasi-testamentary" matters: the appointment of guardians, directions with regard to disposition of the body and funeral directions. It may be useful to have some terms defined — "per stirpes" or "children". Some practitioners deal with these matters at the beginning of the document, some at the end. Either way works. We prefer to insert the definitions early and the guardians, *et cetera* late. Just don't sprinkle them through the document, forcing the reader to hunt for them.

5. The Grammar of Wills

While the intention of the will-maker is paramount in interpreting a will, some words have known and commonly agreed meanings. You must either use them in their commonly understood way or define them. For instance, if you want to use "issue" to mean only "children", you should make that clear. Some of the most common errors arise from simple slips in grammar, so the following is a guide to some of the perennial posers:

    a. "and" and "or" — These words are conjunctions, meaning that they join two or more words or phrases. "And" can be either joint or several. For example, "My trustee may pay the income to my niece Hana and my nephew Hari". What does this mean? If the phrase "my niece Hana and my nephew Hari" is read as **joint**, it means that both Hana and Hari are included — in this case that they will share the income. If "my niece Hana and my nephew Hari" is read as **several**, either one of Hana or Hari could receive the income, and the trustee would have discharged her obligation if she paid it to Hana alone.

    The rule is that when "and" joins nouns it is several, as in the sentence above. The exception is when the sense is mandatory. Thus, in the sentence: "My Trustee *shall* pay the income to my niece Hana and my nephew Hari", the "and" is joint, and both Hana and Hari should receive income.

---

[15] And, finally, specific legacies abate. That is, they will be reduced proportionately: "In the law of wills, the principle of 'abatement' dictates that the residuum of a testator's estate must first be exhausted to pay the testator's debts; second, to pay general legacies; third, to pay demonstrative and specific legacies; and finally to effect devises. Each payment ratably diminishes the amount available to satisfy the lower-ranking categories of payments", *Mickler v. Larson Estate* (2000), 35 E.T.R. (2d) 258, 198 Sask. R. 146, 2000 SKQB 426 (Q.B.). See also *Lindsay v. Waldbrook* (1897), 24 O.A.R. 604 (S.C.O.).

When "and" joins two adjectives, as in "my acrylic and framed paintings", it is joint. That is, the paintings in question will be both acrylic and framed, and any that is, for example, acrylic but unframed would not be included in the gift. If the intention was several, the correct phrase would be "my acrylic paintings and my framed paintings".

"Or" can be either inclusive or exclusive. For example: "My trustee shall pay the residue of my estate to charitable or educational institutions". If the phrase "charitable or educational" is read as **inclusive**, the payment can be made to a charitable institution, to an educational institution or to an institution that is both charitable and educational. If the phrase "charitable or educational" is read as **exclusive**, the payment must be made to a charitable institution, or to an educational institution, but not to an institution that is both charitable and educational.

The rule is that "or" is taken as inclusive, unless the context clearly indicates otherwise. If you think this is too fine a distinction for a busy practitioner to waste precious time on, consider *Re Diplock*.[16] The will in that case directed the executors to use the residue of the estate "for such charitable institution or institutions or other charitable or benevolent objects in England as they in their absolute discretion think fit". The executors dutifully distributed the funds of about £203,000 to 139 charities. When the will was challenged by the family, however, it turned out that the charitable trust was not valid, since it was for mixed charitable and non-charitable purposes ("charitable *or* benevolent"). The money had to be recovered from the charities, and the case became the leading case on proprietary trust remedies. Had the will read "charitable *and* benevolent objects", the objects would have had to be both, the trust would have been valid, the gifts to charity would have stood and the executors would surely have slept better.

b. **among v. between** — "Between" should be used only when there are two items or two beneficiaries. When there are more than two, the proper word is "among". Thus, "*between* my nephew Ziggy and my nieces Yvonne and Xena equally" means that Ziggy gets half and Yvonne and Xena get a quarter each. If the wording were "*among* my nephews Ziggy and my nieces Yvonne and Xena equally", each of Xena, Yvonne, and Ziggy would take a third.

---

[16] *Re Diplock*, [1948] Ch. 465, [1948] 2 All E.R. 318; affirmed (sub nom. *Min. of Health v. Simpson*), [1951] A.C. 251, [1950] 2 All E.R. 1137 (H.L.).

c. Doublets and Triplets — The story is that English has two roots — Anglo-Saxon and Norman French — so that early lawyers wanted to make sure that what they drafted worked for both groups, and employed terms derived from both sources (a bit like the Charge/Mortgage and Transfer/Deed that we register now).[17] The result was that legal drafting seemed to require that each thing be described by at least two (and preferably more) variants. You will recognize these phrases easily once you start to look: "cease and desist", "null and void".[18] Here is a list of doublets and triplets that recur in wills:

▶ do, execute and perform

▶ documents, instruments and writings

▶ levies, assessments and impositions

▶ lien, charge and encumbrance

▶ loans, borrowings and advances

▶ mend, repair and maintain

▶ nominate, perform and carry out

▶ rest, residue and remainder

▶ right, title and interest

▶ sell, call in and convert

▶ sell, alienate and dispose of

▶ signed, published and declared

▶ term, stipulations and conditions

▶ will, direct and declare

▶ give, devise and bequeath

▶ goods, chattels and effects

▶ have, hold and possess

▶ lands, tenements and hereditaments

▶ each and every

---

[17] An unkinder theory is that lawyers simply learned to hide what they were doing in a cloak of verbosity and mumbo-jumbo.

[18] See Robert C. Dick, *Legal Drafting* (Toronto: Carswell, 1972); Reed Dickerson, *The Fundamentals of Legal Drafting* (Boston: Little, Brown, 1965), and E.L. Piesse, *The Elements of Drafting, 6th ed.* (Sydney: Law Book Co., 1981) for extensive lists of common pairs and triplets of words.

- ▶ have and obtain
- ▶ any and all
- ▶ authorize and direct
- ▶ by and under
- ▶ from and after
- ▶ authorize and empower
- ▶ deemed and considered
- ▶ due and owing
- ▶ by and with
- ▶ final and conclusive
- ▶ chargeable and accountable
- ▶ full and complete
- ▶ relieve and discharge
- ▶ full force and effect
- ▶ shall and will
- ▶ shall have and exercise the power
- ▶ sole and exclusive
- ▶ kind and character
- ▶ then and in that event
- ▶ null and void
- ▶ true and correct
- ▶ null and of no effect
- ▶ order and direct
- ▶ over and above
- ▶ perform and discharge
- ▶ when and as
- ▶ power and authority

Let one word suffice.

d. Tense   — Use the present tense as the ordinary tense of the will. A will speaks from death, and using the present tense allows the will-maker to speak with one tense both when the will is drafted and when it is effective, on death. Consider the following clause:

> "to divide the residue of my estate into as many equal shares as there shall be children of mine who survive me, *provided that* if any child of mine *shall have predeceased me* but shall have issue living at my death, such deceased child of mine shall be considered alive for the purpose of such division"

The phrase "shall have predeceased me" invites the interpretation that children of a child of the testator who died before the making of the will are not to inherit. This is avoided where the present tense is used.[19] The clause can be clearer:

> "to divide the residue of my estate into as many equal shares as there are children of mine who survive me, but if any child of mine *dies before me* and has issue living at my death, that deceased child shall be considered alive for the purposes of the division"

Two other errors — the false proviso and the false demonstrative "such" — have also been corrected.

e. Provisos   — In the words of the great grammarian Fowler,[20] "Provided is a small district in the kingdom of if". You will almost always be able to replace "provided that" with "if", and "except that" with "but" or "however", and the change will almost certainly be an improvement.

f. False Demonstrative Adjectives   — "Said", "aforesaid", and "such" should not be used as adjectives. They give an illusion of precision rather than real precision. Since a testator normally has only one wife, it is mere surplusage to refer to "my said wife". "My wife" is

---

[19] The example comes from Robert Dick via the Bar Admission Course material written by James P. Taylor and Fred Irvine, "Form/Syntax and Problems with Language", *Estate Planning and Administration: Reference Materials: 43rd Bar Admission Course*, (Toronto: Dept. of Education, Law Society of Upper Canada, 2001), p. 85.

[20] Sir Ernest Gowers, ed. Fowler's *Modern English Usage* (2nd ed.), Oxford: OUP, 1983.

perfectly clear.[21] If more precision is thought necessary, use the wife's name. Also, "to hold the capital for such child" might better be written as "to hold the capital for that child".

6. Paragraphing: Use It to Your Advantage

Every paragraph in the will should be numbered, except for the very first paragraph and the testimonium. This makes it easier and more accurate, later on, to reference one part of the will for codicils or court application.

Avoid long blocks of text which are intimidating to read, and therefore more likely to result in something being overlooked or omitted. Sometimes long blocks are broken into sub-paragraphs, which is fine, as long as you make sure each one is numbered. Unnumbered paragraphs within a will clause are orphans that will be hard to refer to precisely in subsequent documents.

Finally, giving clauses titles will help readers of the will to find passages quickly, and to comprehend the structure of the will better.

7. Use Words Consistently

Do not start referring to shares, and then begin to call them "parts".

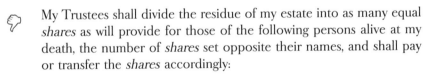

My Trustees shall divide the residue of my estate into as many equal *shares* as will provide for those of the following persons alive at my death, the number of *shares* set opposite their names, and shall pay or transfer the *shares* accordingly:

    i. To JAMES, One (1) *part*;

    ii. To JULIA, One (1) *part.*

On the other hand, you can and should use different terms to distinguish different things.

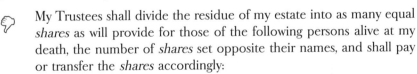

My Trustees shall divide the residue of my estate into as many equal *shares* as will provide for those of the following persons alive at my death, the number of *shares* set opposite their names, and shall pay or transfer the *shares* accordingly:

    i. To JAMES, One (1) share;

    ii. To JULIA, One (1) share.

---

[21] Taylor and Irvine, *supra*, note 17, at p. 8-11. It is sometimes raised that "said wife" is necessary to distinguish the named wife from any future wife, but since marriage revokes a will, the will-maker will have to make or re-make his will if he acquires a new wife.

However, if either JAMES or JULIA dies before me leaving issue alive at my death, the *share* to which he or she would have been entitled if he or she had survived me shall be divided among his or her issue in equal *shares* per stirpes, and those *shares* shall be held according to the terms of paragraph X of my Will.

> My Trustees shall divide the residue of my estate into as many equal *parts* as will provide for those of the following persons alive at my death, the number of *parts* set opposite their names, and shall pay or transfer the *parts* accordingly:
>
> i. To JAMES, One (1) *part*;
>
> ii. To JULIA, One (1) *part*;
>
> but if either JAMES or JULIA dies before me leaving issue alive at my death, the *part* to which he or she would have been entitled if he or she had survived me shall be divided among his or her issue in equal *shares* per stirpes, and those *shares* shall be held according to the terms of paragraph X of my Will.

8. Define and Capitalize

This principle is really a variant of using words consistently. You can be precise in your references, yet avoid repeating long phrases, by using a defined word. Indicate early in the will, or in the clause where the term is used, what the word or phrase means, and in subsequent occurrences, capitalize it to show that it is being used as a defined term.

9. Write Transparently

Clients often want to see a "simple" will, and what they mean by simple can result in a document that simply doesn't cover the bases. We are not advocating that kind of simplicity. The "plain language" movement in legal (and other) drafting has helped to remind us all of the benefits of clarity (and the pitfalls of obscurity). Nevertheless, it has met a certain resistance from those who equate "plain" with "simple minded".[22] For this reason, we prefer the term "transparent", since the point of good writing is always to draw attention to the meaning being conveyed, and not to the language

---

[22] They are wrong, of course: Professor Robert Eagleson, a Professor of English at the University of Sydney, is the leading Australian advocate of the use of plain language. He says:

(continued on next page)

itself. Any time your reader is aware of the language and the style, you are failing to focus attention on the subject itself.

A Little Diversion on Rhetoric

We have some sympathy, however, for the sense of many drafters (and clients) that the making of a will requires a more elevated style than the making of a grocery list. We have all experienced the dilatory client, who can't quite seem to bring himself to sign the document. His caution will be easier to understand if we remember that he is contemplating his own mortality. A client who was a Chaplain, and therefore used to dealing with death, once remarked that when the friend whom he was appointing as executor read the will, he himself would be dead. Similar thoughts probably lie inchoate in the minds of most of our clients. Making a will is a somber occasion. Tycho Brahe, the great astronomer, is said to have put on his court robes every time he went up into his observatory to view the stars, he so felt the solemnity of the act. We, too, should honour the gravity of what is probably the most solemn document our clients ever sign.

In classical rhetorical theory, good writing had *decorum* — that is, it was appropriate in tone, diction and style to the writer, the audience and the subject — so, for example, a writer might write one way for his child and another way when addressing his king, and it would be (and still is) a serious error to confuse the two styles. The more solemn, formal, and public an occasion, the higher the style. So, while many of the points made by the plain language movement are most useful and valuable, we believe that the solemnity of the occasion may require and justify a more formal style when drafting a will than in (for example) a business contract.

High style, however, should not mean obfuscation. *Any* style should be clear. The formality of the occasion of making a will, and thereby contemplating your own death, will support the inverted syntax and elevated diction of a phrase such as: "This is the Last Will of me, Jennifer Corinne Smith, of

---

(continued from previous page)
"Plain language" is the opposite of obscure, convoluted, entangled language. It's the opposite of language that takes a lot of effort and energy to understand and unravel. Plain language should not be equated with "simple" in the sense of simple minded. Nor should it be equated with "simple" in the sense of "childish" or broken language — a kind of pidgin. Nor should it be equated with "simple" or "simplified" in the sense of a reduced document that only gives part of the message.

Plain language, on the contrary, makes use of the full resources of the language. It's good, normal language that adults use every day of the year. It lets the message come through with the greatest of ease. That's the best definition and the best way we should look at plain language.

Robert D. Eagleson, *The Case for Plain Language* (Toronto: Canadian Law Information Council, Plain Language Centre, 1989).

the City of Toronto, in the Province of Ontario, made this 15th day of October, 2003". It will not support meaningless jargon or verbosity such as: "This 15th day of October, 2003, Jennifer Corinne Smith, of the City of Toronto, in the Province of Ontario, being of sound mind and body, does as her Last Will and Testament hereby make, publish, and execute the within document".

There is nothing wrong with a little formality, especially when you are drafting a will. The object is not to produce something that might have been tossed off to the neighbour over the backyard fence. But, however low or high your style, the most important thing is that it allow the meaning to shine through. A transparent document will make a better will because:

a. It will please your client.

b. It will also help to ensure that your client understands the document, so that the requirement of knowledge and approval is fulfilled.

c. It will help your client to identify a problem, if the will does not accomplish what she wants.

d. It will help executors and beneficiaries to understand what their rights and duties are, and how the estate will be handled.

e. Finally, it will assist you in spotting errors in your own drafting.

10. Two Exercises

Try this exercise: Take a long paragraph out of the last will you wrote. Underline the subject of the first sentence. Double underline the verb. If the verb is transitive, circle the object. Now you have the bare bones of the sentence. The subject should be a person. The verb should be an action, and the object should be a concrete thing. How much of the rest of the sentence is really essential to the meaning you are conveying?

You could also try this: Take the same sentence, and circle all versions of the verb "to be" (is, were, are, etc.), then all words ending in "ation", and every "said", "such", "that" and "which". How many can you eliminate? Is the writing now more transparent? One of the risks of making your writing transparent, of course, is that it may become clear that you do not know what you are saying. It is better to find out now, however, than in front of a judge in a negligence suit.

11. The Last Word

Wills are dual-natured documents. Just as people have a physical presence and a spirit, the will has business to do with the material possessions of the will-maker, but it is also the last word that she may leave for those who love her. Sometimes clients want to put spiteful or angry messages in their wills, and we discourage this, not only on humane grounds, but also knowing that such a will is much more likely to be challenged. It is not an error, however, to let the personality of the will-maker shine through the document you draft. If the cottage is important, explain why. If the will-maker loves his son, even though he is not leaving him anything, why not say so, and say why? Many lawyers seem to think that the more arid the document they produce, the better the job they have done. On the contrary, a document that is personal is not only less likely to be challenged, but the personal context may allow the court to understand the will-maker's intentions more accurately if it is challenged, and such a will serves your client's interests, by letting her feel that she has "put her house in order".[23]

Here is a home-made will, typed by the will-maker and full of his character. While we do not offer it as a precedent — its weaknesses in that regard will be apparent — we do offer it as a model of a will that speaks clearly of more than the wealth of the maker.

---

[23] There is a movement that encourages people to write "ethical" wills, to pass on not only their wealth, but their values as well. This is not drafting that you are likely to be involved in, but the growth of the movement may say something about the failure of the legal wills we draft to address the real needs of our clients. See Scott C. Fithian, *Values Based Estate Planning* (John Wiley & Sons, 2000); Barry K. Baines, *Ethical Wills: Putting Your Values on Paper* (Harper Collins, 2001) and Jack Reimer and Nathaniel Stampfer, *So That Your Values Live On: Ethical Wills and How to Prepare Them* (Jewish Lights Publishing, 2002).

Sept. 7......1988

I GEORGE HAROLD ROSS GOLDTHORPE I wish for my check account
to go to my brother REGINALD C. GOLDTHORPE and this family as
we were a split up after our mothers dieth,Reg. and I were
close,our young brother and our older sister went to stay with
our Grang-parents,our baby sister went with Mothers Sister
as they were 2,4,6,years old.our oldest broyher was four years
older that I. Reg. and I went to school to-gether,we stayed with
our Father,Thomas Our oldest brother,soon when down to TORONTO
to our Grandparent and two spinsters Aunt- Thomes soon got work
in Tpronto, It was tough time for us in those days,Dad did his
best,but it was so lonly, We made it Reg. and Myself came down
in 1938 to see if we could fine work,in march which we found out
later, was an of season,But we found work and did good,

I went back home after har vest,Reg. took other work and stay down
here.In 1940 He Married,Maryann and had two children,how have been
very good to Me,Maryann,has the busnes head of the family, She has
promise me that she will see that My wish are cared out.

Reg,Lloyd,and Edith will get what I wished,I am in sound ########
Mind and body, In other woords I know what I am talking about.
I hope this does not give Reg, and Maryann any trouble,I will not
know at this time,just how much the bank account will be.

Signed- George H. R. Goldthorpe

CHAPTER 2

INTRODUCTORY CLAUSES

Like any good introduction, the introduction to a will "clears the board" preparatory to the dispositions that follow.

Introductory clauses are fairly standard, but they do basic work: identify the nature of the document, identify the will-maker, set out the context and the property the will covers, and revoke prior wills.

Identifying the Will-Maker (Name)

Clients may use more than one name. Not only do women change their names on marriage (and again on divorce), but immigrants adopt new names, and people have nicknames. Often, when asked, clients will wave away an alternate name saying, "But I never use that". Make the life of the executor, who has to match the will to the names on other legal documents and records, easier; include *all* your client's names.

> This is the Last Will of me, CHARLES CLIENT, also known as CHARLEY CLIENT, also known as CHARLIE CLIENT, of the City of Kingston in the County of Frontenac, Province of Ontario.

Identifying the Will-Maker (Residence)

While it is not necessary to include his place of residence in order to identify the will-maker, it is helpful in making sure the will is the correct one. The place of residence may also be significant for income tax and probate purposes. A will has to be probated in the county where the deceased had her last place of residence.[24] Of course, people often move between the time they make the will and the time the will is probated.

In some situations, the domicile of your client (rather than his residence) is what matters. For example, taxing statutes in some jurisdictions are based on domicile, as is the law governing the disposition of movables, under international private law.[25] For any of these reasons, it may be important to identify the domicile of the will-maker.

> This is the Last Will of me, WILHEMINA WILLMAKER, resident in the City of Sydney, Australia, but domiciled in the Province of Ontario, Canada.

The Property the Will Covers

A will may not necessarily cover all of the will-maker's property. Frequently, assets in different jurisdictions are disposed of in different wills. Sometimes a particular asset (such as copyrights) needs the care of a special executor. Finally, it is increasingly common to make two or more wills in order to avoid paying Estate Administration Tax on all assets.

> I, THERESA TRAVELLER, of the City of Ottawa, in the County of Carleton, in the Province of Ontario declare that this is my Last Will, made this 29th day of May, 1997, by which I intend to dispose

---

[24] (1) An application for a grant of probate or letters of administration shall be made to the Ontario Superior Court and shall be filed in the office for the county or district in which the testator or intestate had at the time of death a fixed place of abode.

(2) If the testator or intestate had no fixed place of abode in Ontario or resided out of Ontario at the time of death, the application shall be filed in the office for the county or district in which the testator or intestate had property at the time of death.

(3) In other cases the application for probate or letters of administration may be filed in any office. *Estates Act*, R.S.O. 1990, c. E.21, as amended.

[25] See Margaret R. O'Sullivan, "The Role of Domicile and Situs in Succession Matters" (1996), 15 E. & T.J. 236. See also, Donovan Waters, Explanatory Report, Hague Convention on Private International Law, *Proceedings of the Sixteenth Session, Tome II, Succession to Estates — Applicable Law* (1989), p. 525. The Hague Convention would abolish this distinction. Since it has not been ratified by Canada, or, indeed, most states, the Convention is of little practical importance.

of my assets situated in Canada. I will refer to this Will as my "Canadian Will", to my assets situated in Canada as my "Canadian Assets" and to my estate to be administered in Canada as my "Canadian Estate".

Error #1: "Will and Testament"

 This is the Last Will and Testament of me, CLAUDE CLIENT, of the City of Sarnia in the County of Lambton, Province of Ontario.

The phrase "Will and Testament" is redundant.[26] For all purposes of the law of wills in Ontario, "will" suffices.

Solution: Keep it Simple (A) and (B)

Here are two fairly standard, and clean, beginnings to a will:

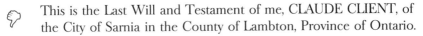 This is the Last Will of me, CHARLES CLIENT, of the City of Kingston in the County of Frontenac, Province of Ontario.

 I, CLARISSA CLIENT, of the City of Toronto, in the Province of Ontario, declare that this is my Last Will, made this 17th day of April, 2002.

Error #2: Will Date Omitted or Entered Twice

In addition to identifying the testator, the introduction may give the date that the will is made. Sometimes the date appears on the signature page, and sometimes on the front page of the will. We prefer to have the date on the last page, right above the signature, so the client will be sure to see it when he signs. The advantage of having it on the front page, however, is that the date is immediately visible to anyone looking at the will.

Here's what matters: make sure the date is on the will somewhere. If it appears twice, check that the dates agree. The possibility of dates that do not agree is a good reason to use the date only once.

---

[26] Historically "testament" is a disposition of personal property, and "will" a disposition of real property. *The Succession Law Reform Act*, s. 1(1) states:

    will includes,

    (a) a testament,

    (b) a codicil,

    (c) an appointment by will or by writing in the nature of a will in exercise of a power, and

    (d) any other testamentary disposition.

R.S.O. 1990, c. S.26, as amended.

☞   **Some computer programs for generating wills enter the date automatically. This can be very helpful, but be sure to check that the correct date has been entered. Your program may enter the month and year that the draft will is generated, which may not be the same month and year in which it is executed.**

Solution: Use the Same Place for the Date in All Your Wills

    This is the Last Will of me, CLAUDETTE CLIENT, of the City of Timmins, in the County of Cochrane, and Province of Ontario, made this 1st day of February, 2003.

☞   **Leave the date blank, and have the will-maker fill it in when the will is executed. This serves several functions: it evidences that the will is actually signed on the date indicated, and it provides a safety measure that the date will be entered when the will is signed. It may also help to establish capacity and knowledge and approval of the contents if the will is challenged, by showing that the will-maker was oriented as to the date when the will was signed.**

Error #3: Prior Designations Revoked

It may not be necessary to revoke previous wills, since the making of a new will under the *Succession Law Reform Act* revokes them.[27] A formal revocation, however, leaves no doubt about the intention of the testator in this regard.[28] Without a formal revocation of the prior will, both wills may be admitted to probate, the former will being revoked only to the extent of any inconsistency with the later will.[29]

---

[27] A will or part of a will is revoked only by,

(a) marriage, subject to section 16;

(b) another will made in accordance with the provisions of this Part;

(c) a writing,

  (i) declaring an intention to revoke, and

  (ii) made in accordance with the provisions of this Part governing making of a will; or

(d) burning, tearing or otherwise destroying it by the testator or by some person in his or her presence and by his or her direction with the intention of revoking it.

Succession Law Reform Act, R.S.O. 1990, c. S.26, s. 15.

[28] See A. H. Oosterhoff, *Oosterhoff on Wills and Succession*, 5th ed. (Scarborough, Ont.: Carswell, 2001), Ch. 7 "Revocation of Will" for a good summary of the law in Ontario in this regard.

[29] See *Re Davies*, [1928] Ch. 24 (Ch. D.).

The standard phrase revoking "all former wills and other testamentary dispositions" may be problematic since it is uncertain whether testamentary dispositions will include designations made outside the will, such as on the plan documents when an RRSP is purchased.

Simple Revocation

 I revoke all former wills and other testamentary dispositions made by me.

 I revoke all former wills and codicils made by me.

Solution: Affirm Designations

The following clause will not change the designations, and may be beneficial in reminding clients that they need to consider those designations. It also evidences the clients' awareness of the designations.

 This Will does not alter any designation of a beneficiary I may have made prior to the date of this Will, and other than by will, under any policy of life insurance, pension, registered plan, annuity, or other plan or policy under which I am competent to designate a beneficiary other than by will.

Error #4: Marriage not Specifically Described.

Marriage revokes a will, unless the will is made in contemplation of the marriage.[30] The will must be made with the clear intention that it remain valid after a *particular* marriage. This requires that:

1. a specific marriage, and not just marriage in general, should be referred to, and

2. the will should state that it is in contemplation of that marriage. A will must not only be made in contemplation of marriage, but must be "expressed to be made" in contemplation of the partic-

---

[30] A will is revoked by the marriage of the testator except where,

(a) there is a declaration in the will that it is made in contemplation of the marriage;

(b) the spouse of the testator elects to take under the will, by an instrument in writing signed by the spouse and filed within one year after the testator's death in the office of the Estate Registrar for Ontario; or

(c) the will is made in exercise of a power of appointment of property which would not in default of the appointment pass to the heir, executor or administrator of the testator or to the persons entitled to the estate of the testator if he or she died intestate. *Succession Law Reform Act,* R.S.O. 1990, c. S.26, s. 16.

ular marriage that took place.[31] As a drafter, you actually have to say that it is a will made in contemplation of the marriage.

 This is the last will of me, CLAUDE CLIENT, of the City of Kingston in the County of Frontenac, Province of Ontario, made in contemplation of marriage.

What does your client want if the marriage does not happen? Your client, if love has not blinded him completely, should be asked to consider both contingencies. Should the will be made conditional on the marriage actually taking place? Remember, a will made in contemplation of marriage is still valid, even if the marriage does not actually take place.

☞   **A client who is about to marry should review the beneficiaries designated on insurance policies and RRSPs. Marriage does not revoke beneficiary designations.[32]**

Solution: Be Specific (Contemplation of Marriage)

👍   This is the Last Will of me, TERRENCE TESTATOR, of the City of Windsor, in the County of Essex, made in contemplation of my marriage to SYLVIA SPOUSE of the City of Kingston, in the County of Frontenac, which marriage is planned to take place on the 22nd of February, 2003. [I intend this will to take effect whether or not the contemplated marriage takes place.] OR [I intend that if the contemplated marriage does not take place within thirty (30) days of the 22nd of February, 2003, this Will shall be void, and my earlier will, made the 12th day of September 1999, shall be revived.]

☞   **Will envelopes that include a warning to clients that a marriage or re-marriage revokes the will are available from legal stationers. Even if the information is included on an envelope, it is a good idea to warn single clients about the effects of marriage in your reporting letter. See the reporting letter in Chapter Thirteen, "Practice Matters".**

---

[31] See *Re Coleman*, [1976] Ch. 1, [1975] 1 All E.R. 675, [1975] 2 W.L.R. 213, (1974) 119 S.J. 86, for a good discussion of the significance of that little word "the" before "marriage" in the statute.

[32] *Kang v. Kang et al.*, unreported, 2002 BCCA 696, 19 December 2002 (B.C.C.A.).

Multiple Wills

A will may cover some but not all of the will-maker's property. The law has long recognized the possibility of bifurcating an estate, but until recently the device of multiple wills was used most commonly by those who had property in another jurisdiction. Since the *Granovsky* case[33] approved the use of multiple wills as a means of probate planning, however, they have become common in Ontario. The two wills must be drafted so as to mesh with each other seamlessly.[34]

> **Identify the two wills consistently. It doesn't matter what you call the two wills, as long as you are consistent. We have seen: Ontario Will and Foreign Property Will, Limited Property Will and General Will, Corporate Properties Will and General Will, Primary Will and Secondary Will, and Public Will and Private Will.**

Error #5: Revoking One of Two Double Wills

PRIMARY WILL

This is the Last Will of me, CLAUDE CLIENT, of the City of Ottawa in the County of Carleton, Province of Ontario with respect to all of my property except my Secondary Estate (as defined below), made this 4th day of March, 2003.

I revoke all former wills made by me.

SECONDARY WILL

This is the Last Will of me, CLAUDE CLIENT, of the City of Ottawa in the County of Carleton, Province of Ontario with respect to my Secondary Estate (as defined below), made this 4th day of March, 2003.

I revoke all former wills made by me.

---

[33] *Re Granovsky Estate* (1998) 156 D.L.R. (4th) 557, 21 E.T.R. (2d) 25 (Ont. Gen. Div.).

[34] See Chapter Twelve "Multiple Wills" for the basic rules on drafting double wills. See also the discussions and precedents in Jordan M. Atin, "Probate Issues", *Estates News: Of Plans, Issues, Schemes, Strategies, Plots and Conspiracies*, Canadian Bar Association — Ontario, 2001 Institute of Continuing Education, 1 February 2001; Susan A. Easterbrook, "Drafting Issues and Developments", *Estate, Trusts and Capacity Law: A Decade in Review*, Ontario Bar Association Annual Institute, 25 January 2002.

Solution: No Revocation in Second Will

If the first will revokes all former wills, and deals with only the assets for probate, the second will does not have to contain a revocation. Between the signing of the first and second wills, the unprobated assets would pass on an intestacy. All the second will must do is fill in the gap, by disposing of the unprobated assets.

> **SECONDARY WILL**
>
> This is the Last Will of me, CHARLIE CLIENT, of the City of Ottawa in the County of Carleton, Province of Ontario with respect to my Secondary Estate (as defined below), made this 4th day of March, 2003.
>
> I have an existing Will executed on the 4th day of March, 2003, which Will deals with all of my property except for my Secondary Estate, which Will I do not intend to revoke.

Solution: Limited Revocation in Both Wills

> **If you use this method, you must be sure that the asset description is complete, and that every asset is caught by one will or the other; if not, there will be a partial intestacy as to the undescribed assets.**

> **PRIMARY WILL**
>
> Subsequent to the execution of this Will, I will execute a Secondary Will dealing with certain of my assets defined in that Will as my Secondary Estate.
>
> **SECONDARY WILL**
>
> This is the Last Will of me, WILMA WILLMAKER of the City of Windsor in the County of Essex, with respect to my Secondary Estate (as defined below), made this 4th day of March, 2003. I revoke all former wills made by me *regarding those assets that form part of my Secondary Estate, to the extent that the will or wills deal with those assets and to the extent of any inconsistency with this Will.*
>
> I declare that I have an existing Will executed on the 4th day of March, 2003, dealing with certain assets defined in that Will as my Primary Estate, and which Will I do not intend to revoke.

If one will revokes all prior wills, and the other revokes only those wills dealing with the special property, the order in which the wills are executed matters. Make sure that you or your assistant sets up the execution so that the wills are signed in the right order.

Solution: Revocation Limited by Date

PRIMARY WILL

>I revoke all wills made by me at any time before the 4th of March, 2003 and I declare this to be my Last Will with respect to all of my property other than my Secondary Estate (as defined below). I declare that this document is the only executed copy of my Last Will with respect to my property other than my Secondary Estate.

SECONDARY WILL

>I revoke all wills made by me at any time before the 4th of March, 2003, and I declare this to be my Last Will with respect to my Secondary Estate (as defined below). I declare that this document is the only executed copy of my Last Will with respect to my Secondary Estate.

Error #6: Tainting the Unprobated Will

Be clear about which will is to be submitted for probate, and keep the assets covered by the probated will to a minimum. If even one of the assets covered in the secondary or special will cannot be transferred without a Certificate of Appointment as Estate Trustee, you may be compelled to probate the secondary will, thus defeating the purpose of the double wills.

You will want to avoid tainting the unprobated will by including an asset that will require probate. Consider using a disclaimer clause, to allow the trustees of the secondary will to disclaim any property that might compel an application for probate.

Solution: Disclaimer

> I authorize my Trustees to disclaim entitlement to receive any property listed in the definition of my Secondary Estate, and any property so disclaimed by my Trustees [within sixty days following the date of my death] shall not form part of my Secondary Estate, but shall be part of my Primary Estate to be dealt with under my Primary Will. My Trustees may disclaim property for any reason that they in their absolute discretion consider appropriate, including, without derogating from the scope of that discretion, securing the result that my Secondary Will does not have to be submitted to the Court for the granting of Letters Probate or a Certificate of Appointment of Estate Trustee.

In some circumstances (e.g. polluted property that carries liability under the *Environmental Protection Act*; or real estate where the probate status is unclear because it is in an area being converted from *Registry Act* to Land Titles) you may make a tertiary or third will.

Error #7: Domestic Contracts Overlooked

Don't overlook the terms of your client's co-habitation or separation agreement. If the agreement differs from the will, the intended effect of the will may be radically altered.

Domestic contracts intersect with wills in three ways:

- a domestic agreement may oblige the will-maker to leave property in a certain way or to designate beneficiaries irrevocably;

- the spouse may contract not to contest the will; or

- the will-maker may agree not to change a mutual will.

Drafting a domestic contract to protect the will from attack by a surviving spouse is a topic that intersects in complex ways with family law, beyond the scope of this book.[35]

Solution: Marriage Contract (Mutual Wills)

Let's get some terminology straight:

▶ Mirror wills — If a couple makes a pair of wills, one each, and the wills leave all to each other and have identical dispositions in the

---

[35] See David Simmonds, "Accomplishing Estate Planning Objectives by Marriage Contracts" in *Marriage Contracts*, ed. By Evita M. Roche and David C. Simmonds (Toronto: Carswell,1988).

alternative that the other party has predeceased, those are "mirror wills". They are by far the commonest arrangement when a couple makes wills together.

▶ Joint wills — If two people make one will together, that is a joint will. Some jurisdictions allow joints wills. Ontario has no statutory or common law basis for a joint will, which will simply be treated as the will of each party.

▶ Mutual wills — A couple makes wills and each of them agrees not to change the wills during their joint lives without the other's consent, and not to change at all after one party has died. Courts will enforce a mutual will in equity, even if the surviving will-maker makes a new will with different dispositions. The new will is a "fraud on the deceased". Although legal title to the property will follow the disposition in the new "fraudulent" will, it will be impressed with a trust for the beneficiaries under the mutual will.[36]

If the parties want to make mutual wills, and bind themselves not to change the will without the other's consent, the following is a simple contract that might be used. The will-makers should be aware, however, that remarriage or *inter vivos* gifts can still undo the arrangement.

BETWEEN: ALLAN ADVOCATE (the husband)

AND: BERNICE BROKER (the wife)

Background

a. ALLAN ADVOCATE and BERNICE BROKER are spouses of one another, having their domicile and habitual residence in the Province of Ontario.

b. ALLAN ADVOCATE and BERNICE BROKER have each made disclosure to the other of their significant assets, liabilities, income and debts existing as of the effective date of this contract. ALLAN ADVOCATE confirms the accuracy of his Net Worth Statement attached as Schedule I to this Agreement, and BERNICE BROKER confirms the accuracy of her Net Worth Statement attached as Schedule II to this Agreement.

---

[36] See *The University of Manitoba v. Sanderson Estate* (1998), 155 D.L.R. (4th) 40 (B.C.C.A.), 20 E.T.R. (2d) 148, 120 B.C.A.C. 186, 166 W.A.C. 186, [1998] 7 W.W.R. 83, 47 B.C.L.R. (3d) 25, for a good discussion of the theory of mutual wills. See also *Edell v. Sitzer.*, (2001), 55 O.R. (3d) 198 (Sup. Ct. Just.).

c. ALLAN ADVOCATE and BERNICE BROKER have been informed of their obligations toward and rights against each other.

d. This contract is intended to take effect as a domestic contract within the meaning of the *Family Law Act*, R.S.O. 1990, c.F.3, as amended.

e. Each of ALLAN ADVOCATE and BERNICE BROKER considers this contract to be fair and reasonable, and is signing this contract voluntarily. Each party further acknowledges that he or she:

   (A) has had independent legal advice, or the opportunity to obtain such advice;

   (B) understands the nature and the consequences of this marriage contract;

   (C) is signing this marriage contract voluntarily without undue influence, fraud, coercion or misrepresentation of any kind; and

   (D) is prepared to execute this marriage contract based upon the information and disclosure made to date.

Therefore this Agreement witnesses that in consideration of the marriage of the parties, mutual love and affection, the recitals made immediately above, and the mutual promises made immediately below, ALLAN ADVOCATE and BERNICE BROKER agree as follows:

1. Within ten (10) days of the date of this Agreement, ALLAN ADVOCATE will execute a Will substantially in the form of the Will annexed as Schedule III to this Agreement.

2. Within ten (10) days of the date of this Agreement, BERNICE BROKER will execute a Will substantially in the form of the Will annexed as Schedule IV to this Agreement.

3. While they are both alive, neither of ALLAN ADVOCATE or BERNICE BROKER will alter or revoke the Wills referred to in paragraphs 1 and 2 ("the Wills") without the written consent of the other party.

4. After the death of either one of ALLAN ADVOCATE or BERNICE BROKER, the survivor will not alter or revoke his or her Will.

5. Should the Will of either ALLAN ADVOCATE or BERNICE BROKER be revoked by operation of law, he or she will execute a new Will upon the same terms and conditions as are contained in the Wills.

6. This Agreement shall enure to the benefit of and be binding upon the Parties and their respective personal representatives and assigns.

To evidence their agreement ALLAN ADVOCATE and BERNICE BROKER have signed four copies of this contract on the 20th day of December, 2003, under seal.

CHAPTER 3

BENEFICIARY DESIGNATIONS

Life insurance contracts and registered plans (both Registered Retirement Savings Plans and Registered Retirement Income Funds) are frequently dealt with in a will. For one thing, the *Succession Law Reform Act* allows a designation of beneficiary to be made in a will,[37] and the *Insurance Act*

---

[37] 51. (1) A participant may designate a person to receive a benefit payable under a plan on the participant's death,

> (a) by an instrument signed by him or her or signed on his or her behalf by another person in his or her presence and by his or her direction; or
>
> (b) by will, and may revoke the designation by either of those methods.

Succession Law Reform Act, R.S.O. 1990, c. S.26, s. 51(1), as amended.

implies that a beneficiary can be named in a will.[38] For another, changing or confirming the designated beneficiary under policies and plans is often part of the complete plan for the distribution of the will-maker's assets.

Designations of beneficiaries should not be routinely included in a will. Unless you are varying the existing arrangements, or making more complex provisions than the plan or policy form allows, leave them out.

Error #1: Misplaced Designation

Insurance proceeds and registered plan benefits are paid to a named beneficiary and, thus, are not usually treated as part of the estate (unless the estate is named as beneficiary). There may still be some doubt as to whether the proceeds of a registered plan payable on the death of a plan holder are included in the deceased's estate,[39] but the general rule is that, since they never pass into the hands of the executor, they are not included in the probateable estate. Designating a beneficiary is, therefore, a very simple way to reduce probate tax. However, if the designation or declaration appears in a will after the clause formally vesting the estate in the executor, the will may appear to include the proceeds in the estate.

Solution: Put Designations First

The best practice, if the will is to include beneficiary declarations or designations, is to make them before vesting the estate in the executor. Designations may come before or after the executor is named, but they should definitely not be in the body of the will.[40]

---

[38] 190. (1) An insured may in a contract or by a declaration designate the insured's personal representative or a beneficiary to receive insurance money.

(2) Subject to section 191, the insured may from time to time alter or revoke the designation by a declaration....

192. (1) A designation in an instrument purporting to be a will is not ineffective by reason only of the fact that the instrument is invalid as a will or that the designation is invalid as a bequest under the will.

(2) Despite the *Succession Law Reform Act*, a designation in a will is of no effect against a designation made later than the making of the will.

(3) Where a designation is contained in a will, if subsequently the will is revoked by operation of law or otherwise, the designation is thereby revoked.

(4) Where a designation is contained in an instrument that purports to be a will, if subsequently the instrument if valid as a will would be revoked by operation of law or otherwise, the designation is thereby revoked.

Insurance Act, R.S.O. 1990, c. I.8, s. 192, as amended.

[39] *Canadian Imperial Bank of Commerce v. Besharah* (1989), 68 O.R. (2d) 443, 33 E.T.R. 186, 58 D.L.R. (4th) 705 (H.C.).

[40] See Chapter One on the Architecture of a Will.

How particularly do you need to describe the plan or policy? Financial institutions prefer that it be identified precisely with an account or policy number, but if you do include the number make sure you get it right.[41]

Registered Plans

Error #2: Survivorship in Designations

To include a 30-day survivorship clause in a registered plan designation creates a vacuum in the legal ownership. If the beneficiary can only receive the proceeds if he survives for 30 days, who owns the proceeds (or who is the owner in equity of the beneficial interest) in the interim? Remember that certainty of objects is required for a valid trust.

> I designate my wife, JANE SMITH, *if she is living on the thirtieth day following the date of my death*, to receive all refunds of premiums or contributions payable upon or as a result of my death, out of any registered retirement income fund that I may own at the time of my death.

The survivorship condition here is simply unnecessary since double probate is not an issue for designated funds.

Solution: Immediate Vesting

> I designate my wife, JANE SMITH, if she survives me, as beneficiary to receive all benefits payable after my death under any [Registered Retirement Savings Plan], [Registered Retirement Income Funds], [Deferred Profit Sharing Plans], or [Pension Plans] that I may own at my death, including my plan with ABC Inc., Account Number 123, and my plan with DEF Ltd., Account Number 456. This is a designation within the meaning of Part III of the *Succession Law Reform Act*, R.S.O. 1990, c. S.26.

Since the designation in a will only binds those plans in existence at the time the will is made, there is no need for overly inclusive language, such as you would employ to capture post-will changes in other assets. Name the particular plans and leave it at that.

---

[41] *Waugh Estate v. Waugh* (1990)37 E.T.R. 146 63 Man. R. (2d) 155 (Q.B.) held that a general designation of "any RRSP owned by me at my death" was effective.

Solution: Life Insurance RRSPs

If there are RRSPs held by the will-maker which are also governed by the *Insurance Act*:

> I designate my husband, JOSHUA SMITH, if he survives me, as beneficiary to receive all benefits payable after my death (including payments made as a consequence of my death as well as contractual payments continuing after my death) pursuant to any [Registered Retirement Savings Plan], [Registered Retirement Income Fund], [Deferred Profit Sharing Plan], or [Pension Plans] that I may own at my death, including my plan with ABC Inc., Account Number 123, and my plan with DEF Ltd., Account Number 456. In this designation, the terms "Registered Retirement Savings Plans" o[r "Registered Retirement Income Funds"] shall have the same meaning as in the *Income Tax Act* (Canada). This is a designation within the meaning of the *Succession Law Reform Act*, and, to the extent that these Plans [or Funds] are governed by the *Insurance Act*, this shall also be a declaration within the meaning of the *Insurance Act*.

Error #3: Minor Beneficiaries

If the beneficiary of a registered plan is a minor at the time the planholder dies, the proceeds cannot be paid to the minor. The financial institution will pay them into court, unless there is a guardian of property appointed for the child who is able to claim them.[42] Once paid into court, they are available for maintenance on application to the Children's Lawyer, and (often a result the clients want very much to avoid) when the child turns 18, it is all his.

> I designate my wife, JANE SMITH ("JANE"), if she survives me, to receive all benefits payable after my death under any Registered Retirement Savings Plan, Registered Retirement Income Funds, Deferred Profit Sharing Plans, or Pension Plans ("the Benefits") that I may own at my death. If my wife, JANE, does not survive me, the Benefits shall be paid to my children who survive me in equal shares.

---

[42] Amounts under $10,000 can be paid to a parent or custodian under s. 51(1) of the *Children's Law Reform Act*, R.S.O. 1990, c. C.12.

Solution: An Alternate Designation to the Estate

The following clause replaces a predeceased spouse with living children, and provides that if any of the children are minors, the executor can receive the funds.[43]

> (a) I designate my wife, JANE, if she survives me, as beneficiary to receive all benefits payable after my death under any [Registered Retirement Savings Plan], [Registered Retirement Income Funds], [Deferred Profit Sharing Plans], or [Pension Plans] that I may own at my death, including my plan with ABC Inc., Account Number 123, and my plan with DEF Ltd., Account Number 456 (collectively referred to as "the Benefits").
>
> (b) If JANE dies before me the Benefits shall be paid to my estate. This is a designation within the meaning of Part III of the *Succession Law Reform Act.*
>
> (c) If JANE dies before me and if, at my death, any child of mine is a minor, I authorize my Trustees, on behalf of my children, to deal with the Benefits in compliance with the provisions of section 60(1) of the *Income Tax Act.* An annuity purchased pursuant to this clause shall be an authorized investment of my estate, and I relieve my Trustees of liability for purchasing it. The receipt of my Trustees shall be a sufficient discharge to the institution or institutions paying the Benefits.

The clause above refers to subsection 60(l) of the *Income Tax Act,* which allows a dependent child to convert the proceeds of a registered plan into an annuity. It has been little used, given the restriction of this conversion option to minors and disabled beneficiaries. The February 2003 budget makes it slightly easier for a disabled child to qualify as a dependant, but the annuity provisions remain of limited use. Nevertheless, for those who have children who are or may be "dependent by reason of physical or mental infirmity",[44] the following clause gives very specific directions about how to handle the proceeds of registered plans.

---

[43] RRSP proceeds passing to the estate will, however, be subject to Estate Administration Tax.

[44] See the *Income Tax Act,* R.S.C. 1985, c. 1 (5th Supplement), s. 60(l), as amended; also IT-500R "Registered Retirement Savings Plans — Deat of an Annuitant", December 18, 1996.

Solution: Adult Dependent Child

> (a) I designate my son, RICHARD SMITH, (referred to as "my Son") if he survives me, as beneficiary, to receive all benefits payable after my death pursuant to any Registered Retirement Savings Plan or Registered Retirement Income Fund of which I am the annuitant, as defined in the *Income Tax Act* ("the Benefits"). This is a designation within the meaning of Part III of the *Succession Law Reform Act.*
>
> (b) If my Son is mentally incapable, I direct the person paying the Benefits to pay them to my Trustees to be dealt with in accordance with the terms of paragraph (c) below. The receipt of my Trustees shall be a sufficient discharge to the person or institution paying the Benefits.
>
> (c) If, at the date of my death, my Son is dependent on me by reason of physical or mental infirmity as defined in the *Income Tax Act,* I direct my Trustees, on behalf of my Son, to deal with the Benefits in compliance with the provisions of section 60(1) of the *Income Tax Act.*

Solution: An RRSP Trust

Although the *Succession Law Reform Act* does not (as the *Insurance Act* does) make specific reference to payment to a trustee, there appears to be no reason why the payment of proceeds could not be directed to an adult, to hold in trust for minor children.[45]

> (a) I designate SAM SMITH and JUNE SMITH to receive all benefits payable after my death pursuant to the following Registered Retirement Savings Plans [or Registered Retirement Income Funds]: my plan with ABC Inc., Account Number 123, and my plan with DEF Ltd., Account Number 456 ("the Benefits").
>
> (b) I direct that the Benefits shall be held by SAM SMITH and JUNE SMITH (referred to as the "RRSP/RRIF Trustees") as the Trustees of a separate trust, to be known as "the Children's RRSP/RRIF Trust". The receipt of the

---

[45] See Technical Interpretation 2002-0143685 (28 February 2003).

RRSP/RRIF Trustees shall fully discharge the institution paying the Benefits, which shall not be required to see to the carrying out of the terms of the trust.

(c) This Trust shall not form part of my estate and shall be administered as a separate trust notwithstanding that the Trustees may be the same persons as the Trustees of my estate.

(d) The RRSP/RRIF Trustees shall have all the same powers and discretions in administering the Children's RRSP/RRIF Trust as the Trustees of my estate have with respect to the administration of my estate.

(e) This is a designation within the meaning of the *Succession Law Reform Act*, and I revoke all prior designations in respect of the Registered Retirement Savings Plans or Registered Retirement Income Funds.

(f) The RRSP/RRIF Trustees shall deal with the Children's RRSP/RRIF Trust on the same terms and in the same manner as I have provided for the residue of my estate, and I hereby incorporate by reference, as terms of the Children's RRSP/RRIF Trust, the provisions of sub-paragraph Y of my Will into this paragraph 2 of my Will with the necessary modifications.

☞ **Like insurance trusts, RRSP trusts can be set up in a free-standing document. To ensure that the proposed trustee is bound by the terms of the trust, and is aware of the arrangements, have the trustee sign the separate deed as well.**

Error #4: Income Tax Ignored

Registered plans are tax-sheltered funds. Although a spouse will be able to take a "rollover" of the funds into his or her own registered plan, if a non-spouse is designated, the beneficiary receives the proceeds but the tax liability is borne by the estate.[46] Although the responsibility for Income Tax is joint and several between the estate and the beneficiary, Canada Customs and Revenue Agency (CCRA) will first look to the estate for payment, and

---

[46] *Fekete Estate v. Simon* (2000), 32 E.T.R. (2d) 202 (Ont. S.C.J.).

only if there are insufficient funds there will CCRA look to the beneficiary for the payment of the tax.

Solution: Beneficiary to Pay the Tax

If the intention of the plan-holder is that the tax is to be paid by the beneficiary who receives the proceeds, this clause may assist, but only if the named beneficiary is also a residual beneficiary under the will. It is probably not possible to force the RRSP beneficiary to pay the tax directly, or to make the receipt of the RRSP proceeds conditional on the payment of the tax.[47]

> (a) I designate my daughter, ANNE SMITH, (referred to as "my Daughter"), if she survives me, to receive all benefits payable after my death pursuant to any Registered Retirement Savings Plan [or Registered Retirement Income Fund] of which I am the annuitant, as defined in the *Income Tax Act* ("the Benefits"). This is a designation within the meaning of Part III of the *Succession Law Reform Act.*
>
> (b) My Daughter shall bring into account and hotchpot, upon the division of the residue of my estate in accordance with the provision of clause X below, the value of the Benefits. [The amount of the Benefits to be brought into account shall be reduced by an amount to be determined by my Trustees, on account of the potential income taxation, regardless of the timing or actual amount of these taxes.]

Error #5: RRSPs in the Estate

Occasionally, the proceeds of a registered plan are to be paid into the estate, rather than directly to a beneficiary. While this may not be in itself an error, not to deal with the consequences would be. If there is a living spouse, it is well to allow for the estate and the spouse to elect to have some or all of the proceeds used to satisfy any share that the spouse has in the estate.

---

[47] If a spouse is the beneficiary under the RRSP, the spouse might elect against the tax deferral and force the tax to be borne by the residue of the estate. Even if the estate is designated as beneficiary, and an election is made to transfer the funds to the spouse, the spouse can still refuse the election and force the estate to be responsible for the income tax so that he or she takes the funds tax free.

Solution: Joint Election

> If my estate is entitled to receive any amount from a Registered Savings Plan, which would have qualified as a "refund of premiums" as that term is defined in subsection 146(1) of the *Income Tax Act* (Canada) as amended, had it been received directly by a beneficiary of my Will, I authorize my Trustees to elect jointly with my beneficiary that any amounts that my Trustees, in the exercise of an uncontrolled discretion, consider appropriate be deemed to have been received directly by my beneficiary. I also direct my Trustees to pay to any beneficiary so electing the amount subject to the election and to add the balance remaining, if any, to the residue of my estate.

Solution: Authority to Purchase an Annuity

A trustee may use RRSP proceeds that have been paid to the estate to purchase an annuity for a minor child, to defer tax and spread it equitably among all of the residual beneficiaries. As a bonus, payments to a minor child will be taxed in the child's tax return at his or her graduated rate. Purchasing an annuity may, however, be an improper delegation of discretion or an imprudent investment.

> My Trustees may acquire an annuity under which a beneficiary, who is a dependent child or grandchild of mine, or a trust for the exclusive benefit of such child or grandchild is the annuitant. An annuity purchased under this clause shall be an authorized investment of my estate.

Solution: RRSP Contributions

Executors have the power to contribute to the RRSP of the deceased. Contributions to a spousal RRSP can also be made, if the surviving spouse will receive the contributed amount outright as all or part of his share of the estate. Where the entire estate is to be held in a spousal trust, no contribution is possible.

> **Executors do not need to be given the authority to make RRSP contributions, since the *Income Tax Act* authorizes them to do so. Consider inserting a gentle reminder to the executors that they have this power to make RRSP contributions. Similar provisions may be inserted to deal with Registered Education Savings Plans.**

> If, at the time of my death, I have not made the maximum contributions which are deductible for income tax purposes in respect of the calendar year in which my death occurs, or in respect of the calendar year immediately preceding, to the Registered Retirement Savings Plans of which I am or my spouse, YOLANDE, is the annuitant, and if YOLANDE survives me I authorize my Trustees in the exercise of an absolute discretion to contribute on my behalf to a Registered Retirement Savings Plan of which I am or YOLANDE is the annuitant, regardless of whether it is in existence at my death.

Solution: RESP Contributions

A subscriber to a Registered Education Savings Plan has the right to receive a return of contributions prior to death. If this right was not exercised, it passes to his or her estate. Accordingly, a will-maker may wish to leave instructions for dealing with his or her rights in an RESP.

> I am a subscriber to a Registered Education Savings Plan (the "RESP"), Account No. 123456 for the benefit of my grandchildren. If, at my death, any of my grandchildren qualify or may qualify for educational assistance payments (as that term is defined in the *Income Tax Act*), I direct my Trustees to take those steps necessary to maintain the RESP for the benefit of my grandchildren, including making contributions from the residue of my estate to the RESP.

Life Insurance

A will may contain a simple declaration as to the beneficiary of a policy of life insurance, or it may set up a trust to hold the proceeds of the insurance policy.[48] A declaration or trust of insurance in the will is vulnerable to revocation, since the *Insurance Act* provides that the revocation of a will

---

[48] Kathryn Bennett, "Insurance and Trust Solutions" in Ontario Bar Association, Continuing Legal Education Program, *Beneficiary Planning 2002: Gifts From Beyond the Grave* (Toronto: Ontario Bar Association, Continuing Legal Education, 2002).

automatically revokes the insurance designation it contains.[49] If your client is one who makes frequent changes to her will, or if she is likely to go off to a less experienced lawyer for her next will, you may prefer not to include any reference to the insurance in her will, especially if you are not changing the designation.

> **Use your reporting letter to remind a client that an insurance designation or trust is revoked if his will is revoked. See the reporting letter in Chapter Thirteen, "Practice Matters".**

> I declare that the proceeds of Perpetual Life Insurance Co., Policy No. 12345 shall be paid and payable to my daughter THERESA. This is a declaration within the meaning of the *Insurance Act.*

A life insurance trust is a useful technique that will avoid Estate Administration Tax (since the proceeds pass directly into the hands of the trustees) but still permit the insurance proceeds to be paid out in accordance with trust provisions in the Insurance Declaration or the Will.

Insurers are only required to pay out to the last person they have on record as beneficiary, so if there is an earlier designation on file, and your will changes that, you must make the insurer aware of the change.

> **Send a copy of the first page of a will, containing the life insurance or plan provisions, and the signature page only to the financial institution. That way, they are notified of the change without being apprised of the whole of the will-maker's dispositions.**

As with any other designation, the declaration of a life insurance beneficiary in a will only binds policies in effect at the date the declaration is signed.

---

[49] 190(3) Where a designation is contained in a will, if the will is subsequently revoked by operation of law or otherwise, the designation is thereby revoked.
Insurance Act, R.S.O. 1990, c. I.8, s. 190(3), as amended.

☞   **Obtain the full particulars — company name, policy number, current beneficiary and ownership — of any policy that the client intends to deal with in the will. The more particular the designation, the less likely that the financial institution will be unco-operative.**

Error #6: Minor Beneficiary

As with a registered plan, funds from an insurance policy cannot be paid directly to the beneficiary if he is a minor. The option — payment into court until the minor is 18 and then full vesting — is not at all attractive, especially if there are large sums involved.

Solution: A Trust for Minor Children

The following is a fairly basic insurance trust for minor children that can be used as part of a will that already contains provisions for holding the residue in trust for minor children.

(a) I hereby designate my wife, LINDA, if she survives me, as beneficiary of the proceeds of all policies of insurance on my life (collectively referred to as the "Insurance Proceeds").

(b) If LINDA dies before me, the Insurance Proceeds shall be paid to the Insurance Trustees (as defined below) and held in a separate trust fund (the "Insurance Trust Fund"). For greater certainty, I designate the Insurance Trustees for purposes of the *Insurance Act* as the recipients of the Insurance Proceeds.

(c) The Insurance Trustees shall invest and reinvest the Insurance Trust Fund for the benefit of my children and their respective issue, upon the same trusts, terms and conditions as to the payment of income and capital of the Insurance Trust Fund as I have provided for the residue of my Estate, and I hereby incorporate by reference the trust and dispositive provisions of clause X of my Will into this paragraph of my Will with the necessary modification as terms of the Insurance Trust Fund.

(d) I authorize the Insurance Trustees, in their absolute discretion, to advance the Insurance Proceeds, or any part of them, by way of loan to my general estate and if the Insurance Trustees consider it desirable to do so, to buy from my general estate whatever assets the Insurance Trustees consider advisable. The Insurance Trustees shall have the same powers and discretions in administering the Insurance Proceeds as the Trustees of my estate have for the administration of my residuary estate.

(e) The Insurance Trustees shall be my brother, LAW-RENCE, and my friend, LAURA. The receipt of the Insurance Trustees fully discharges the institution paying the Insurance Proceeds, which shall not be required to see to the carrying out of the terms of the trust.

(f) This is a designation within the meaning of the *Insurance Act* and I revoke any previous designation to the extent of any inconsistency with this designation.

(g) For greater certainty, the Insurance Proceeds shall not form part of my estate and shall be administered as a separate trust notwithstanding that the Insurance Trustees may be the same persons as the Trustees of my estate.

☞ **If the will may be challenged, do not put beneficiary designations in it. Even if the will is proved, payment of the proceeds of the insurance may be held up, and one of the big advantages of life insurance — immediate payout — will be lost.**

Error #7: Jointly Owned Policy Designation in Will

If the policy is a jointly owned policy, the declaration of designation should not be included in a will. While both owners of the joint policy are alive, neither one can change the designation alone, so any declaration must be executed by both owners. That means that the declaration (and any consequential trust) must be made in a document they can both sign, not in a will. If you do a free-standing insurance trust, the trustee may also sign to accept the terms of the trust.[50]

---

[50] For a full discussion of the problems of designating beneficiaries for jointly owned policies, see Robin Goodman and Joel Cuperfain "Estate Planning with Life Insurance". Estates and Trusts Forum, Law Society of Upper Canada, 2002.

Solution: A Separate Document

Any declaration of the beneficiary of a single life insurance policy can be set out in a will or in a separate document. You should consider a separate document for the same reasons you might prefer to make the beneficiary declaration outside of the will — the possibility that it will be revoked by a later will, and concern about delaying payout if the will is challenged. You will certainly do a separate insurance declaration and trust document when the policy is a jointly owned policy.

Insurance trusts are a complex subject, and the free-standing trust is not really part of a will at all. Nevertheless, we offer an example of a free-standing trust for a jointly owned policy.

THIS AGREEMENT dated the   day of   , 2003

BETWEEN:

ANNE SMITH and STEPHEN SMITH ("the Insured")

and

JAKE GRANT ("the Insurance Trustee")

Background:

1. ANNE SMITH and STEPHEN SMITH have designated and designate the Insurance Trustee, in trust, for their children as the beneficiaries of a joint and last-to-die life insurance policy on their lives being Policy No. 123456 carried by ABC Life ("the Proceeds").

2. The Insured and the Insurance Trustee agree that on the death of the last to die of ANNE SMITH and STEPHEN SMITH, the Proceeds shall be held in trust by the Insurance Trustee and distributed in accordance with the terms of this Agreement.

THIS AGREEMENT WITNESSES THAT the parties agree as follows:

1. The Insurance Trustee shall hold the Proceeds in a separate trust fund (referred to as "the Insurance Trust") for the children of ANNE SMITH and STEPHEN SMITH alive at the death of the last to die of ANNE SMITH and STEPHEN SMITH (the "Division Day") and shall invest and reinvest the Insurance Trust and deal with it on the following terms:

2. Insert whatever terms are to apply to the trust.

3. This is a declaration designating a beneficiary pursuant to the *Insurance Act.* The receipt of the Insurance Trustee fully discharges the institiution paying the Proceeds, which shall not be required to see to the carrying out of the trust.

4. In administering the Insurance Trust, the Insurance Trustees have all the powers and discretions listed in Schedule A, attached to the Agreement.

5. The Insurance Trustee hereby accepts his obligations under this Agreement, and agrees to be bound by the provisions of it and to hold the Insurance Trust upon the trusts here set out.

6. The Insurance Trustee shall be entitled to receive and shall be paid out of the Insurance Trust as compensation for acting as Trustee, the fees and reimbursement and other remuneration provided for in the Fee Agreement dated the   day of   and attached as Schedule B.

In Witness to their Agreement the parties have signed under seal on the date set out above.

SIGNED, SEALED and
DELIVERED

In the presence of _____	)	_____
as to the signature of Anne Smith	)	Anne Smith
_____	)	_____
as to the signature of Stephen Smith	)	Stephen Smith
_____	)	_____
as to the signature of Jake Grant	)	Jake Grant

Do not settle an insurance trust with a nominal amount (a gold coin, or a ten-dollar bill) as you would another *inter vivos* trust, in order to ensure that the trust is properly constituted, and that the beneficiaries are not mere volunteers. An insurance trust is an executory testamentary trust, complete except for the final settlement, which will happen inevitably when the insured dies and the policy is paid out.[51] While settling it with a nominal

---

[51] The *Insurance Act* also provides specifically for the rights of suit:

195. A beneficiary may enforce for the beneficiary's own benefit, and a trustee appointed pursuant to section 193 may enforce as trustee, the payment of insurance money made payable to him, her or it in the contract or by a declaration and in accordance with the provisions thereof, but the insurer may set up any defence that it could have set up against the insured or the insured's personal representative. R.S.O. 1990, c. I.8, s. 195.

amount will not invalidate the trust, it will affect its tax status, making it an *inter vivos* trust subject to the top marginal tax rates.

Error #8: No Commingling Allowed

For administrative ease, a trustee may wish to hold the insurance trust fund and the general estate in the same account. Equity would consider commingling as a breach of trust, unless authorized by the trust document.

Solution: Commingling Provisions

> IN THE WILL
>
> (a) If any insurance proceeds are being held in trust (the "Established Trust") for a beneficiary who becomes entitled under my Will to a share of my estate, my Trustees may hold that share in the same manner and subject to the same trust terms and conditions as the Established Trust and my Trustees may, in their absolute discretion, add the share to the Established Trust or maintain it as a separate trust.
>
> (b) My Trustees may, in their discretion, commingle and pool assets comprising my estate with other monies or assets held by my Trustees, either in my estate or under a trusteeship of my Trustees outside of my estate, subject to the investment provisions of my Will.
>
> (c) Whenever my Trustees pay capital out of the pooled fund, my Trustees' valuation of the fund for the purpose of that payment shall be final and binding. My Trustees may maintain a common fund or set aside as many separate funds for the beneficiaries of my Will as my Trustees in their discretion consider advisable, and they may re-allocate assets from one fund to another or discontinue funds established and re-establish separate funds as my Trustees from time to time deem advisable.

Although the beneficiary of a life insurance policy or a registered plan can be changed in a will, sometimes there is no intention to make a change. The will-maker is content with the status quo, and merely wants to confirm that she is aware of the designations and has taken them into account in making the provisions in the will.

Confirmation of Designations

I confirm all designations and declarations in respect of policies of insurance on my life or registered plans made by me during my lifetime [in favour of my spouse and children]. I declare that any insurance monies or refund of premiums payable to any beneficiary is in addition to and not in substitution for the benefits given to them by my Will.

CHAPTER 4

APPOINTMENT OF EXECUTOR AND TRUSTEE

Even if the terms of a will are well-crafted and precise, the selection of an inappropriate executor may impede the administration of an estate. The choice of executor will depend on the will-maker's assets, her personal circumstances, and the dispositive provisions in the will. If the will is fairly straightforward and the distribution is outright, family members are a good choice. If there are more complex assets, testamentary trusts, or complicated family dynamics, a more experienced and objective third party should be considered. Sometimes a corporate trustee together with a family member or friend is appropriate. If all of the executors are individuals, possible conflicts of interest should be canvassed, and elderly executors should be avoided. If any executor will charge a fee, compensation and a fee agreement must be discussed.

Error #1: Sole Reference to "Estate Trustee"

When the generic term "estate trustee" was introduced, some lawyers assumed that the term included both the executor and the trustee. The executor is responsible for gathering assets, paying debts, and distributing the estate in the first year after death. The trustee, on the other hand, is responsible for administering the trusts established under the will. Under 74.01 of *The Rules of Civil Procedure*, the term "estate trustee" means "executor, administrator, or administrator with the will annexed". The defined meaning does not include the trustee.

    I appoint my brother, ALLAN, and my spouse, CARA, to be the Estate Trustees of this Will.

Although arguably the intent of the will-maker can be gleaned, a specific reference to the appointment of a trustee is clearer.

Solution: Complete Appointment

> (a) I appoint my brother, ALLAN, to be the Estate Trustee, Executor and Trustee of this Will, but if ALLAN dies before me or is or becomes unwilling or unable to act as my Estate Trustee, Executor and Trustee before the trusts set out in this Will have been fully performed, I appoint my brother, SAM, and my sister, PATRICIA, to be the Estate Trustees, Executors and Trustees of this Will in the place of ALLAN.
>
> (b) I refer to my Estate Trustee, Executor and Trustee or Estate Trustees, Executors and Trustees, original, substituted or surviving as "my Trustees".

Since Ontario statutes (apart from the Rules) have not yet been amended to make reference to "Estate Trustee", include both "Executor" and "Estate Trustee" in any definition.

Error #2: No Provision for Incapacity

There is an old precedent that continues to circulate. An initial executor and trustee is appointed. If the first appointed executor dies before the will-maker (and only in that case), a successor is named. No provision is made, however, if the first appointed executor survives but is unable or unwilling to act.

 (a) I give all my property wheresoever situate, including any property over which I may have a general power of appointment, to my spouse, HARRY, *if he survives me*, and I appoint him to be the Executor of my Will. I expressly authorize him to sell all or any of my property, real or personal, at such time or times, for such price or prices and upon such terms as he may consider advisable.

(b) If my husband should *die before me or die at the same time or in circumstances rendering it uncertain which of us survived the other*, I appoint my brother, SAM, and my sister, PATRICIA, to be the Executors and Trustees of this Will and I refer to them as my Trustees. I give all my property to my trustees upon the following trusts, namely.. . .

If, as might well happen, Harry is not fully competent when the will-maker dies, Sam and Patricia will not be able to act.

Error #3: Survivorship Clause

The appointment of the executor and trustee should speak from the date of death. If a 30-day survivorship clause is included, a third party may not accept the authority of an executor to act until the 30-day period elapses.

(a) I appoint my spouse, ANNE, to be the Estate Trustee, Executor and Trustee of this Will, but if ANNE dies before me *or within a period of thirty (30) days following the date of my death*, or is or becomes unwilling or unable to act before all of the trusts set out in this Will have been fully performed, I appoint my brother, STEVEN, and my sister, TERESA, to be the Executors and Trustees in her place.

(b) I refer to my Executor and Trustee or my Executors and Trustees, original, substituted or surviving as "my Trustees".

Solution: Immediate Unconditional Appointment

> (a) I appoint my spouse, ANNE, to be the Estate Trustee, Executor and Trustee of this Will, but if my spouse, ANNE, dies before me, or is or becomes unwilling or unable to act before all of the trusts set out in this Will have been fully performed, I appoint my brother, SAM, and my sister, TERESA, to be the Estate Trustees, Executors and Trustees in her place.
>
> (b) I refer to my Estate Trustee, Executor and Trustee or my Estate Trustees, Executors and Trustees, original, substituted or surviving as "my Estate Trustees".

Error #4: Foreign Executor

Often the will-maker wants to appoint as executor a person who resides outside Canada. If the suggested executor lives in a country that is not part of the Commonwealth (such as the United States) the executor may be required to post a bond in order to act. Section 6 of the *Estates Act*[52] provides:

> "Letters probate shall not be granted to a person not resident in Ontario or elsewhere in the Commonwealth unless the person has given the like security as is required from an administrator in case of intestacy or in the opinion of the judge such security should under special circumstances be dispensed with or be reduced in amount."

Solution: Consulting Clause

If a will-maker wants the non-Commonwealth resident to be involved in the administration, but because of concerns about bonding does not actually want to appoint him as executor, the following precatory clause may be included.

> It is my wish that my Estate Trustee, Executor and Trustee consult my son, JOHN, in making decisions with respect to my Estate.

---

[52] Estates Act, R.S.O. 1990, c. E.21, as amended.

Solution: Successor Executor

Sometimes there is uncertainty as to where the chosen executor will reside at the time of the will-maker's death. One option is to appoint the non-Commonwealth resident and an alternate in the event that the non-Commonwealth resident renounces the appointment. An executor may renounce the appointment under section 34 of the *Estates Act*:

> Where a person renounces probate of the will of which the person is appointed an executor, the person's rights in respect of the executorship wholly cease, and the representation to the testator and the administration of the testator's property, without any further renunciation, goes, devolves and is committed in like manner as if that person had not been appointed executor.

Solution: Bond Waived

A will can provide that the requirement to post a bond be waived, although the provision is not binding on the court in Ontario. An application to the court to have the bond waived may be stronger if the will-maker has stated her intention that the executor is not to be bonded.

> I declare that no individual acting as an Estate Trustee, Executor or Trustee under this Will shall be required to post a bond or give any security for the performance of his or her duties notwithstanding the laws of any country or jurisdiction.

 The clause waiving a bond is either included in the Executor and Trustee sections as a separate paragraph, or it may be included as a statement in the general administrative provisions.

Error #5: No Successor Executors and Trustees

There should be a comprehensive appointment of executors and trustees, especially if a long-term trust is to be administered. To provide for continuity, the will-maker may:

1. Appoint a series of people who will likely outlive the terms of the trust;

2. Appoint a corporate trustee as a primary or successor trustee, as it does not die; or

3. Give the executors and trustees the power to appoint further executors and trustees.

Solution: One Substitute in the Order of Priority

> (a) I appoint one of the following persons, in the following order of priority, as my Estate Trustee, Executor and Trustee, each individual to be appointed in the event that the individual named before him or her dies before me or is or becomes unwilling or unable to act as my Estate Trustee, Executor and Trustee before the trusts set out in this Will have been fully performed, namely my spouse, ANNE, my son, BILL, my daughter, CAREN, and ABC Trust Corporation.
>
> (b) I hereinafter refer to my Estate Trustee, Executor and Trustee, original, substituted or surviving, as "my Trustee".

Solution: Minimum Number of Trustees

> (a) I appoint my spouse, ANNE, to be my Estate Trustee, Executor and Trustee of this Will. If ANNE dies before me or is or becomes unwilling or unable to act as my Estate Trustee, Executor and Trustee before the trusts set out in this Will have been fully performed, there should be at all times two (2) Estate Trustees, Executors and Trustees, and I appoint, in the following order of priority, those of the following persons who are not already acting and are able and willing to act to fill the vacancy so created, namely BILL, CAREN, DONNA and EDMUND.
>
> (b) I refer to my Estate Trustee, Executor and Trustee or Estate Trustees, Executors and Trustees, original, substituted or surviving, as "my Trustees".

Solution: Appointment of Child at age of 21 years

An executor must be the age of majority in order to act. If a sole executor is a minor at the will-maker's death, the grant of probate may be made to the guardians until the minor attains the age of majority. [53]

---

[53] Section 26 of the *Estates Act* sets out as follows:

(continued on next page)

If a minor is appointed with an adult, the adult may apply for probate with the minor's right to apply reserved until he or she attains the age of majority.

 Make sure the age at which the child will become a trustee is rationalized with the age when she gets a vested interest in the estate. Having a 21-year-old trustee holding assets for herself and her siblings to age 35 may be setting the wolf to mind the sheep.

> (a) I appoint my sister, ANNE, and each child of mine upon that child attaining the age of twenty-one (21) years to be my Estate Trustees, Executors and Trustees of this Will; but if ANNE dies before me or is or becomes unwilling or unable to act as my Estate Trustee, Executor and Trustee before the trusts set out in this Will have been fully performed and should there be no child of mine alive who has attained the age of twenty-one (21) years, then I appoint my friend, BOB, to be the Estate Trustee, Executor and Trustee of this Will in place of ANNE.
>
> (b) I refer to my Estate Trustee, Executor and Trustee, or Estate Trustees, Executors and Trustees, original, substituted or surviving, as "my Trustees".

 It is generally better not to appoint minor children — at the time the will is made, it may be very difficult to predict how much responsibility a child will subsequently develop.

Solution: Power to Appoint Successor Trustee

> (a) I appoint my sister, ANNE, to be the Estate Trustee, Executor and Trustee of this Will, but if ANNE dies before me

(continued from previous page)

26.(1) Where a minor is sole executor — Where a minor is sole executor, administration with the will annexed shall be granted to the guardian of the minor or to such other person as the court thinks fit, until the minor has attained the full age of 21 years, at which time and not before, probate of the will may be granted to the minor.

(2) Power of administrator in such case — The person to whom such administration is granted has the same powers as an administrator has by virtue of an administration granted to an administrator during minority of the next of kin.

> or is or becomes unwilling or unable to act as my Estate Trustee, Executor and Trustee before the trusts set out in this Will have been fully performed, ANNE may by instrument in writing during her lifetime or by her will appoint some person or persons, including a trust company, to act as the Estate Trustee, Executor and Trustee or Estate Trustees, Executors and Trustees of this Will together with her or in her place.
>
> (b) I refer to my Estate Trustee, Executor and Trustee or my Estate Trustees, Executors and Trustees, original, substituted or surviving, as "my Trustees".

Include the ability to appoint trustees when the will-maker wants the trustees to be able to vary the situs of any trust. It is particularly relevant if any beneficiaries reside outside of Ontario.

Solution: Power to Appoint, Remove and Substitute Trustees

> (a) My Trustee who is an individual or a majority of my Trustees who are individuals may, by instrument in writing, appoint a trustee to fill the vacancy resulting from the resignation, death, removal or inability to act of any of my Trustees.
>
> (b) My Trustees shall also have the right at any time when in their absolute discretion they consider it advisable by instrument in writing to appoint ABC Trust Company as an additional Estate Trustee, Executor and Trustee of this Will. My Trustee who is an individual or a majority of my Trustees who are individuals may at any time by instrument in writing remove ABC Trust Company for the time being acting as one of my Trustees and appoint another trust company as Trustee in its place.
>
> (c) Any corporate trustee acting under this Will shall have charge of all accounts and shall keep in its custody all the assets of my estate and may cause to be registered in its name solely any assets held in connection with or forming part of my estate.

Solution: Non-resident Beneficiaries

If there are non-resident beneficiaries, the will-maker may want to confer on the trustees the power to allow the administration of the estate or any assets to be transferred to another jurisdiction.

> I authorize my Trustee to appoint any one or more trustees in another jurisdiction, either in place of or in addition to my Trustee, so that any of the trusts in this Will may be administered in another jurisdiction. My Trustee may appoint by deed any person or corporation that in his absolute discretion he deems advisable. Thus, separate trusts may have different trustees. Anyone so appointed who accepts the office shall have the same powers, duties, discretions and authorities as my originally appointed Estate Trustees, Executors and Trustees have under this Will.

Error #6: No Successor (Professional)

If an acting co-executor or a co-trustee dies, the surviving co-executor and co-trustee continues to manage the estate unless a substitute is provided for in the will. If the sole surviving executor and trustee dies during the administration of the estate, her executor and trustee becomes responsible for the administration of the estate.[54]

If a will-maker is the sole executor of an estate under administration, the executorship will devolve to his or her executors. The spouse of a lawyer or an accountant could thus end up administering dozens of estates.[55]

Solution: Executor for Non-Family Members (Professional)

> For those estates of which I am the sole Estate Trustee, Executor or Trustee (except for the estates of my spouse and any other person

---

[54] *Bruce (Twp.) v. Thornburn* (1987), 26 E.T.R. 96 (Ont. H.C.) the authority given to a surviving or continuing trustee to appoint a new trustee by deed extends to a sole trustee appointing a successor; *Re Moorehouse*, [1946] O.W.N. 789, 4 D.L.R. 542 (H.C.) — section 3 does not empower a retiring trustee to appoint a successor.

[55] Section 46 of the *Estates Act* sets out the following:

Survivorship

46.(1) Where there are several personal representatives and one or more of them dies, the powers conferred upon them shall vest in the survivor or survivors, unless there is some provision to the contrary in the will.

(2) Until the appointment of new personal representatives, the personal representatives or representative for the time being of a sole personal representative, or, where there were two or more personal representatives, of the last surviving or continuing personal representative, may exercise or perform any power or trust that was given to, or capable of being exercised by the sole or last surviving personal representative.

> related to me by blood or marriage), I appoint my colleague, SARA, to be the successor Estate Trustee, Executor or Trustee. [56]

Error #7: Too Many Executors

Some individuals refuse to pick favourites and insist on appointing all of their children. The *Trustee Act*[57] places no restriction on the number of trustees who may be originally appointed. There is also no limitation on the number of new trustees who may be appointed — whether non-judicially[58] or judicially.[59] However, the practicality of appointing many trustees must be considered.[60]

Solution: Majority Decision Provision

Unless the will provides otherwise, if more than one executor is appointed, the general rule is that co-executors are regarded in law as one person and they all must act jointly.[61] The rule for trustees is the same in that they must all act unanimously.[62] As a result, for practical purposes it is better not to have more than three individuals. If the will-maker decides to appoint three executors, he may want to provide for a 2/3 majority clause to deal with a potential stalemate.

> (a) If at any time my Trustees are unable to agree regarding any matter in connection with my estate, I declare that the decision of the majority of my Trustees [of which my wife, CATHERINE, shall be one] shall be binding upon all persons concerned. Any Trustee who does not form part of the majority shall execute all documents necessary to give effect to the decision but shall not be deemed to concur in the decision by virtue of so doing.
>
> (b) Any one or more of my Trustees who acts in good faith and does not form part of the majority decision shall not

---

[56] *Re Laking* (1971), 24 D.L.R. (3d) 5, [1972] 1 O.R. 649 (Ont. Surr. Ct.).held that where a will-maker appoints her husband as executor, and another person to act in her place with respect to another estate, effect will be given to the appointment.

[57] *Trustee Act*, R.S.O. 1990, c. T.23 as amended.

[58] Section 3.(1) of the *Trustee Act.*

[59] Section 5 of the *Trustee Act.*

[60] The Ontario Law Reform Commission recommended that a trust not be able to have more than four trustees except with a court order, notwithstanding the terms of the trust agreement. This recommendation did not extend to executors. Ontario Law Reform Commission, *Report on the Law of Trusts* (Toronto, Ont.: The Commission, 1984), at p. 123.

[61] *Ex part Rigby*, 19 Ves 462.

[62] *Gibb v. McMahon* (1905) 9 O.L.R. 522 (C.A.), affirmed (1906), 37 S.C.R. 362.

> be personally liable for any loss suffered by my estate by reason of the acts or omissions which result from that majority decision.

☞ **If a Trust Company is appointed, it will typically require that it must be part of the majority for any decision for liability reasons.**

Error #8: No Power to Resign

An executor may wish to resign for various reasons. Section 2 of the *Trustee Act* does not apply to the resignation of an executor under a will.[63] Without the express provision in the will for resignation, therefore, the executor would be required to obtain court approval and prepare accounts for her administration.

Solution: Permit Resignation

 A trustee may resign on thirty (30) days' written notice to the other trustees and to the next-appointed trustees. No trustee who resigns shall be required to pass accounts, and the next-appointed trustees shall only be liable for the assets which are delivered to them by the trustee so resigning.

☞ **In some instances, a succeeding trustee will require the prior trustee to pass accounts in order to make certain that the succeeding trustee is not inheriting any problems and starts the administration with a clean slate.**

Error #9: Equalization Ignored

If a surviving spouse[64] elects for an equalization of net family property, he cannot act as executor and trustee of the deceased spouse's estate, subject to the terms of the will.[65]

---

[63] *Re McLean* (1982), 37 O.R. (2d) 164, 11 E.T.R. 293, 135 D.L.R. (3d) 667 (Ont. H.C.).

[64] *Walsh v. Bona* held that it was not discriminatory for common law spouses to be excluded from the provincial property regimes applicable to married spouses. *Walsh v. Bona* (sub nom. *Nova Scotia (Attorney General) v. Walsh*) (2002), 32 R.F.L. (5th) 81, 221 D.L.R. (4th) 1, 297 N.R. 203 (S.C.C.).

[65] *Reid Martin v. Reid* (1999), 35 E.T.R. (2d) 267, 11 R.F.L. (5th) 374 (Ont. Div. Ct.).

Solution: No Appointment

If there is a real possibility of an election by the spouse under the *Family Law Act,* do not appoint the spouse as executor.

Solution: Spouse Deemed to Predecease

 If my spouse elects, under the provisions of the *Family Law Act,* for an equalization of net family property my spouse shall be deemed to have died before me for all purposes of this Will.

Error #10: No Adaptation for Professional Trustee

If a trust company is to be appointed, you should contact the trust company prior to the execution of the will. In this way, you can confirm that the trust company will accept the appointment and that the required clauses are included in the will.[66] Typically, trust companies request the draft be reviewed to ensure that the provisions comply with their administrative requirements.

Burden of Administration

Burden of Administration and Custody of Estate Assets

A trust company usually wants a statement included that gives it charge of all accounts and custody all the assets of the estate.

 I direct that if ABC Trust Corporation is acting as one of my Trustees, it shall have charge of all of my accounts and shall keep in its custody all of the assets of my estate.

Compensation Issues   The right to executor's compensation is recognized in the *Trustee Act:*

> 61(1) A trustee, guardian or personal representative is entitled to such fair and reasonable allowance for the care, pains and trouble, and the time expended in and about the estate as may be allowed by a judge of the Superior Court of Justice.

---

[66] Will-makers sometimes appoint a trust company without consulting the trust company. On the will-maker's death, the trust company may decline to act because the estate is not large enough or the estate plan will be difficult or impossible to administer. It is important, therefore, that the trust company be contacted when the will-maker is preparing the documentation to make certain that the will-maker is properly protected.

In *Re Toronto General Trusts Corp. and Central Ontario Railway Co.*,[67] the Court elaborated "care, pain and trouble", and set out the factors to be considered in fixing compensation.

These percentages merely represent a general convention and may be varied by the court.[68] A trustee is also entitled to out-of-pocket expenses without the approval of the beneficiaries or court order.[69] Nothing in the legislation precludes the executor's compensation from being fixed by the instrument creating the trust.[70]

Ability to Pre-take

Ability to Pre-take Compensation

Pre-taking refers to the taking of compensation after the performance of executors' duties, but before compensation has been approved by the court or the competent beneficiaries. Despite the traditional prohibition against pre-taking, some recent cases allowed it.[71] Until their right to pre-take is certain, however, a professional trustee will want a clause included to avoid having to pass accounts simply to fix compensation.

> If ABC Trust is appointed as one of the Estate Trustees, Executors and Trustees of this Will or the sole Estate Trustee, Executor and Trustee of this Will, I authorize ABC Trust to take and transfer to itself at reasonable intervals from the income and/or capital of my estate amounts on account of compensation which my Trustees reasonably anticipate will be required at the end of the accounting period in progress, either upon the audit of the estate accounts or on approval by the beneficiaries of my estate, but if the amount

---

[67] *Re Toronto General Trusts Corp. and Central Ontario Railway Co.* (1905), 6 O.W.R. 350 (Ont. H.C.).

[68] There is a substantial amount of case law on the relationship and application of these percentages and the factors to be considered in establishing the remuneration for trustees which are beyond the scope of this book. Frederick D. Baker, *Widdifield on Executors' Accounts: Being a Treatise on the Administration of Estates*, 5th ed. (Toronto: Carswell, 1967), and Laura M. Tyrrell, "The Exercise of Discretion by a Trustee: When is an Absolute Discretion Not?" in *The Pitfalls of Being an Executor and Trustee* (Toronto, Ontario: Canadian Bar Association — Ontario, Continuing Legal Education, 1999).

[69] Section 23.1(1) *Trustee Act*: Expenses of Trustees — A trustee who is of the opinion that an exspense would be properly incurred in carrying out the trust may pay the expense directly from the trust property or pay the expense personally and recover a corresponding amount from the trust property. Later disallowance by the court — The Superior Court of Justice may afterwards disallow the payment or recovery if it is of the opinion that the expense was not properly incurred in carrying out the trust.

[70] *Trustee Act*, section 61(5): "Where allowance fixed by the instrument — Nothing in this section applies where the allowance is fixed by the instrument creating the trust".

[71] *Re William George King Trust*, (1994), 2 E.T.R. (2d) 123, 113 D.L.R. (4th) 701 (Ont. Gen. Div.).

> subsequently awarded on court audit or agreed to by the beneficiaries is less than the amount pre-taken, the difference shall be repaid forthwith to my estate without interest. [The compensation of co-executors, if any, will be in addition to the fees states above.]

Fee Agreements

Fee Agreements

A trust company will generally require a compensation agreement. The fee agreement should be clear.[72] The will-drafter should also confirm if there is to be more than one fee agreement.[73] All agreements should be executed prior to the will and incorporated into the will by reference.[74]

> I direct that if ABC Trust Corporation is appointed an Estate Trustee, Executor and Trustee of this Will, then it shall be entitled to receive and shall be paid out of my estate as compensation for its acting as Estate Trustee, Executor and Trustee of this Will, the compensation provided for in the memorandum annexed to this Will dated July 23, 2003, and signed by me, prior to the execution of this Will which memorandum is hereby incorporated into this Will.

Other Compensation Issues

If the executor is also the solicitor, the lawyer will want to carefully delineate the legal functions for which she can charge hourly rates, and her trustee's duties which are compensated in accordance with the *Trustee Act.* For clarity, a clause should be included in the will which allows both legal fees and executor's compensation to be charged.[75]

---

[72] In *Re Andrachuk Estate,* a clause authorized the trustees to take a reasonable *per diem* rate. Greer J. held that this wording did not fix compensation. In order for it to be fixed, it must be by way of a "fixed amount or a liquidated amount". *Re Andrachuk Estate* (sub nom. *Andrachuk Estate v. Van Beurden*), [2000] O.T.C. 34, 32 E.T.R. (2d) 1 (Sup. Ct. Just.).

[73] Some trust companies have different agreements depending on the nature of services they are to provide: eg. 1. Fee for Acting as Executor; 2. Fee for Acting as Trustee of Testamentary Trust: Trust Company to Manage; 3. Fee for Acting as Trustee of Testamentary Trust: Investment Management to be delegated to Approved Portfolio Manager.

[74] *Re Robertson,* [1949] O.R. 427; , 4 D.L.R. 319 (Ont. H.C.) *Re Anderson* (1985) 53 O.R. (2d) 36 (Ont. Surr. Ct.) — In order that a compensation agreement be binding, it must either be contained in the will or trust instrument or directly related to the will or trust.

[75] *Trustee Act,* section 61.(4) Allowance to barrister or solicitor trustee for professional services — Where a barrister or solicitor is a trustee, guardian or personal representative, and has rendered necessary professional services to the estate, regard may be had in making the allowance to such circumstances, and the allowance shall be increased by such amount as may be considered fair and reasonable in respect of such services.

I direct that if my solicitor, JILL, is retained to do necessary legal work in connection with my estate, she, or any firm of which she may be a partner, shall be entitled to charge and be paid for her or their professional services for acting on behalf of my estate in addition to the fees charged by my solicitor in acting as Executor, Trustee and Estate Trustee of this Will.

Trustee to Serve Without Compensation

 I direct that my Executor and Trustee shall serve without compensation.

Legacies

Legacies in lieu of Executor's Compensation

On occasion, a will-maker wants to leave a friend or a family member a legacy in lieu of executor's compensation. This has two advantages: the executor (who may be a family member and not inclined to request compensation) will receive compensation and it will be received by the executor tax free. A legacy given to an executor is presumed to be in lieu of executor's compensation,[76] but this presumption is rebuttable. The same presumption does not exist if the trustee receives an interest in the residue.[77] To remove doubt, the intent of the will-maker should be specified in the will.

 I direct that each of my Trustees shall receive $X in lieu of any compensation which might otherwise be awarded to them by the court.[78]

---

[76] D.W.M. Waters, *The Law of Trusts in Canada*, 2nd ed. (Toronto: Carswell, 1984), at p. 954.

[77] Jordan M. Atin, "Executor's Compensation" in *The Grateful Dead: How to Keep Estate Accounting on Track* (Toronto, Ont.: Canadian Bar Association — Ontario, Continuing Legal Education, 2000).

[78] There is occasional concern expressed that the CCRA could argue that this should be included by the Executor as income. See also Jordan M. Atin, "Protection of Trustees", in *Drafting Wills to Avoid Litigation* (Toronto, Ont.: Dept. of Education, Law Society of Upper Canada, 2000), at pp. 6–2 to 6–4.

Benefits in Addition to Compensation

> I declare that any benefits received by JIM under the provisions of this Will shall be in addition to any remuneration to which JIM may be entitled for services rendered as a trustee [or as solicitor] for my estate.

Error #11: No Powers to Special Trustees

In certain circumstances, the will-maker may appoint a "special trustee" to be the trustee of a particular trust. For example, funds may be set aside for a child and transferred to a parent or guardian to hold as special trustee, or a share for a challenged beneficiary is paid to a particular person to hold as special trustee. A common error is to direct that funds be paid to the special trustee, but to omit to confer the powers and discretions required to administer the funds.

Solution: Appointment of Special Trustees

> (i)   For the purpose of the trusts established under this paragraph X of my Will, I appoint my daughter, TERESA as Special Trustee of these Trusts.
>
> (ii) [Insert trust provisions for grandchildren.]
>
> (iii) I declare that the Special Trustee of the trusts established under this paragraph X of this Will shall have with the necessary modifications, all the same powers, authority and discretions granted to the Trustees of my general estate under the provisions of this Will.
>
> (iv) Once the trust funds have been paid over to my Special Trustee, my Trustees shall be under no obligation to see to the carrying out of the terms of the trusts. The receipt of the Special Trustee shall be a sufficient discharge to my Trustees.

CHAPTER 5

PERSONAL PROPERTY

Personal Effects

Personal property means all property that is not real property. In practice, choses-in-action, such as shares or bank accounts, are treated separately from "personal effects" — the household items and mementos that will-makers usually think of as personal property.

 If you use a term like "personal effects", rather than a list of the kind of property that is being covered, consider defining it in the will, and make sure that the client reads the definition. Does it include the garden tractor? Is it clear one way or another? The advent of word processing makes it easy to adapt the definition to address a client's particular concerns and assets.[79]

Sometimes articles are defined by where they are located: "in storage or in or about or belonging to, or generally used in connection with, any and every dwelling house, apartment and recreational residence I may own or in which I may reside at my death".

Definition (Comprehensive)

 In my Will, the term "Personal Effects" means all articles of personal, household and gardening use or ornament including all automobiles (including any car collection I may own), snowmobiles and accessories, boats, motors and accessories, garden implements and vehicles, domestic animals, sports equipment and machinery, guns and accessories, brass, silver, plate and plated articles, linen, china and glass, books (except books of account), pictures, paintings and prints, furniture, jewellery, wearing apparel, musical instruments, articles of virtu, antiques and curios, manuscripts (but not

---

[79] The term "personal effects" in a farmer's will would not normally include grain, livestock, farm machinery, equipment or implements, or other assets related to the business or operation of the will-maker's farm: *Surminsky (Litigation Guardian of) v. Ulmer Estate*, [1998] 2 W.W.R. 692, 19 E.T.R. (2d) 287, (sub nom. *Surminsky v. Ulmer Estate*) 159 Sask. R. 217, 1997 Carswell Sask. 523 (Q.B.).

any copyright that I may own), wines and liquors, consumable stores and provisions in storage or in or about or belonging to, or generally used in connection with, any and every dwelling house, apartment and recreational residence that I own or in which I reside at my death.

Error #1: No Provision for Personal Effects

If no disposition is made of personal effects, they may be sold under the executor's general power (and obligation) to convert assets to cash.[80] Most will-makers prefer to have their intimate items pass to family and friends. Although the monetary value may be relatively small, personal effects are often bitterly contested because they have great sentimental value. Moreover, sometimes will-makers have very valuable personal effects such as paintings, antique furniture, or vintage cars.

Don't assume personal and household effects are too small to worry about.

Solution: A Single Article to a Particular Person

My Trustee shall transfer and deliver to my cousin, JAMES, if he survives me, my Stradivarius violin.

Solution: General Gift of All Personal Effects

My Trustees shall deliver all articles of personal, domestic and household use or ornament belonging to me at my death, including consumable stores, and all automobiles, vehicles, boats, motors and accessories then owned by me to my husband, RICHARD, if he survives me, but if he dies before me, my Trustees shall divide these articles among my children alive at my death as my Trustees in their absolute discretion consider appropriate.

Ademption

A gift of a particular piece of personal property is a specific gift, subject to ademption; that is, it will fail if the article described in the will cannot be found after the will-maker's death.[81]

---

[80] A well drafted will should give the executor an option to pass assets "in specie" — see Chapter Ten, "Executors and Trustees' Powers and Rights".

[81] See Ralph E. Scane, "Specific Gifts: Some Problem Areas" (1982-84), 6 E. & T.Q. 217.

A will speaks from death, so if an article is subject to a contract for sale at the time of the will-maker's death, the equitable doctrine which treats "as done that which ought to have been done" means that the article is treated as already sold, and hence as no longer part of the estate.[82] The proceeds of the contract for sale, on the other hand, are not what the will-maker described in the gift, and will not pass to the named beneficiary either.

Subsection 20(2) of the *Succession Law Reform Act*, "Rights in place of property devised", allows a beneficiary to take the proceeds of an insurance policy in place of a destroyed article, or the benefit of a contract for sale, where the particular article has been sold.

The *Substitute Decisions Act* also contains a specific exception to the doctrine of ademption for property disposed of by an attorney under a Power of Attorney:[83]

> 36. The doctrine of ademption does not apply to property that is subject to a specific testamentary gift and that a guardian of property disposes of under this Act, and any one who would have acquired a right to the property on the death of the incapable person is entitled to receive from the residue of the estate the equivalent of a corresponding right in the proceeds of the disposition of the property without interest.

If the intention of the will-maker is that ademption is to apply to articles disposed of by the attorney, consider inserting a clause such as the following:

> If, at my death, I do not own any item listed in clause X of my Will or in any memorandum made subsequent to my Will, the gift of that item shall adeem, notwithstanding any statutory provision to the contrary. This clause shall indicate the contrary intention pursuant to the *Substitute Decisions Act.*

---

[82] See *Re Church* (sub nom. *Church v. Hill*), [1923] S.C.R. 642, 3 W.W.R. 405, 3 D.L.R. 1045.

[83] *Substitute Decisions Act,* S.O. 1992, c.30, as amended.

Make sure specific gifts are described with sufficient particularity to be identifiable. Avoid ambiguous terms such as "contents"[84] and "money".[85]

Error #2: Improper Descriptions

Choses-in-Action

Shares and bank accounts are choses-in-action, a form of personal property that will-makers often wish to give to particular people, or to have used as a fund. For example, an inheritance may be held in a separate account, and the will-maker's intention is to pass it directly to her children, although the residue is passing to the spouse.

 I direct my Trustee to transfer to my daughter, TAMMY, if she survives me, my Guaranteed Investment Certificate Number 123456789 with the Paragon Bank.

A specific gift of a chose-in-action will not ordinarily be traced into another chose-in-action. In the clause above, if funds in the GIC in question had been transferred, on maturity, to another GIC bearing a different number, the gift would be subject to ademption, since a court would presume that the will-maker, having moved the assets knowingly, no longer intended Tammy to benefit.[86]

Solution: State the Intention

I direct my Trustees to transfer to my son, MARTIN, if he survives me, my bank account with Empire Bank of Canada, Account Number 123456789. If I no longer have that account at my death, this gift shall adeem unless in the opinion of my Trustees (which shall be conclusive and not subject to challenge in any way) the proceeds of this bank account should be traced to another fund.

---

[84] A gift in a will of the "contents" of the dwelling house of the will-maker included a diamond ring on the finger of the deceased at the time of his death in *Re Tremaine*(1929), 37 O.W.N. 186 (H.C.), but a clause in a will giving the husband of the will-maker a life interest in a house, "also contents of same", then making specific bequests of jewellery and clothing to other beneficiaries will operate to give the husband the "contents" of the house minus the jewellery and clothing: *Re Baumann* (1924), 27 O.W.N. 209 (H.C.).

[85] See *Perrin v. Morgan*, [1943] A.C. 399, [1943] 1 All E.R. 187 (H.L.): "In the case of an ordinary English word like 'money', which is not always employed in the same sense, I can see no possible justification for fixing on it, as the result of a series of judicial decisions about a series of different wills, a cast-iron meaning ... the word 'money' has not got one natural or usual meaning. It has several meanings, each of which in appropriate circumstances may be regarded as natural...."

[86] See *Re Hubert* (1975), 13 N.B.R. (2d) 257 (Q.B.).

A general gift of shares in a company is not a specific gift, but a gift of "my" shares is.[87] Generally, any gift of something described with the article "my" betokens a specific gift.

 I direct my Trustees to deliver 200 shares of Here Today Hi-Tech Limited to my friend BETTY.

This clause could be interpereted as a direction to the trustee to purchase Here Today High-Tech Limited shares if there were none in the estate.

Solution: Use "My" to Describe the Asset

> I direct my Trustees to transfer to my friend, BETTY, if she survives me, all of *my* shares in the capital stock of Here Today High-Tech Limited. If, at my death, my shares in Here Today High-Tech Limited are represented by a different capital holding, as the result of a change in the structure or a sale of Here Today High-Tech Limited or its assets to another corporation, then the reference to my shares in the capital stock of Here Today High-Tech Limited means the capital holding or holdings that, as a result of that change, took the place of the shares I own at the date of making this Will.

Error #3: No Condition or Gift Over

Gifts of personal property are subject to anti-lapse provisions in the *Succession Law Reform Act*:[88]

> 31. Except when a contrary intention appears in the will, where a devise or bequest is made to a child, grandchild, brother or sister of the testator who dies before the testator, either before or after the testator makes his or her will, and leaves a spouse or issue surviving the testator, the devise or bequest does not lapse but takes effect as if it had been made directly to the persons among whom and in the shares in which the estate of that person would have been divisible,

---

[87] See *Re Millar* (1927), 60 O.L.R., 434 (H.C.), [1927] 3 D.L.R. 270 ; *Re McLean* (1969), 1 N.B.R. (2d) 500 (*sub nom. Larlee v. Earle*), 4 D.L.R. 617 (C.A.). The latter case held that a gift of shares could not be saved by legislation very similar in wording to s. 31 of the *Succession Law Reform Act* because the shares were subject to a single contract for sale, but destined in the will to several different beneficiaries. Since the legislation spoke of a monolithic "right", it could not be divided and sub-stitued for the shares that were to be sold. The gift adeemed.

[88] *Succession Law Reform Act*, R.S.O. 1990, c. S.26.

     (a) if that person had died immediately after the death of the testator;

     (b) if that person had died intestate;

     (c) if that person had died without debts; and

     (d) if section 45 [preferential share] had not been passed.

 I direct my Trustee to deliver to my beloved son, ROBERT, my antique gold watch that I received from my grandfather, and that has been in the family for seven generations.

In this clause, if Robert dies before the will-maker, the cherished item would end up passing to Robert's wife. A simple condition would prevent that mishap.

Solution: Item falls to residue if the donee has predeceased:

 I direct my Trustee to deliver to my beloved son, ROBERT, if he survives me, my antique gold watch that I received from my grandfather, and that has been in the family for seven generations.

Solution: Item passes to another if the donee has predeceased:

 I direct my Trustee to deliver my antique gold watch that I received from my grandfather, and that has been in the family for seven generations, to my beloved son ROBERT or, if he dies before me, to my beloved son, STEPHEN, if he survives me.

Methods of Dividing Personal Effects

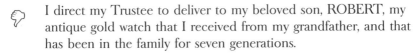 **Where the effects are to be divided among more than one person (such as the will-maker's children), there is often a desire that they be divided equitably. Beware, however, of obligating the executor to make an equitable distribution, since it may give disgruntled beneficiaries an opportunity to challenge the executor's administration of the estate.**

Error #4: No Method for Distributing Personal Effects

The maxim "equality is equity" requires executors to divide equally among a class of beneficiaries where there is no other indication of how things are to be divided. In the following clause, the operation of the maxim could require every article to be valued and an exact division by value to be made among the children.

 I direct my Trustee to divide all articles of personal, domestic, household, and garden use or ornament, including consumable stores and all automobiles, boats, motors, and accessories owned by me at my death equally among my children alive at my death.

The simplest ways of dividing personal effects are (1) by agreement and (2) by the trustees' discretion, or by some combination.

Solution: Division by Agreement, Then by Trustee's Discretion

 I direct my Trustee to divide all articles of personal, domestic, household, and garden use or ornament, including consumable stores and all automobiles, boats, motors, and accessories owned by me at my death among my children alive at my death as they agree or, failing agreement, as my Trustees in their absolute discretion deem advisable, and not necessarily in equal shares.

If the children are the Trustees, however, some other method is needed. A slightly more formal division is by lot.

Solution: Division by Lot

I direct my Trustee to divide all articles of personal, domestic, household and garden use or ornament, including consumable stores, automobiles, boats, motors and accessories owned by me at my death among my children alive at my death by lot. My Trustee shall list all the articles to be divided, and shall draw straws to determine the order in which my children shall choose. My Trustee may sort the articles to be divided into as many lots as he wishes. Each child shall then choose, in the order determined, one lot of articles by rotation, until all of the lots have been selected.

Solution: Division by Lot (Alternate version)

 My Trustees shall divide all articles of a personal, domestic and household use or ornament belonging to me at my death including consumable stores, and all automobiles, vehicles, boats, motors and accessories then owned by me among my children alive at my

death as my children agree. But if there is disagreement, I recommend to my Trustees a process of dividing by lots, as follows. My
Trustees shall sort the articles to be divided into as many lots as
they deem appropriate. My eldest living child has the first choice to
select a lot, followed by my second eldest living child, after which a
new round will begin again with my eldest living child and so on,
until all the lots have been selected. My Trustees shall transfer the
articles so chosen to the child who has chosen them.

Sometimes, the will-maker prefers to let friends and relations choose
for themselves some small piece or memorabilia that may have memories
for the chooser.

Solution: Right to Select

My Trustees shall allow my friend, POLLY, if she survives me, to
choose any articles of personal and household use or ornament
belonging to me at my death and shall transfer the articles chosen
to POLLY. The articles which POLLY does not want shall become
part of the residue of my estate.

**Solution: Right to Select One or More Articles
(More than One Person)**

My Trustees shall allow each of my cousins, ANNE, BETTY and
CAROL, who survives me, to choose three articles of my jewellery
belonging to me at my death, and shall deliver each piece so
chosen to the person who has chosen it. The jewellery which my
cousins do not choose shall become part of the residue of my
estate.

Where the will holds the residue in trust for a spouse, specify on what
terms the personal effects are held, and also that they are not to be sold.

Solution: A Spousal Trust

> I direct my Trustees to hold for my husband, GREGORY, during his lifetime, if he survives me, all articles of personal, domestic and household use or ornament belonging to me at my death, and to allow GREGORY the use of these articles. During his lifetime, GREGORY shall maintain the articles in good repair and insure them to their full value in the name of my Trustees. My Trustees shall not be responsible to see to the repair or insurance of these articles, nor shall they be liable for any loss or damage if GREGORY fails to maintain the insurance on them or to maintain them in good repair. Upon GREGORY's death or whenever he advises my Trustees in writing that he no longer desires the use of these articles, or whenever my Trustees in their absolute discretion determine that GREGORY no longer has use of them, these articles shall be divided among my children then alive as they may agree, or, failing agreement, as my Trustees in their absolute discretion deem advisable, not necessarily in equal shares. Any articles not transferred to my children shall fall into and form part of the residue of my estate to be dealt with as part of it.

Where the will-maker is concerned that the division among children may be unequal, it is possible to equalize the shares, without binding the trustee to an impossible task.

Solution: Equalizing Shares

> My Trustees shall dispose of all articles of personal, domestic and household use or ornament belonging to me at my death, including consumable stores, and all automobiles and accessories then owned by me, among my children XENA, YENTA and ZOE alive at my death, as my Trustees in their absolute discretion deem advisable. If in my Trustees' opinion the distribution results in a significant inequality among my children, then my Trustees, in their absolute discretion, may adjust the proportions of the residue of my estate in order to pay a larger portion to any child who in their opinion has been disadvantaged in the distribution. I do not intend to achieve absolute equality of benefit among my children, but only to relieve a significant disproportion. The decision of my Trustees as to when a disproportion is significant shall be final and binding on all parties.

Error #5: Stickers

Will-makers are sometimes advised — not, we trust, by solicitors — to go around their house and stick labels on property indicating to whom they would like it delivered.

> I direct my Trustees to deliver to my niece JANET, if she survives me, those of my oil paintings as shall be marked with labels bearing her name.

There are two problems here:

- The reference to property that "shall be marked" is or can be taken to be a reference to an event that will happen after the making of the will. Thus, when he places stickers on the paintings, the will-maker is making a testamentary action without proper formalities. That portion of the will could not be admitted to probate.[89]

- More practically, stickers are far too easily removed or moved after the death of the will-maker to be reliable.

However, will-makers do not have to list everything they want to make a specific gift of in the will. Such lists are cumbersome. For a will-maker who wants to designate property to a number of beneficiaries, the memorandum is better than stickers. Generally, such a memorandum can be either legally binding or precatory.

Solution: A Legally Binding Memorandum Incorporated by Reference

> My Trustees shall dispose of all articles of personal, domestic and household use or ornament belonging to me at my death, including consumable stores, and all automobiles and accessories then owned by me, in accordance with a memorandum which I have signed prior to this Will, which memorandum is incorporated into this Will.

The memorandum will not cover all of the will-maker's personal effects, so the will should go on to state what to do with any items not disposed of in the memorandum.

> Any remaining articles not disposed of in accordance with the memorandum shall be divided among my children and grandchildren alive at my death as my Trustees in their absolute discretion deem advisable, and not necessarily in equal shares.

---

[89] *In the Goods of Sunderland* (sub nom. *Re Sunderland*) (1866), 1 L.R.P.& D. 198.

If you use a legally binding memorandum, make sure it is dated so the evidence is available to establish that it was prepared before the will. Clients are often dilatory about producing the memorandum. If you have set a day for the will to be executed, verify in advance that the memorandum exists and is described with sufficient particularity to make it identifiable when the will is probated. Store the memorandum with the original will.

To be binding, a memorandum must be incorporated by reference; that is, it must be created before the will, and referred to specifically in the will. Like a list, it may generate repeated revisions to the will, as family members fall in and out of favour, or the will-maker changes his mind. A precatory memorandum, that does not bind the executors, can be changed from time to time without necessitating a change in the will. It does not bind the executors, but acts as a guide to their discretion.

 Including items of significant value on a precatory memorandum is an invitation to litigation.[90]

Solution: A Precatory Memorandum for Spouse

 My Trustees shall give to my wife, LORNA, if she survives me, all articles of personal, domestic, household and garden use or ornament belonging to me at my death, including consumable stores and including all automobiles, boats, motors and accessories owned by me at my death. I am confident, and it is my wish, that LORNA give effect to any memorandum I may leave with my Will as to the disposition of these articles and to any wishes I may have expressed orally regarding their disposition.

Solution: A Precatory Memorandum for Trustee

 My Trustees shall dispose of all articles of personal, domestic and household use or ornament belonging to me at my death, including consumable stores, and all automobiles and accessories then owned by me, among my children, LINDA, MARILYN and NANCY, alive at my death as my Trustees in their absolute discretion deem

---

[90] See *Thomas Estate v. Gay* (1996), 14 E.T.R. (2d) 229, (sub nom. *Re Thomas Estate*) 11 O.T.C. 16.(Ont. Gen. Div.).

advisable. Without in any way limiting the discretion of my Trustees hereunder, it is my wish that in disposing of these articles they give effect to my wishes as expressed in any memorandum which I may leave with this Will.

Trustees can only exercise discretion within the binding terms of the gift. Thus, the clause above would be incorrect if the will-maker intended to put anyone other than Linda, Marilyn or Nancy in the memorandum.

Solution: A Power of Appointment

My Trustees shall dispose of all articles of personal, domestic and household use or ornament belonging to me at my death, including consumable stores, and all automobiles and accessories owned by me at my death, among my children and grandchildren then alive as my daughter, ELIZABETH, may appoint.

Error #6: Non-existent Memorandum

If there is any doubt at all that there will be a memorandum, refer to it as a possibility, not a certainty.

My Trustees shall divide my Personal Effects among my children and grandchildren alive at my death as my Trustees in their absolute discretion deem advisable. I desire that in disposing of these articles, my Trustees give effect to the wishes expressed in *a memorandum that I will make and store with this Will.*

My Trustees shall divide my personal effects among my children and grandchildren alive at my death as my Trustees in their absolute discretion deem advisable. It is my intention to leave a memorandum of my wishes regarding the disposition of these articles, and I request my Trustees to abide by the wishes I have expressed there. If I do not leave a memorandum or to the extent that the memorandum I leave does not deal with any articles, I desire my Trustees to abide by the wishes I have expressed in other ways, including orally, and I express my confidence that my Trustees will follow what they are able to determine about my preferences and will exercise their best judgment.

Error #7: Trustees Lack Discretion

If the memorandum does not cover all of the will-maker's personal effects, it may be necessary to deal with them by default. Often the clothing and linen of a deceased without close family will be donated to charity. This would, however, be improper if the Trustees do not have the requisite discretion.

Solution: A Wide Discretion to go with the Memorandum

> My Trustees shall divide and distribute any remaining articles not disposed of in accordance with my memorandum among those persons and institutions that my Trustees in their absolute discretion appoint. I authorize my Trustees, in their discretion, to sell any of these articles and the proceeds of the sale shall fall into the residue of my estate.

Error #8: No Allowance for Minor Beneficiaries

Sometimes, especially when there are minor beneficiaries, it may be necessary to store personal effects for some time. Consider the liability of the trustee, in that case, if the goods are damaged or lost.

Storage and Insurance

> If my Trustees are of the opinion that any child or other issue of mine is not old enough to make use of an article, they may sell the article and add the proceeds of sale to the residue of my estate or hold the article until the child for whom it is set aside is old enough to make use of it.

Sometimes the will-maker is uncertain about the ultimate destination of a particular piece of property.

My Trustees shall deliver my grandmother's wedding ring to a member of my family who will keep it as an heirloom and not sell it.

My Trustees shall deliver to my sister, TINA, my grandmother's wedding ring. TINA is not to sell the ring, but to keep it as an heirloom to be given from one generation to another. When she no longer needs it, TINA shall deliver the ring to her eldest daughter, or to her eldest granddaughter if she has no daughter.

The ring shall be kept in the family and passed to the eldest
female child of each generation.

You cannot give something outright and then purport to place restrictions on its use. The instruction in the clause above would not be binding,
so the drafter should make that clear.

Solution: Expression of Wishes

> I intend that my grandmother's wedding ring not be sold for any
> reason whatsoever, but that it be kept as an heirloom given from
> one generation to another. I therefore direct my Trustees to deliver
> my grandmother's wedding ring to my daughter, TERESA, if she is
> alive at my death. It is my wish that:
>
> (a) My daughter, TERESA, give the ring to her eldest
>   daughter, if she has a daughter, or to her eldest grand-
>   daughter if she has no daughter, or to her eldest son, if she
>   has no granddaughter.
>
> (b) If TERESA has no children, she may give the ring to
>   whatever member of our family she thinks fit.
>
> (c) I wish that whenever possible the ring stay with a female
>   relative, rather than a male relative, and that each person
>   to whom the ring passes be given, with the ring, a copy of
>   this clause of my Will.

Solution: Early Distribution

> My Trustees shall hold all my jewellery for my niece HANNAH, if
> she survives me, until she attains the age of eighteen (18) years,
> when my Trustees shall deliver the jewellery to her. My Trustees
> may at any time or times that they in their discretion consider it
> advisable, deliver any or all of the jewellery to my niece for her own
> use absolutely, and I authorize my Trustees to deliver the jewellery
> to HANNAH and accept her receipt as a sufficient discharge not-
> withstanding that she may not have attained the age of majority. If
> HANNAH should die before having received all of my jewellery,
> any jewellery she has not received shall fall into the residue of my
> estate.

Solution: Option to Sell

> If my Trustees are of the opinion that any child or other issue of mine is not old enough to make use of an article, they may either sell the article and add the proceeds of sale to the residue of my estate or hold the article until the child is old enough to make use of it. I authorize my Trustees to deliver any article to my children or other issue of mine whenever my Trustees consider advisable notwithstanding that the recipient may be under the age of majority. The actual delivery of any article to a recipient shall be a complete release to my Trustees.

Solution: Gift to Parent

> My Trustees may deliver any article being held for a minor beneficiary to a custodial parent or guardian of the minor, or to another person to whom my Trustees in their absolute discretion deem it advisable to deliver the article, whose receipt shall discharge my Trustees.

Error #9: No Shipping and Handling

If personal effects are going to beneficiaries at a distance, consider who will pay the cost of transporting them.

Solution: Shipping Paid by Estate

> (a) My Trustees shall divide my Personal Effects among my children and grandchildren alive at my death as my Trustees in their absolute discretion deem advisable.
>
> (b) It is my intention to leave a memorandum of my wishes expressed regarding the disposition of these articles, and I request my Trustees to abide by the wishes I have expressed there. If I do not leave a memorandum or to the extent that the memorandum I leave does not deal with any articles, I ask my Trustees to abide by the wishes I have expressed in other ways, including orally, and I express my confidence that my Trustees will follow what they are able to determine about my preferences and exercise their best judgment.

> (c) If my Trustees are of the opinion that any child or grandchild of mine is not old enough to make use of an article, they may either sell the article and add the proceeds of sale to the residue of my estate or hold the article until the child pr grandchild is old enough to make use of it.
>
> (d) I authorize my Trustees to deliver any article to my children or grandchildren whenever my Trustees consider it advisable notwithstanding that the recipient may be under the age of majority. The actual delivery of any article to a recipient shall be a complete release to my Trustees.
>
> (e) *I direct my Trustees to pay all necessary packing, insurance and delivery charges, if any, incurred in connection with giving effect to the provisions of this paragraph, out of the capital of my general estate, and also the costs (if any) of insurance and storage pending the delivery.*

Error #10: Animal Trusts

Despite the great emotional importance they may have for a will-maker, animals have no legal status as persons, but are considered property. Many will-makers will want to make some provision to ensure that an animal is cared for properly. It is, however, an error to treat an animal as a proper object of a trust.

 I direct my Trustees to set aside $10,000 in trust for my dog Digger for his natural life, to ensure that he is properly and humanely cared for.

Solution: (A Fixed Sum):

> My Trustees shall deliver to my wife's friend CARL, if he survives me, any pet or pets owned by me at the time of my death, and if he agrees in writing to provide lifetime care for my pet or pets, to pay the sum of $15,000 to CARL for each pet owned by me at the time of my death for which he assumes the care, to assist CARL in ensuring that my pet or pets are well fed and cared for and receive all necessary veterinary services. In the event that CARL dies before me or survives me but is unable or unwilling to care for my pet or pets, this legacy shall lapse and fall into the residue of my estate.

Sometimes, more elaborate provisions must be made for the care of animals.

Solution: A Discretionary Amount:

(a) If either of my dogs, namely TWEEDLEDUM and TWEEDLEDEE, being two spayed female Chocolate Labradors (hereinafter referred to as "the Dogs") is alive at my death, my Trustees shall give the Dogs to OONA, if she survives me. If more than one of the Dogs is then alive, OONA must agree in writing to take both Dogs, and that they will be kept together. Oona must agree in writing that any Dog she receives under this clause of my Will, will be provided with good care for that Dog's natural life.

(b) If OONA is unable or unwilling for any reason, including being unable to give the written assurances required, to accept the Dogs on these terms, I direct my Trustees to use their discretion in finding a person or persons (the "Replacement Owner") to provide a suitable home for the Dogs. Anyone who, in the opinion of my Trustees, is able to provide a good home for the Dogs and to give the same assurances required of OONA shall be the Replacement Owner and shall take the gift intended for OONA. My Trustees shall deliver the Dogs to OONA, or to the Replacement Owner as soon as is reasonably possible after receiving the written assurances. I direct that all shipping, insurance, board and other charges incidental to the delivery of the Dogs to OONA or to the Replacement Owner shall be borne by my estate.

(c) It is my intention by making these provisions, to ensure that the animals that have given me so much affection and joy are treated well and have as happy an existence as possible. While I recognize that this gift does not impose any obligation on OONA or the Replacement Owner, it is my strong wish and desire that OONA or the Replacement Owner care for the Dogs personally, and I trust that whoever takes on the care of my beloved animals will follow my wishes in this regard.

(d) My Trustees shall set aside and invest a sum (the "Dogs' Fund") in an amount that my Trustees, in the exercise of an absolute discretion, consider to be sufficient to provide full care for the Dogs for the remainder of their natural lives.

(e) My Trustees shall hold and keep invested the Dogs' Fund, and so long as there is a Dog alive, my Trustees shall pay to OONA or the Replacement Owner as much of the net income and capital as they, in their absolute discretion, consider necessary or advisable for the care of the Dogs. Any net income that is not paid out in any year shall be accumulated and added to the capital of the Dogs' Fund. After the expiration of the maximum period permitted by law for the accumulation of income, all of the net income shall be paid to OONA or the Replacement Owner.

(f) My Trustees shall not be required to see to the carrying out of the undertakings given by OONA or the Replacement Owner, whose receipt for any payments shall be sufficient discharge to my Trustees.

(g) On the death of the survivor of the Dogs, my Trustees shall pay the portion of the Dogs' Fund then remaining to X Charity for Dogs. The receipt of the person purporting to be the proper officer of a charitable institution is a sufficient discharge to my Trustees who need not see to the application of the funds.

Error #11: Missed Opportunities

Some assets, like art work and environmentally sensitive real estate, can generate a tax receipt, but only if they are donated to the proper place.

Solution:

 I authorize my Trustees to donate to Waterside University or any other institution or public authority in Canada designated at the time of the donation under subsection 26(2) of the *Cultural Property Export and Import Act*, R.S. 1985, c. C-51, as amended from time to time such of my material as described in the preceding paragraph as they in their absolute discretion see fit.

Error #12: Legal Restrictions Ignored

Some assets, like firearms, cannot be transferred without proper authorization. Others, like alcohol, are subject to restriction on how they can be transferred. Generally, a careful drafter will provide the tools necessary to assist the executor in making the transfer of articles of personal property as painless as possible. There is an additional benefit, in that extra costs associated with the acquisition of permits and licences may be obviated.

Solution:

> I direct my Trustees to transfer any firearms I own at my death (the "Gun Collection") to my brother, JOE, if he survives me. But if JOE is not able to accept the Gun Collection within a reasonable period following my death for any reason, including his inability or unwillingness to obtain the requisite certificates and registrations, my Trustees shall arrange for the sale of the Gun Collection and shall pay the net proceeds, if any, to JOE if he is then alive. It is my wish that if my gun collection must be sold, my Trustees consult with JOE in order to arrange for the sale of my Gun Collection.

Shares are an example of a kind of personal property that may be subject to restrictions on how they can be disposed of, for example in a shareholder agreement.

If your client is a shareholder in a small business, ask about shareholder agreements, and make sure you review the agreement for restrictions on the transfer of shares that may conflict with the plan in the will.

Solution: Shareholder Agreement

> An agreement (the "Shareholder Agreement") was made by me, my spouse, SONJA, and my brother, PHILLIP, being all of the shareholders of Holdco, on the 11th day of May, 2003 with regard to the shares of Holdco. Pursuant to the terms of the Shareholder Agreement, I direct that my Trustees shall abide by and be bound by the terms of the Shareholder Agreement and my Trustees shall have whatever powers are necessary or desirable to give effect to the terms of the Shareholder Agreement.

Solution: Gift of Shares

(a) My Trustees shall transfer to my daughter RACHEL, if she survives me, all of my shares of Holdco, together with all dividends accruing thereon at my death. If at my death these shares, as the result of any change in the capital structure or sale of the company to any other company, are replaced by a different capital holding, then the bequest shall take effect as if it had been a bequest of the replacement capital holding or holdings which, as the result of the change, took the place of the original shares.

(b) If, for any reason, including the terms of the Shareholder Agreement, my shares in Holdco may not be transferred to RACHEL, I direct my Trustees to take whatever steps are required to see that there vests in RACHEL an interest in Holdco equivalent as to value and control to that which, at the time of my death, I enjoyed by virtue of my ownership of my shares in Holdco, or the equivalent value from the residue of my estate.

Since the estate will bear the cost of any capital gains tax on the shares, the will-maker should consider how to deal with the tax burden.

CHAPTER 6

REAL PROPERTY

Real estate is one of the most difficult assets to plan for, since sentimental attachments can drive drafting to undesirable levels of complexity.

Theoretically, describing real property should be a simple matter; directly-owned interests are described by a municipal address or legal description, condominiums are described in terms of units (do not forget parking units and common elements) and co-operatives are left as shares in the corporation with the devise subject to the by-laws and any shareholders' agreements.

Error #1: Mis-description of the Real Property

Unfortunately, describing real property turns out to be tricky and a significant source of potential liability. You must first establish that the will-maker has an interest that can be devised. In *Earl v. Wilhelm*,[91]for example, a gift of land to a beneficiary failed because the property was held by a corporation. The beneficiaries that received the shares of the corporation got the land, and the solicitor was found liable to the disappointed beneficiary. In *Carr-Glynn v. Frearsons*,[92] a will devised property to a beneficiary which turned out to be held jointly with right of survivorship with another party. On appeal, the court criticized the lawyer for allowing the client to execute the will when the nature of ownership was unknown, notwithstanding that the 81-year-old client was cautioned as to the impact of rights of survivorship and actually refused the lawyer's offer to search title.

Solution: Review the Deed

Clients are often uncertain of particulars with respect to their real estate holdings. The deed *must* be reviewed.

 If you acted on the real estate purchase, it should be fairly easy to access the deed and any other information required. Otherwise, the clients should be told, in preparation for their meeting, to bring a copy of all deeds that can be located. In Chapter Thirteen "Practice Matters", you will find a list that can be mailed or e-mailed to a client setting out the documents that clients should bring with them to the meeting.

---

[91] Earl v. Wilhelm (1997), 18 E.T.R. (2d) 191 (Sask. Q.B.), reversed in part (2000), 31 E.T.R. (2d) 193, 183 D.L.R. (4th) 45 (Sask. C.A.), affirmed (2000) 34 E.T.R. (2d) 238, 199 Sask. R. 21, [2000] 9 W.W.R. 196, 232 W.A.C. 21 (Sask C.A.).

[92] Carr-Glynn v. Frearsons, [1999] Ch. 326, [1999] 2 W.L.R. 1046, [1998] 4 All E.R. 225, [1999] 1 F.L.R. 8, (1998) 148 N.L.J. 1487, [1998] N.P.C. 136.

Error #2: "My Principal Residence", "My Home", "My Matrimonial Home" or "My House"

These terms can be problematic if a client owns more than one real property at his death. "Principal Residence" may mean the city dwelling or a cottage property. Similarly, "my Home" and "my House" do not necessarily refer to one real property. There can be more than one "Matrimonial Home" as defined in the *Family Law Act*[93]. The following clause may include a cottage and a house, even though the will-maker expected to own only one property as his death and intended to pass only one residence:

 My Trustees shall transfer any residence that I may own and be using at my death to my daughter, MARGARET, if she survives me.

Solution: Provide Description

If the will-maker has or may have more than one residence, provide the municipal address of the property, and describe it with sufficient accuracy to exclude other properties.

 My trustees shall transfer any interest I may own at my death in my residence, being the lands and buildings municipally known as 78 Water Street, Elora, Ontario ("the Residence") to my daughter, MARGARET, if she survives me.

Solution: Define Terms

The clause above will not, of course, suffice if the named property has been replaced by a later residence. If the will-maker wants to cover any residence she has at the time of her death, and only that piece of property, the term can be defined.

 My trustees shall transfer to my daughter, MARGARET, if she survives me, any interest I may own at my death in the lands and buildings I own and use as my primary personal residence at my death ("the Residence"). For clarity, "primary personal residence" does not to include any cottage, farm, cabin, or chalet, or any residence located outside Ontario.

---

[93] Section 18. (1) reads: "Every property in which a person has an interest and that is or, if the spouses have separated, was at the time of separation ordinarily occupied by the person and his or her spouse as their family residence is their matrimonial home". *Family Law Act*, R.S.O. 1990, c. F.3, as amended.

Error #3: Joint Tenants or Tenants in Common Not Indicated

If real property is devised to two or more people, the clause should set out whether the beneficiaries should receive it as tenants-in-common or as joint tenants.[94]

Subject to a contrary intention, the property will be presumed to be held as tenants-in-common.[95]

Error #4: No Contingency

Some drafters assume that if real property is conveyed to two people as tenants-in-common and one of them dies, the whole property will pass to the survivor. There is no such presumption. The share devised to a beneficiary who dies before the will-maker, as a tenant-in-common, will fail and either be distributed in accordance with the anti-lapse provisions or devolve on an intestacy.[96] A gift of real property to two or more people jointly with right of survivorship, however, signifies that if a beneficiary has predeceased the interest will be divided among the surviving named beneficiaries.

 My Trustees shall transfer any interest I may own at my death in my residence, being the lands and buildings municipally described as 113 Hurst Street, North Bay, Ontario ("the Residence"), to my sister, EMILY, and my brother, BRAD, in equal shares as tenants-in-common.

In this clause, if either Emily or Brad dies before the will-maker, the anti-lapse provisions[97] will apply unless a contrary intention is expressed elsewhere in the will.

Solution: A Contrary Intention

Contents

 My Trustees shall transfer any interest I may own at my death in my cottage, being the lands and buildings municipally known as RR#1,

---

[94] "Share and share alike" refers to ownership as tenants in common

[95] *The Conveyancing and Law of Property Act*, s. 13. (1): Where by any letters patent, assurance or will, made and executed after the 1st day of July, 1834, land has been or is granted, conveyed or devised to two or more persons, other than executors or trustees, in fee simple or for any less estate, it shall be considered that such persons took or take as tenants in common and not as joint tenants, unless an intention sufficiently appears on the face of the letters patent, assurance or will, that they are to take as joint tenants. R.S.O. 1990, c. C.34, as amended.

[96] For further discussion of the anti-lapse rules, see Chapter Seven, "Legacies".

[97] See Chapter Seven "Legacies" for further information on the application of the anti-lapse provisions.

Lake Cushing, Ontario, ("the Cottage Property") to those of my siblings, namely EDWARD, ROBERT, and SUSAN, then alive equally as tenants-in-common; but if two of my siblings die before me, to my sole surviving sibling. If all of EDWARD, ROBERT, and SUSAN die before me, the Cottage Property shall be sold and the net proceeds added to the residue of my estate to be dealt with as part of it.

Error #5: Contents Ignored

If the will-maker wants the contents of a residence to be included, the will must say so. Otherwise, the contents will be disposed of in accordance with the personal property or residue provisions.

If my spouse, BERTRAM, dies before me, my Trustees shall transfer any interest I may own at my death in my cottage located on Herring Lake, being the lands and buildings municipally known as 111 Herringway Drive, Muskoka, Ontario ("The Cottage") together with all household goods, chattels, furniture and articles of domestic and household use or ornament located in and used in connection with it to my son, CARL, if he survives me. Any items of personal property not delivered to CARL pursuant to this paragraph shall be dealt with under paragraph X of this my will.

If the will-maker intends to include boats or other equipment not actually kept in the building, they should be specified. The personal effects can also be more generally described as those "in or about or belonging to or generally used in connection with" the cottage.

On occasion, personal property not normally located in a home or cottage is located there on the will-maker's death. This personal property will be included in the gift. You should draw to your client's attention the possibility that if he tends to leave the golf cart at the cottage, it may be included in the gift of the cottage to his non-golfing son.

Error #6: Unequal Treatment

Some will-makers want to leave a cottage or home to one child but ultimately desire that these benefits be equalized among the children. A hotchpot provision effects this result. The same device, used when the will-maker wants advances, debts or other interests in property taken into account, is discussed in Chapter Seven "Legacies". The beneficiary "brings into account and hotchpot" the fair market value of the item received.

Here is an example of how the hotchpot calculation works. The value of the realty (in this instance) is added to the value of the residue. This inflated residual amount is then divided among the beneficiaries in accordance with the will's terms. Once the respective amounts are determined for each beneficiary, based on this inflated amount, the value of the item is deducted from the real estate beneficiary's share.

Facts	Residual beneficiaries: Samantha, Arthur and Thomas equally
	Value of real estate transferred to Thomas: $200,000.00
	Value of the residue of estate: $1,000,000.00
Step #1:	Value of residue + Value of real estate = $ 1,200,000.00
Step #2:	1,200,000.00 divided by 3 = $400,000.00
Step #3:	Thomas' share ($400,000.00) - Value of real estate ($200,000.00) = $200,000.00
Result:	Thomas receives $200,000.00 of the residue and the real estate (worth $200,000)
	Samantha receives $400,000.00 of the residue
	Arthur receives $400,000.00 of the residue

 Hotchpot does not work for beneficiaries who are not also residual beneficiaries. It also cannot be used if the value of the real property exceeds the value of the beneficiary's share in the residue.

Solution: Realty brought into Hotchpot

 II. My Cottage — If my daughter, MARGARET, survives me, my Trustees shall transfer to MARGARET any interest I may own at my death in my cottage located on Lake Agatha, being the lands and building municipally known as 111 Petty Coat Lane, Surrey, Ontario ("the Cottage").

    III. Residue

       (a) My Trustees shall divide the residue of my estate among my children alive at my death in equal shares per capita.

> (b) Before taking any share in the residue of my estate under clause III(a) of this will, my daughter, MARGARET, shall bring into account and hotchpot without interest the value as at my death of the Cottage received pursuant to paragraph II of this Will.

Error #7: Income Tax Liability

If realty that does not qualify as a principal residence is devised to a spouse or to a qualifying spousal trust, capital gains tax is deferred. Otherwise, it must be paid by the estate. Most will-makers assume that the recipient of real property will be responsible for the capital gains tax. It is the estate, however, and not the beneficiary, who bears the tax.

For example, if a cottage is conveyed to a child and there is $100,000.00 in taxable capital gains, the residue of the estate will be responsible for the payment. If the residue is being divided among 4 children equally, they will all bear the tax — even though the property is only to be received by one child. If this result accords with the intent of the will-maker, fine. But if the will-maker wants the child receiving the property to be responsible for the capital gains tax, it must be dealt with in the will.

☞ **There is no capital gain if a principal residence is transferred. Before 1972, there was no capital gains tax at all; and between 1972 and 1981, married couples could each claim one tax-exempt principal residence. Since 1982, married couples have been allowed only one principal residence, and since 1993, the same restriction applies to common-law couples. Accordingly, each married couple is entitled to designate a tax-exempt principal residence for the period 1972 to 1981, and each common-law partner for the period 1972 to 1993. Therefter, only one principal residence can be designated per family unit.**

Solution: Liability Hotchpot

If the devisee of the real property is also a residual beneficiary, the tax liability can be brought into account and hotchpot. You must make certain, however, that the value of the recipient's share of the residue will be sufficient to offset the capital gains tax.

Solution: Reimbursement of Tax or Sale of Property

> If my daughter, MARGARET, survives me, my Trustees shall transfer to MARGARET any interest I may own at my death in my cottage, being the lands and buildings municipally known as 111 Lakeview Street, in the Township of Tiny, Ontario ("The Cottage") on condition that MARGARET pay any income tax owing by my estate as a consequence of the deemed disposition of the Cottage at my death (the "Tax Liability"). I direct my Trustees as soon as possible following my death to determine the Tax Liability of the Cottage and to notify MARGARET in writing of the Tax Liability. If payment of the Tax Liability is not made to my Trustees within one (1) month from the date that my daughter, MARGARET, receives the notice of the Tax Liability, my Trustees shall sell the Cottage and pay the net proceeds to my daughter, MARGARET.

Error #8: Mortgage Ignored

The *Succession Law Reform Act* sets out that, subject to a contrary intention, any mortgage debt is to be paid out of an interest in the land.[98] Thus, if the will-maker wants the mortgage to be discharged by the estate, she must say so in the will.[99]

Solution: Mortgage Discharged By Estate

> If my spouse, ANNE, survives me for a period of thirty (30) days, my Trustees shall transfer to ANNE, free of any mortgages, whatever lands and buildings I own and which I am using as my primary personal residence at my death.

Solution: Devise Subject to Mortgage

> If my spouse, ANNE, survives me for a period of thirty (30) days, my Trustees shall transfer to ANNE, subject to any mortgages, whatever

---

[98] See s. 32(1): "Primary liability of real property to satisfy mortgage — Where a person dies possessed of, or entitled to, or under a general power of appointment by his or her will disposes of, an interest in freehold or leasehold property which, at the time of his or her death, is subject to a mortgage, and the deceased has not, by will, deed or other document, signified a contrary or other intention, (a) the interest is, as between the different persons claiming through the deceased, primarily liable for the payment or satisfaction of the mortgage debt; and (b) every part of the interest, according to its value, bears a proportionate part of the mortgage debt on the whole interest." R.S.O. 1990, c. S.26, as amended.

[99] *Perry v. Hicknell* (1981) , 34 O.R. (2d) 246, (sub nom. *Re Hicknell*) 10 E.T.R. 288, 128 D.L.R. (3d) 68 (H.C.).

> lands and buildings I own and which I am using as my primary
> personal residence at my death.

House Trusts

As house trusts are usually administered for several years, they must be
carefully crafted to anticipate future complications. Financial considerations,
such as the availability of funds to provide for a property's upkeep and the
responsibility for ongoing expenses, must be examined. Considerations of a
non-financial nature are also critical; family dynamics and the residence and
mobility of the beneficiaries all play a part. Flexibility should be one of the
hallmarks of a house trust. Never recommend a trust where it is unlikely that
the estate (or beneficiaries) will be able to support it. It may be very difficult
for the trustees to have the life tenant vacated from the premises.

Error #9: A White Elephant

As people are living longer, house trusts should set out what will happen
if a life tenant is no longer able or willing to reside in a house held for him.
Older precedents regularly fail to consider this contingency, with the result
that the life tenant cannot afford to move out of the house that he is no
longer able to enjoy.

 If my spouse, ADAM, survives me, my Trustees shall hold any
interest I may own at my death in my residence, being the lands
and buildings municipally known as 123 Appleway Street, Sudbury,
Ontario ("the Premises"), until the death of ADAM. Upon the
death of the survivor of ADAM and me, the Premises fall into and
form part of the residue of my estate to be dealt with as part of it.

Solution: Disposition Date With Contingency

When should the house be sold? Here are some events that might
trigger the sale: remarriage or cohabitation of the life tenant, her failure to
pay for expenses, or her desire to move to a smaller home or a facility with
nursing care. Some will-makers also give the trustee a power to sell the
property at their absolute discretion — just in case the house trust is creating unworkable problems.

 The Disposition Date shall be the first to happen of:

>   (i)   The date of the death of my spouse ADAM;
>
>   (ii) The date ADAM remarries or begins cohabiting in a con-
>   jugal relationship;

> (iii) The date upon which ADAM (or his attorney for property or guardian for property is ADAM does not have capacity) notifies my Trustees in writing that he no longer requires the Premises held for him;
>
> (iv) The date when, in the opinion of my Trustees, ADAM has failed to pay any expenses with respect to the Premises as provided in paragraph X; and
>
> (v) The date my Trustees in their absolute discretion determine that the Premises should be sold.

Error #10: Expenses Not Assigned

Real property is expensive to maintain, and the trust should set out who will be responsible for expenses. There are two kinds: capital expenditures and expenses for maintenance and day-to-day upkeep. The life tenant is generally responsible for maintenance and day-to-day upkeep, but not for capital expenditures. In the case of a cottage trust, however, a will-maker may want his estate to be responsible for all expenses, for fear that the life tenant cannot afford the upkeep.

Error #11: No Discretion To Set Aside Expense Fund

Trustees should always have the ability to set aside an expense fund if a house trust may be administered under the terms of a will. Without this authorization, there is no express authority to set aside the funds. Even if the life tenant is directed to pay for upkeep, there may be necessary capital expenditures. The Trustees should also be empowered to access the expense fund for the payment of upkeep if the life tenant fails to pay and the estate becomes legally responsible. At a minimum, a house fund should: (1) provide for the accumulation of unused income, (2) provide for the payment of income after 21 years,[100] and (3) dispose of the fund on the termination of the house trust.

 If there will likely be disagreement among beneficiaries and trustees, you may want to specify a minimum amount to be set aside in the house fund.

---

[100] If it is not possible that the fund will be held for more than 21 years from the death of the will-maker, a provision for the payout of income after the accumulations period is not necessary.

Error #12: House Expenses Paid from Spousal Trust

If the trustees are not empowered to carve out an expense fund from the residue initially, they must pay the expenses directly out of the residue. If the residue is held in a spousal trust, however, the payment of expenses out of the spousal trust may taint it, since someone other than the spouse — the capital beneficiaries — may benefit.

Error #13: Right to Collect Rents or Right to Occupy

Is the beneficiary a true life tenant, with the right to collect the rents if he ceases to occupy the property, or does he only have a right to occupy the property? The will should make it clear.

If the beneficiary (usually a spouse) who is to reside in the property may want to move to a different home, you must give the trustees the ability to sell and purchase a substitute property. The will-maker may also want the trustees to be able to lease a residence and use any proceeds from selling the house to pay rent. This power may be particularly useful if the will-maker wants her spouse to be provided with a residence, but the trustees find they do not have sufficient funds to maintain the house she owned at death.

Solution: House Trust

I. If my spouse, ANNE, survives me, my Trustees shall hold for ANNE, rent free during her lifetime, whatever interest I own at my death in my residence being the lands and buildings municipally known as 33 Moster Street, Elliot Lake, Ontario ("the Residence").

Right to Collect Rents, Purchase Replacement Residence or Lease a Residence

II. My Trustees may, upon the written direction of ANNE (or her attorney for property or guardian of property if ANNE does not have capacity):

a. lease all or any portion of the Residence on the terms and conditions that my Trustees determine and ANNE approves, and pay the net rentals to ANNE in convenient instalments to be determined by ANNE and my Trustees;

b. dispose of the whole or any part of the Residence on the terms that my Trustees determine and ANNE approves. My Trustees shall invest the net proceeds of the sale and pay the net income therefrom to or for ANNE in convenient instalments as my Trustees determine; or

c. sell the Residence and with the net proceeds of sale provide by purchase or lease another residence for ANNE from time to time. If prior to ANNE's death, any part of the net proceeds of sale is not used for the purchase or lease of a residence for ANNE it shall be added to the Residence Fund (as defined hereunder).

Expenses

III. ANNE shall, while she resides in the Residence, be responsible for the payment of all expenses for the following purposes:

a. insurance of the Residence against damage or destruction as well as public liability indemnity insurance;

b. local and municipal taxes related to the Residence;

c. maintenance costs and ordinary repairs;

d. the cost of all utilities and telephone expenses; and

e. all common element, usage or like fees; (collectively referred to as the "Residential Payments").

Expense Fund

IV. My Trustees may set aside a sum of money from the capital of my general estate ("the Residence Fund") which, in their absolute discretion, they consider sufficient to pay all capital expenses with respect to the Residence. My Trustees shall pay the capital expenses and may in their absolute discretion pay any Residential Payments which are not paid by ANNE and become the responsibility of my estate and any expenses or rent for a replacement residence under clause 2.c. The Residence Fund shall be held on the following terms:

a. Any expenses may be paid out of the net income or the capital of the Residence Fund as my Trustees in their absolute discretion determine. b. Any net income not used in any year shall be accumulated and added to the capital of the Residence Fund;

b. After the expiration of the maximum period permitted by law for the accumulation of income, any net income from the Residence Fund not used to pay Residence Expenses in any year shall be paid to ANNE.

Disposition

V. Upon ANNE's death, the Residence, any net proceeds from the sale of any residence and the balance of the Residence Fund shall be divided equally among my children alive at ANNE's death; but if any child of mine is not then living and leaves issue then living, that deceased child's share shall be divided among his or her issue in equal shares *per stirpes*, subject to clause X dealing with the shares of grandchildren.

Estate to Pay Expenses

Variations of House Trust Solution

1. Right to Occupy Only

If my spouse, ANNE, survives me, my Trustees shall allow ANNE, during her lifetime, the exclusive use and occupation rent free of whatever interest I own at my death in my home being the lands and buildings municipally known as 33 Moster Street, Elliot Lake, Ontario ("the Residence").

No further reference would be made to additional powers.

2. Estate to Pay Expenses

While my Trustees are holding the Residence, all taxes, insurance, all ordinary and structural repairs, condominium management fees or costs, mortgage interest and principal payments, the cost of all utilities and any and all other charges or amounts necessary for the general upkeep of the Residence (collectively the "Residential Payments") shall be paid by my estate.

Gift Over To Unascertainable Beneficiaries

Error #14: Saunders v. Vautier

Sometimes, the house trust can be terminated at an earlier time, if all the beneficiaries of the trust are ascertainable and competent.[101] The will-maker may not be overly concerned if the trust is terminated at an earlier time if everyone is in agreement.

 If my spouse, BETTY, survives me, my Trustees shall hold the Property as a home for BETTY, until the Disposition Date. Upon the Disposition Date, my Trustees shall transfer the Property to my son, BARRY, *if he is alive at my death.*

If an earlier termination is undesirable, however, there should be a gift over to unascertainable beneficiaries.

Solution: Gift Over To Unascertainable Beneficiaries

> If my spouse, BETTY, survives me, my Trustees shall hold the Property as a home for BETTY, until the Disposition Date. Upon the Disposition Date, my Trustees shall transfer the Property to my son, BARRY, if he is alive at the Disposition Date, but if he dies before the Disposition Date, to his issue then living in equal shares *per stirpes.*

Error #16: Neglecting the Long View

In certain instances, will-makers want the trustees to hold a property (usually a cottage that has sentimental value) for several generations.

Solution: Cottage Trust for Children and Grandchildren

> I. My Trustees shall transfer any interest I may own at my death in my cottage, being the lands and buildings municipally described as RR#1, Lake Cushing, Ontario ("the Cottage") as a cottage residence for my children and grandchildren until the Disposition Date as defined below.
>
> II. Disposition Date — The Disposition Date shall be the first of the following dates:

---

[101] See the discussion on the Rule in *Saunder v. Vautier* in Chapter Nine "Trusts".

a. The date upon which my children living at the time direct my Trustees in writing to sell the Cottage;

b. The date when there is no longer a grandchild of mine alive and under the age of thirty (30) years; and

c. The date that my Trustees in their absolute discretion consider it advisable to dispose of the Cottage.

III. Cottage Expenses — While the Cottage is held by my Trustees, all taxes, insurance, all ordinary and structural repairs, condominium management fees or costs, mortgage interest and principal payments, the cost of all utilities and any and all other charges or amounts necessary for the general upkeep of the Cottage (collectively the "Cottage Expenses") shall be paid by my estate.

IV. Cottage Fund — My Trustees may set aside a sum of money from the capital of my general estate ("the Cottage Fund") which, in their absolute discretion, they consider sufficient to pay all the Cottage Expenses.

a. the Cottage Expenses shall be paid out of the income or the capital or both of the Cottage Fund as my Trustees in their discretion deem advisable;

b. any income not used in any year shall be accumulated and added to the capital of the Cottage Fund;

c. After the expiration of the maximum period permitted by law for the accumulation of income, any net income from the Cottage Fund not used to pay Cottage Expenses in any year shall divided equally among my issue in equal shares per stirpes.

d. Any amount remaining in the Cottage Fund on the Disposition Date shall fall into the residue of my estate to be dealt with as part of it.

V. Disposition

a. If the Disposition Date is the date upon which my children alive at the time direct my Trustees in writing to sell the Cottage [or the date my Trustees in their absolute discretion consider it advisable to dispose of the Cottage,] my Trustees shall sell the Cottage and divide the net proceeds of the sale among my issue in equal shares

> *per stirpes* subject to the trusts set out for my grandchildren in paragraph X below.
>
> b. If the Disposition Date is the date when there is no longer a grandchild of mine alive and under the age of thirty (30) years, my Trustees shall convey the Cottage to my grandchildren then alive as tenants in common.

Error #16: House Trust for Minor Children

On occasion, a parent desires that the home be retained for his children. Such a trust, however, is often impractical. Unless a guardian agrees to continue to reside in the home with the children, chances are that the home will be sold. In each of the following provisions, there is sufficient flexibility that the trustees at their discretion can retain the real estate or sell it — depending on the needs of the children and their overall circumstances from time to time.

Solution: House Trust for Mother and Minor Children

> I. If my spouse, ANNE , dies before me or dies within a period of thirty (30) days after my death, and if at the death of the survivor of ANNE and me any child of mine is alive and under the age of eighteen (18) years, my Trustees may, in their absolute discretion, hold any interest I may own at my death in lands and buildings which at the time of my death are used by me as family residences ("the Residence"), as a home for my mother SARA, my children alive from time to time, or any one or more of them until the Disposition Date.
>
> II. The Disposition Date shall be the first to happen of the following events:
>
> a. the date that there is no longer a child of mine alive and under the age of 18 years; and
>
> b. the date my Trustees in their absolute discretion determine that it is no longer advisable to hold the Residence.
>
> III. [Assignment of Expenses] See above.
>
> IV. [Creation of Residence Expense Fund] See above.
>
> V. Disposition —

a. If the Disposition Date is the date there is no longer a child of mine alive and under the age of eighteen (18) years, on the Disposition Date, my Trustees shall transfer the Residence to my children alive on the Disposition Date in equal shares as tenants in common.

b. If the Disposition Date is the date my Trustees in their absolute discretion determine that it is no longer advisable to hold the Residence, on the Disposition Date, my Trustees shall sell the Residence and the net proceeds of sale shall fall into the residue of my estate to be dealt with as part of it.

Solution: House Trust for Minor Children

I. If my spouse, ANNE, dies before me or dies within a period of thirty (30) days after my death, and if any child of mine is then alive and under the age of eighteen (18) years, my Trustees may, in their absolute discretion, make whatever provisions (if any) for a home for any one or more of my children, including those over the age of eighteen (18) years, that my Trustees in their absolute discretion consider advisable from time to time. My Trustees may retain any property I own at the time of my death or obtain another property by purchase or by rental.

II. [Assignment of Expenses] See above.

III. [Residence Expense Fund] See above.

Error #17: Missed Opportunities

There are other ways to handle real property than an outright gift or a trust. For those will-makers who do not want to transfer a real property or set up a house trust, the following are further options:

Solution: Declaration of Intent Regarding Right of Survivorship

If jointly held property is intended to pass by right of survivorship, and that has been taken into account in planning the will, a statement to that effect may prevent misunderstanding and suspicion when the estate comes to be administered. The statement should be placed prior to the executor's appointment, since the realty does not pass through the will.

> I confirm my intention that if my spouse, BRUCE, survives me any beneficial interest I may have in any residence that I hold jointly with BRUCE as a joint tenant shall, along with legal title, pass to BRUCE as sole owner by virtue of right of survivorship.

Solution: Direction To Sell Real Property

A direction to sell a certain property is sometimes included to compel a sale and forestall the potential for conflict among family members.

> If my spouse, BRUCE, dies before me, my Trustees shall sell whatever residence I may own or have an interest in and be occupying as my home at my death and shall add the net proceeds from the sale to the residue of my estate to be dealt with as part of it.

Solution: Option to Purchase

An option to purchase is given to beneficiaries if the will-maker suspects that one beneficiary, more than another, will want the cottage (it is usually a cottage), but does not want to presume the beneficiary's preference with an outright gift.

> I. If my son, BRUCE, survives me, my Trustees shall obtain an appraisal by a certified independent real estate appraiser (the cost which is to be paid by my estate) as soon as possible following my death of the fair market value of any interest I may own at my death in my cottage being the lands and buildings municipally known as 56 Lakeside Drive, RR#1, Whitefish Lake, Ontario, ("the Cottage"). Upon receipt of the appraisal, my Trustees are to notify BRUCE that he has the option, on the terms set out in the notice, to purchase the Cottage for the fair market value as appraised. The option to purchase the Cottage shall be exercised by BRUCE by notice in writing to my Trustees within ninety (90) days following the date on which notice was given to BRUCE by my Trustees.
>
> II. If BRUCE fails to exercise to exercise the option to purchase the Cottage provided for in this paragraph or notifies my Trustees in writing that he does not want to purchase the Cottage, BRUCE's right to exercise this option shall expire and the Cottage shall fall into and form

part of the residue of my estate. If BRUCE exercises the option set out in this paragraph, my Trustees, subject to the receipt of the purchase price and subject to the usual adjustments, shall convey to BRUCE all my interest in the Cottage. The purchase price, subject to the usual adjustments, shall be added to the residue of my estate to be deal with as part of it.

You can set out a formula or process to be used to ascertain the fair market value. However, if a trust company is acting as trustee, the strategy must be approved ahead of time to avoid conflict with the trustee's internal policies.

Solution: In Kind Option with Hotchpot

Sometime, the will-maker wants the beneficiary to be able to apply his or her share of the residue to the purchase of the real property.

I. If my son, CALVIN, survives me, as soon as possible following my death my Trustees shall obtain an appraisal by a certified independent real estate appraiser (the cost which is to be paid by my estate) of the fair market value of any interest I may own at my death in my cottage being the lands and buildings municipally known as 987 Hobson's Lane, RR#1, Buck Lake, Ontario, ("the Cottage").

II. Upon receipt of the appraisal, my Trustees are to notify CALVIN that he has the option, on the terms set out in the notice, to receive the Cottage as part of his distributive share in the residue of my estate. The option to receive the Cottage shall be exercised by CALVIN by notice in writing to my Trustees within ninety (90) days following the date on which notice was given to CALVIN by my Trustees.

III. If CALVIN does not exercise the option to receive the Cottage, or advises my Trustees in writing that he does not want to receive the Cottage as part of his distributive share of the residue, the option to receive the Cottage shall cease and the Cottage shall fall into the residue of my estate to be dealt with as part of it.

IV. If CALVIN exercises this option, my Trustees shall convey the Cottage to CALVIN, subject to the following provisions. The fair market value of the Cottage shall be brought into account and hotchpot in the division of the residue of my estate against CALVIN, but if the fair market value exceed CALVIN's share in the residue of my estate, CALVIN's right to take the Cottage as part of the distributive share of the residue shall be conditional on CALVIN's delivery to my Trustees of a promissory note or notes in an amount equal to the difference between the fair market value and CALVIN's distributive share. The promissory note or notes shall evidence a debt payable in a number of equal annual installments without interest, the number of installments to be determined by my Trustees in their absolute discretion. I authorize my Trustees to assign the promissory note or notes so delivered to the remaining beneficiaries of the residue of my estate in accordance with their proportionate interest in the residue. No promissory note need be secured by a mortgage or other interest in property.

Solution: A Formula for Fair Market Value

For the purposes of this paragraph, the fair market value of my Cottage shall be determined by obtaining two appraisals from certified real estate appraisers, and using the average value given by such appraisers, if the lower appraised amount is within 5% of the higher appraised amount. If there is a disparity in value greater than 5% of the higher amount, then I direct my Trustees to obtain a third appraisal and establish the fair market value of the Cotttage as the average value between the closest two of the three appraisals.

Solution: First Refusal for Each Child In Order of Priority

Where more than one beneficiary may be interested in the property, or where relations are not really harmonious, give beneficiaries the option to purchase a property in an order of priority.

I. If my son, ALFRED, survives me, as soon as possible following my death, my Trustees shall obtain an appraisal by a certified independent real estate appraiser (the cost which is to be paid by my estate) of the fair market value of any interest I may own at my death in my cottage , being the lands and buildings municipally known as RR#1, Thunder Bay, Ontario ("The Cottage") .

II. Upon receipt of the appraisal, my Trustees are to notify ALFRED that he has ninety (90) days to enter into a binding contract to purchase the Cottage for the fair market value asappraised and on such further terms and conditions set out in the notice Failing agreement within ninety days, the option to purchase given to ALFRED shall expire.

III. If ALFRED has given notice in writing that he does not wish to purchase the Cottage, or if his option to purchase has expired, or if for any reason he fails to complete the transaction, my children BRENDA and COLIN, in that order, shall be given the opportunity to purchase the Cottage on the same terms and conditions set forth in the notice given to ALFRED, except that BRENDA and COLIN shall have only thirty (30) days from receiving notice from my Trustees to enter into a binding contract to purchase the Cottage.

IV. Failing agreement within thirty (30) days, the option to purchase given shall expire, and the next in line shall be given the option to purchase on the terms above set out, and so on from time to time.

V. If no child of mine purchases the Cottage as above provided, the Cottage shall fall into the residue of my estate to be dealt with as an original part of it.

VI. For clarity, any child who accepts the option to purchase shall be responsible for the payment of his or her solicitor's fees, disbursements incurred in connection with such transfer, and payment of the land transfer tax and any other taxes which are usually the responsibility of a purchaser. The purchase price, subject to the usual adjustments, shall be added to the residue of my estate to be dealt with as part of it.

CHAPTER 7

LEGACIES

A legacy is a gift of money or money equivalents, as opposed to a bequest (a gift of personal property) and a devise (a gift of real property). Legacies can be general, demonstrative or residual. Residual legacies are discussed in Chapter Seven, "Residue"; in this chapter we will be discussing demonstrative and general legacies.

Error #1: Insufficient Funds

Insufficiency of funds can be a problem with general as well as demonstrative legacies. As clients plan to avoid probate by using joint tenancy and beneficiary designations, they move assets out of the residue of their estate from which they had planned to pay legacies. They are often not aware that they cannot control the destination of these funds by will.

 Make enquiries about the ownership of property and beneficiary designations, and make sure the clients have sufficient funds to pay the legacies they plan to leave. Since they may be tempted to change these arrangements after making the will, include a reference to the fund that is to satisfy the legacies in your reporting letter.

A shortage of funds may also arise because the client has followed a gifting program, rather than waiting for assets to pass by will. Consider using a clause to take into account *inter vivos* gifts. Sometimes a will-maker actually intends to make *inter vivos* gifts, and wants them taken into account in calculating the amount of a legacy.

Solution: *Inter Vivos* Gifts

The following clause restricts the gifts to be taken into account to those made after the will, since all of the gifts from a parent to a child (for example) in the course of the parent's long life are probably too many for any executor to be asked to track down.

 My Trustees, when determining the amount of the legacies in Clause X of this Will, shall take into account the gifts I have made after the date of this Will to any of the legatees (including charitable institutions) named there, and my Trustees shall reduce the amount of any legacy in Clause X by the amount of the gifts received by the legatees from me during my lifetime and after the date of this Will. For greater certainty, it is my intention that each legatee receive in total the amounts provided in Clause X by way of *inter vivos* and testamentary gifts.

If gifts made before the will are to be taken into account, they should be listed and referred to specifically in the will. Clients should also be encouraged to make the executor's life easier by keeping track of post-will gifts in a record book.

Multiple wills can raise similar problems with regard to payment of legacies. If the assets passing in the probatable will are kept minimal (as is intended) but the estate covered by that will contains the liquid assets from which legacies are most easily paid, there may be insufficient assets to pay for the legacies in the probateable will. One solution is to include in the non- probate will a "top-up" provision, so that any deficiency is paid from the other estate.

Solution: Double Wills: Incorporation by Reference (In Non-Probate Will)

> To the extent that the assets of my Primary Estate are insufficient to satisfy in full the legacies set out in Clause X of my Primary Will, I direct the Trustees of my Secondary Estate to satisfy those deficiencies from my Secondary Estate and to that extent I incorporate Clause X of my Primary Will into this my Secondary Will by reference, with the necessary modifications.

Error #2: Double Legacies

Survivorship clauses (typically 30 days) in mirror wills prepared for a couple can result in a legacy being paid out twice if both spouses die within the survivorship period. The following clause, if it appeared in both spouses' wills, would result in $200,000 being paid out to Josiah if the spouses died within 30 days of each other:

> If my spouse HILARY dies before me or survives me, but dies within a period of thirty (30) days from the date of my death, my Trustee shall pay to my friend, JOSIAH SAMUELS, if he is alive at the death of the survivor of me and my spouse, the sum of $100,000.

Solution: Allow for Payment from Both Estates

> If my spouse HILARY dies before me or survives me but dies within thirty (30) days after my death, my Trustees shall pay to my friend, JOSIAH SAMUELS, if he is living at the death of the survivor of HILARY and me, the sum of $100,000; but if HILARY and I die within thirty (30) days of each other, and as a consequence JOSIAH SAMUELS is also entitled to receive the sum of $100,000 in HILARY'S Will, I direct that the legacy here provided for be reduced to $50,000, it being my intention and expectation that in those circumstances the legacy will be paid equally from the two estates; but if the gift from HILARY'S estate is more or less than $50,000, the amount payable from my estate shall be adjusted so that the total sum of $100,000 is paid to my friend JOSIAH SAMUELS from the two estates.

Solution: Modified Survivorship Clause

The same problem will arise if the survivorship provision is contained in a general clause later in the will. In that case, the general survivorship clause should be modified so that it does not apply to any paragraph dealing with a legacy.

> (a) In this Will and any Codicil, all references to an interest passing to a beneficiary include a condition that the beneficiary must survive the date of my death by thirty (30) clear days, failing which the gift shall not pass to the beneficiary and this Will and any Codicil shall be construed as if the beneficiary had died before me. For greater certainty, phrases such as "dies before me" or "survives me" shall include the condition of survivorship by thirty (30) clear days.
>
> (b) Wherever I have made a gift to a person whose will contains an identical gift (of the same amount to the same person or institution) to a gift in my Will, however, if I die within thirty (30) days of the death of that person, or in circumstances where the order of our deaths cannot be determined, the identical gift shall be made once only either out of that person's estate or out of my estate, and I direct my Trustee to make such arrangements as are necessary and advisable to give effect to that intention.

Solution: Refer to the Complementary Will (Trustee's Discretion)

> I wish to advise my Trustee that my husband HUBERT's Will makes provision for a similar legacy to that here provided. If my husband HUBERT and I die within thirty (30) days of each other or in circumstances such that the order of our deaths cannot be determined, we intend that legacy to be paid once only either out of my husband's estate or out of mine, and I direct my Trustee to make such arrangements as are necessary to give effect to that intention.

Error #3: Lapsing Gifts

A gift to a person who has died before the will-maker usually fails. As a drafter, you have to know what your client intends in that event.

My Trustees shall pay the following cash legacies as soon as possible after my death:

(a) to my sister ANNA, the sum of $10,000;

(b) to my friend BETTA, the sum of $10,000; and

(c) to my friend CORA, the sum of $10,000.

If a beneficiary has predeceased, her legacy will lapse, unless: (1) it is a residual gift, (2) a contrary intention appears in the will,[102] or (3) it is saved by s. 31 of the *Succession Law Reform Act* (the "anti-lapse provisions").[103] The following gift might have unintended consequences if the named sister died before the will-maker.

My Trustees shall pay the sum of $150,000 to my sister CHAR-LOTTE SIMPKINS, in recognition of the many years she has stood

---

[102] One common law exception to the doctrine of lapse holds that a will-maker who leaves a legacy to someone to whom she owed a moral obligation does not intend it to lapse, so the gift will pass to the estate of the predeceased legatee. See *Re Mackie* (1986), 54 O.R. (2d) 784, 28 D.L.R. (4th) 571, 22 E.T.R. 66 (H.C.J.). See also T.G. Youdan, Annotation, "The Doctrine of Lapse: The Ambit and Applicability of Common Law Exceptions" (1980), 6 E.T.R. 95.

[103] Substitutional gifts — Except when a contrary intention appears by the will, where a devise or bequest is made to a child, grandchild, brother or sister of the testator who dies before the testator, either before or after the testator makes his or her will, and leaves a spouse or issue surviving the testator, the devise or bequest does not lapse but takes effect as if it had been made directly to the persons among whom and in the shares in which the estate of that person would have been divisible,

(a) if that person had died immediately after the death of the testator;

(b) if that person had died intestate;

(c) if that person had died without debts; and

(d) if section 45 had not been passed.

R.S.O. 1990, c. S.26, s. 31, as amended.

by me, and to compensate her for the hardship she has endured at the hands of her despicable husband.

By operation of the "anti-lapse" provisions in the *Succession Law Reform Act*, the gift in the clause above might actually go to the husband in question, if Charlotte died before the will-maker.

Solution: A Gift Over

The commonest way to indicate a contrary intention and defeat the operation of the anti-lapse provision is by a gift in favour of an alternate beneficiary if the first beneficiary has predeceased — a so-called "gift over".

> My Trustees shall pay the sum of $150,000 to my sister CHAR-LOTTE SIMPKINS, in recognition of the many years she has stood by me, and to compensate her for the hardship she has endured, but if my sister CHARLOTTE should die before me, the gift shall be paid to her children alive at my death in equal shares per capita.

Sometimes, however, no alternate beneficiary is intended, and the gift is intended to fail completely if the named beneficiary cannot take it.

Solution: Intentional Lapse

> In recognition of the many years she has stood by me, and to compensate her for the hardship she has endured, my Trustees shall pay the sum of $150,000 to my sister CHARLOTTE SIMP-KINS, if she survives me.

Finally, it is possible to put in a general clause that ousts the operation of the anti-lapse provisions.

Solution: A General Lapse Clause

While the following clause may express the general intention of most will-makers, it should not be relied upon for dealing with lapse and anti-lapse problems. It is better to name the person who will take on a gift over or specify that the gift fails if the donee dies first.

> I intend that my Will be construed without regard to section 31 of the *Succession Law Reform Act*, so that no spouse or relation of anyone entitled under my Will shall be entitled to benefit by virtue of section 31. This paragraph shall be construed to be the contrary intention referred to in section 31 of the *Succession Law Reform Act*.

Charitable Gifts

By all means, encourage your client to make charitable gifts where appropriate. For such gifts to be valid, however, they must either be outright gifts to a recognized charitable institution, or trusts for a charitable purpose. Not every worthy cause, however, is legally charitable. The definition of charity derives from a statute passed in the reign of Elizabeth I,[104] and although it has been somewhat rationalized and modified over time,[105] it does not necessarily comply with what a will-maker of the twenty-first century thinks of as charitable. Which of the following would you think are charitable?

- assisting immigrant women to network and find jobs[106]

- a newspaper run by and for homeless people[107]

- a club for model railroaders[108]

- providing free internet access to the public.[109]

Since your and your client's instincts about what is charitable may not be the same as the courts' rulings, it is important to go back to the definition of charity, if you are setting up a charitable trust. As set out in *Pemsel:*

> "'Charity' in its legal sense comprises four principal divisions: trusts for the relief of poverty; trusts for the advancement of education; trusts for the advancement of religion; and trusts for other purposes beneficial to the community, not

---

[104] *The Statute of Charitable Uses,* 1601 (43 Eliz. 1, c. 4). The Preamble to the Statute, which was passed to prevent the misuse of funds that had been meant for charitable purposes and misappropriated, lists those purposes for which gifts said to be charitable had been given. It is, thus, a list of what donors in the 16th Century were willing to give money for: "some for Releife of aged impotent and poore people, some for Maintenance of sicke and maymed Souldiers and Marriners, Schooles of Learninge, Free Schooles and Schollers in Universities, some for Repaire of Bridges Portes Havens Causwaies Churches Seabankes and Highewaies, some for Educacion and prefermente of Orphans, some for or towards Releife Stocke or Maintenance for Howses for Correccion, some for Mariages of poore Maides, some for Supportacion Ayde and Helpe of younge Tradesmen, Handiecraftesmen and persons decayed, and others for releife or redemption of Prisoners or Captives, and for aide or ease of any poore Inhabitants concerninge paymente of Fifteenes, settinge out of Souldiers and other Taxes ...."

[105] In particular in *The Income Tax Commissioners v. Pemsel,* [1891] A.C. 531 (H.L.), sub nom. *Pemsel v. Special Commissioners of Income Tax,* [1891] 3 T.C. 53, [1891-94] All E.R. 28 (H.L.).

[106] *Vancouver Society of Immigrant and Visible Minority Women v. M.N.R.,* [1999] 1 S.C.R. 10, 59 C.R.R. (2d) 1, [1999] 2 C.T.C. 1. Not charitable.

[107] *Briarpatch Inc. v. The Queen* (1996), 96 D.T.C. 6294, [1996] 2 C.T.C. 94, 197 N.R. 229 (Fed. C.A.). Not charitable.

[108] *National Model Railroad Association, Seventh Division, Pacific Northwest Region v. Minister of National Revenue* (1989), 89 D.T.C. 5133, 3 E.T.R. 268, [1989] 1 C.T.C. 300 (Fed. C.A.) Charitable.

[109] *Vancouver Regional Free Net Assn. v. M.N.R.* (C.A.), [1996] 3 F.C. 880. Charitable.

falling under any of the preceding heads … within the spirit and intendment of the Statute of Elizabeth."[110]

Error #4: Purpose Gifts

My Trustees shall hold the sum of $10,000 and use the interest thereon for the promotion of interest in the Middle Ages, and in particular in the music, dance, clothing, weaponry, and social customs prevalent in Europe from approximately 600 A.D. to 1500 A.D.

This gift purports to create a perpetual gift for a purpose that is not charitable. Although the *Perpetuities Act*[111] would convert it into a power of appointment, allowing the trustees to hold the sum for twenty-one years, and pay it to those beneficiaries they choose, such a clause is an invitation to litigation, especially if significant sums are involved.

Error #5: Improperly Named Charity

Like any other beneficiary, a charity must be correctly named.[112]

☞   **The correct name of a charity can be ascertained by asking the client to provide a receipt from the charity, if they are regular donors, or by checking the website for Canada Customs and Revenue Agency (www.ccra-gcra.ca) under Charities. The website now provides the annual reports of charities online, as well.**

---

[110] *Pemsel v. Special Commissioners of Income Tax, supra,* note 4.

[111] (1) A trust for a specific non-charitable purpose that creates no enforceable equitable interest in a specific person shall be construed as a power to appoint the income or the capital, as the case may be, and, unless the trust is created for an illegal purpose or a purpose contrary to public policy, the trust is valid so long as and to the extent that it is exercised either by the original trustee or the trustee's successor, within a period of twenty-one years, despite the fact that the limitation creating the trust manifested an intention, either expressly or by implication, that the trust should or might continue for a period in excess of that period, but, in the case of such a trust that is expressed to be of perpetual duration, the court may declare the limitation to be void if the court is of the opinion that by so doing the result would more closely approximate the intention of the creator of the trust than the period of validity provided by this section.

(2) To the extent that the income or capital of a trust for a specific non-charitable purpose is not fully expended within a period of twenty-one years, or within any annual or other recurring period within which the limitation creating the trust provided for the expenditure of all or a specified portion of the income or the capital, the person or persons, or the person or person's successors, who would have been entitled to the property comprised in the trust if the trust had been invalid from the time of its creation, are entitled to such unexpended income or capital. R.S.O. 1990, c. P.9, s. 16, as amended.

[112] *Re Carrick* (1929), 64 O.L.R. 39, [1929] 3 D.L.R. 373 (H.C.) This case involved a gift to named charities that did not exist, although at least three charities with similar names did. The court considered the surrounding circumstances.

Solution: A Cy-Près Clause

Charities change, and it is prudent to include a cy-près clause in the gift, if the client would want the gift to go to a successor institution.[113] Cy-Près powers are often combined with a provision that allows the executors to accept the receipt of the treasurer of the institution.

Failure of Charitable Gift

> For the purposes of my Will:
>
> a. The receipt of any person purporting to be the proper officer of the charitable institution named as a beneficiary shall be a full discharge to my Trustees.
>
> b. If, at the time of distribution, any institutional beneficiary never existed or has amalgamated with another institutional beneficiary or has changed its name or objects, any provision for it in my Will shall not fail and I declare that, notwithstanding the particular form of the bequest, my paramount intention is to benefit a general charitable purpose and my Trustees are hereby authorized in their absolute discretion to pay the bequest to the institutional beneficiary that they consider most closely fulfils the objects I intend to benefit.

If the client does not want the gift to go to any other charity, it would be an error to use the clause above. Instead, the will should direct that the gift will fail if the named charity no longer exists.

> If, in the discretion of my Trustees, any charitable institution named in my Will has ceased to operate (as distinct from changing the location of its work, changing its name, amalgamating or uniting with another organization or organizations) the gift to the organization shall lapse.

There are tax advantages to donating appreciated securities to a charity, rather than cash. A charitable legacy should advert to the possibility of making such a gift. Although the trustee would have the power to make a gift in kind, the charity might be unwilling to accept marketable securities if the will made a gift of cash.

---

[113] Dennis O'Connor, "Cy-Près Doctrine: Whose Money is it Anyway?", *Adventures in Charitable Giving* (Ottawa: Community Foundation of Ottawa-Carleton, 1999).

Cash or Securities

> My Trustees shall pay to ABC Charity $10,000 in cash or the equivalent value in marketable securities or cash and marketable securities in such proportions as my Trustees in their absolute discretion decide. I declare that the receipt of the person purporting to be the proper officer of the charitable institution shall be a full discharge to my Trustees.

Solution: Gift of Pledged Amounts

> I authorize my Trustees at any time within the five (5) years following my death to exercise their absolute discretion to pay some or all of the amounts that I have pledged to charitable organizations or for charitable objects that are left unpaid at my death, notwithstanding that the pledges may not be legally binding on my estate.

A charity can be named as a beneficiary under a registered plan such as a Registered Retirement Savings Plan. The resultant tax credit, generated by the gift, can relieve some of the tax generated on the sheltered plan by the inclusion of the plan proceeds in income in the year of death.

Legacies in lieu of Compensation

A legacy left to the person who is named as executor will be presumed to be in lieu of compensation.[114] The presumption is easily ousted by any indication of a contrary intention.[115]

> I declare that any benefits received by my friend WINSTON under Clause X of my Will shall be in addition to any remuneration to which he may be entitled for services rendered as a Trustee for my estate.

Demonstrative legacies

A demonstrative legacy is one that is to be paid from a specified fund, rather than being paid from the general residue of the estate.

---

[114] F. S. Baker, ed., *Widdifield on Executor's Accounts,* 5th ed. (Toronto: Carswell, 1967), pp. 311-12.

[115] See *Re Hill Estate,* (1994), 46 A.C.W.S. (3d) 804 (Ont. Gen. Div.).

From the principal and interest due or to become due to me from JOHN SMITH under a mortgage on the premises known as 42B Baker Street in the sum of $40,000 principal, I give the sum of $20,000 to my nephew HENRY, if he survives me, and I give the balance of the principal and the accrued interest to my niece HETTY, if she survives me.

While it usually makes no difference, the demonstrative legacy will not abate with general legacies, but depends on the existence of the fund from which it is to be satisfied. On the other hand, if the fund is not sufficient to pay the demonstrative legacies, they will abate, rather than coming out of residue.[116]

Annuities

An annuity is a particular form of legacy. A direction to an executor to purchase an annuity does not require the beneficiary to take the annuity in that form: she is entitled to request the cash instead.[117]

 If my sister EDITH is alive on Division Day, my trustees shall purchase from the residue of my estate an annuity from a Canadian life insurance company, in an amount sufficient to pay to my sister EDITH or for her benefit, the sum of $2,000 monthly, commencing no later than the second month after my death. On the death of my sister EDITH, if I have issue then living any amount remaining in the guarantee period on the annuity shall be payable to my niece ANGELA.

Since annuities are sometimes used to produce a stream of income for a beneficiary who is thought not to be able to handle lump sums, this result can be avoided by specifying that the annuity be a Government of Canada annuity, which is inalienable.[118]

 If my sister EDITH is alive on Division Day, my Trustees shall purchase an annuity from the Government of Canada under the *Government Annuities Act*, R.S.C. 1970, c. G-6, in an amount sufficient to pay to her or for her benefit, $2,000 monthly, commencing

---

[116] In the law of wills, the principle of "abatement" dictates that the residuum of a testator's estate must firstly be exhausted to pay the testator's debts, secondly to pay general legacies, thirdly to pay demonstrative and specific legacies, and finally to effect devises. Each payment ratably diminishes the amount available to satisfy the lower-ranking categories of payments: *Mickler v. Larson Estate* (2000), 35 E.T.R. (2d) 258, 198 Sask. R. 146 (Q.B.).

[117] See *Lotzkar v. McLean* (1979), 15 B.C.L.R. 259, 6 E.T.R. 245 (B.C.S.C.).

[118] *Re Boxall; Jensen and Cunningham v. Wutzky*, [1946] 3 W.W.R. 413, [1947] 1 D.L.R. 66 (Sask. C.A.).

> no later than the second month after my death. On the death of my sister EDITH , any amount remaining in the guarantee period on the annuity shall be payable to my issue in equal shares per stirpes.

If it is desirable to control the payments out of the fund, a trust may be a better vehicle. Occasionally, an estate has a number of small trusts that are expensive and cumbersome to administer. A clause allowing an annuity to be purchased in their place will assist the executor in winding up the estate. It is important that the clause specify that the annuity be for life or a term of years; otherwise it may be taken to be a perpetual annuity, to which the rule in *Saunders v. Vautier* applies, allowing the beneficiary to take the whole of it immediately.

Optional Annuity

> I direct my Trustees to purchase an annuity for life or for a term of years for any beneficiary, whenever the cost of administration of any trust fund maintained by my Trustees on behalf of that beneficiary has, in the opinion of my Trustees, become excessive compared to the capital and income in the fund.

Perpetuity Clause

Perpetuity Problems

This is not the place for a full discussion of the so-called Rule against Perpetuities.[119] Actually, the rule itself is quite simple: the difficulty comes in working out its application to any particular set of facts. The common-law rule holds that any interest that will not certainly vest within the perpetuity period is void from the start. The period is the extent of a life-in-being plus 21 years. The *Perpetuities Act* has mitigated the rule by allowing a "wait-and-see" approach to gifts that might or might not vest in the period, by creating presumptions about when persons can be deemed to bear children, and by allowing a class to be split, so that some of the gifts can vest, even if they do not all vest. If this is confusing to you, you are probably in the majority. When you are drafting, the golden rule is that whenever gifts are postponed for a period that may be more than 21 years, you must run a perpetuities check. The following is a clause that may assist.

---

[119] See Thomas G. Feeney, *The Canadian Law of Wills*, 3rd ed. (Toronto: Butterworths, 1987), Ch. 9 for a good discussion in detail of the rule.

Notwithstanding anything in my Will, any interest in my estate directed to be held for the benefit of any person shall vest absolutely in the person for whom the interest is held and who, immediately before such vesting, is entitled to receive the income from that interest, on the earlier of the following two dates:

> (a) the date upon which the person is entitled absolutely to that interest, or
>
> (b) the last day of the period which is the longest period under which vesting may be lawfully postponed.

Conditions   If your client instructs you to make gifts conditional, you will have to ensure that the condition proposed will be valid. While most conditions are innocuous, some are contrary to public policy. As a solicitor, you must make clear to your client that even a private document may have such conditions invalidated. The gift will then pass without any conditions, which is probably exactly what your client does *not* intend. A condition is generally contrary to public policy if it requires the beneficiary to commit a prohibited act, or prevents her from doing her duty, including the duty of a parent.[120]

Conditions based on religious and national distinctions are not considered contrary to public policy, unless they contravene an actual statute. A client who wishes to make discriminatory conditions, however, should be warned that conditions that run contrary to Charter values may be vulnerable to attack.

Error #6: *In Terrorem* Clauses

Many will-makers worry about someone challenging their will, or about their spouse remarrying after they are gone. As a result, wills often contain conditions requiring the spouse to remain single, or voiding a legacy if the legatee challenges the will. Such provisions must be drafted with care, because if they are found to be "*in terrorem*" they will fail, with the possible result that the gift passes without any condition.[121] A condition is *in terrorem* if (a) it prohibits either marriage or challenging the will, and (b) it exists solely to prevent the prohibited action.[122] Fortunately, having a clause found

---

[120] See the discussion in Feeney, *supra*, note 15, at pp. 252 ff.

[121] Whether the voiding of the condition results in the gift failing or passing without condition depends on whether it is a gift of personalty or realty, and whether the impugned condition is *malum in se* or *malum prohibitum*. This area of the law is full of fine distinctions that do not always make apparent sense. The best way to avoid having to wander these byzantine pathways is to write conditions that will not be in danger of avoidance.

[122] *Re Kent* [1982] 6 W.W.R. 165, 13 E.T.R. 53, 38 B.C.L.R. 216, 139 D.L.R. (3d) 318 (B.C.S.C.).

to be *in terrorem* is easy to prevent: a gift over to another person or even into the residue of the estate on breach of the condition makes the condition valid. Another device, also effective, is to make an alternative (smaller) gift to the legatee who remarries or challenges the will.[123]

> If your client fears a challenge from someone who would not take on an intestacy (such as a former spouse), it may be better to leave him out of the will altogether than to leave a conditional legacy. A legatee is entitled to see at least part of the will, and to Notice of an Application for Appointment of Estate Trustee with a Will.

Solution: A Condition with a gift over

> If any beneficiary undertakes litigation regarding the provisions in or the validity of my Will other than for judicial interpretation of the Will or for the assistance of the Court in the course of administration, all benefits to which that person would have been entitled shall lapse, and shall fall into the residue of my estate to be distributed as if that person had died before me and had left no issue alive at my death.

Class Gifts   Class gifts are those to be shared by a group of beneficiaries who are identified by characteristic in relation to the donor ("my children", "the nieces of my wife") rather than by name. There may be some confusion if a class gift and a gift to named persons are used together without proper prepositions.

Error #7: Class and Named Gifts Mixed

   My Trustees shall divide the sum of $1,000,000 equally between the children of my niece CANDACE and my nephew KENNETH.

This gift is ambiguous, since it is not clear whether Kenneth or his children are the intended beneficiaries.

Error #8: No Date to Determine the Class

A gift to a class should state the date at which the members of the class are to be determined. In the following clause, the entitlement of a grandchild born between the deaths of the grandparents is uncertain.

---

[123] See Gerry W. Beyer, Rob G. Dickinson, and Kenneth L. Wake, "The Fine Art of Intimidating Disgruntled Beneficiaries with *In Terrorem* Clauses" (1998), 51 SMU L. Rev. 225.

On the death of the survivor of my husband and me, my Trustees shall divide the sum of $40,000 (referred to as the "Grandchildren's Fund") equally among my grandchildren to be used for their education.

The so-called "class closing rules" will be applied when the will does not clearly indicate when the will-maker intends the class to close.

Class Closing Rules

1. Generally, if the gift is:

    a. an immediate gift ("to my grandchildren"):

        i. the class closes on the will-maker's death; but

        ii. if there are no members on the death of the will-maker, the class closes when it is no longer possible for there to be any new members (it is said to "close naturally").

    b. a gift after a prior interest, such as a life interest (to my sister EVELYN for life and after her death "to my grandchildren"):

        i. the class closes when the prior interest terminates (usually on the death of a life tenant, in this case Evelyn);

        ii. if there are no members when the prior interest terminates, the class closes when it is no longer possible for there to be any new members

    c. a conditional gift ("to my grandchildren if they reach the age of 25"):

        i. the class closes on the will-maker's death if any member has fulfilled the condition;

        ii. if there are no members who have fulfilled the condition on the will-maker's death, the class closes when the first member of the class fulfils the condition (as soon as a grandchild turns 25 in this case);

    d. a conditional gift after a prior interest ("to my sister EVELYN for life and then to my grandchildren if they reach the age of 25");

> i. the class closes when the prior interest terminates (Evelyn's death);
>
> ii. if there are no members at that time, it closes when the first member of the class fulfills the condition (as soon after Evelyn's death as a grandchild turns 25).

Solution: A Division Date

> On the death of the survivor of my husband HAROLD and me (the "Division Date"), my Trustees shall divide the sum of $40,000 (the "Grandchildren's Fund") equally among my grandchildren who are alive at the Division Date.

Interest

Interest

The general rule is that interest on a legacy is not payable until the end of the "executor's year", nor can a beneficiary compel the payment of a legacy before the executor's year is out, even when the will directs that it is to be paid "as soon as possible".[124]

> My Trustee shall pay the following legacies without interest:

Forgiveness of Debt I, II, III

Forgiveness of Debt

A debt forgiven is a legacy. A blanket forgiveness may help an executor by relieving her of the obligation to track down loans which, within families, are frequently made casually and without a clear statement about when, if ever, they are to be repaid. If not all debts are to be forgiven, the will should define the ones that are.

> To forgive those debts payable to my estate by my son AARON, but only those debts existing at the date of this Will.

---

[124] *Re Girvin Estate* (1932), 40 Man. R. 481 (K.B.). One exception to this rule is that maintenance for minors may be paid from interest on a legacy where no other provisions have been made for the maintenance of the minor. See *re Mcintyre; Mcintyre V. London and Western Trusts Co.* (1905), 9 O.L.R. 408. K. Thomas Grozinger, "The Ontario Law of Advancement on an Intestacy" (1993) 12 Est. & Tr. J. 396-404.

To forgive those debts payable to my estate by my son AARON, but only those debts that I have not documented or otherwise evidenced in writing.

As a legacy, the forgiven debt is subject to the same rules regarding lapse as any other legacy. The next clause prevents the benefit of the forgiveness from lapsing, or being subject to anti-lapse provisions.

 I forgive my son AARON all sums, whether for principal or interest and whether secured or unsecured, that he may owe me at my death, and I direct my Trustees to cancel all securities, to deliver to my son any evidence of indebtedness, and to pay out of the residue of my estate any expense incidental to this cancellation and discharge. If my son AARON dies before me, his estate shall be entitled to the benefit of this gift as though my son AARON had died immediately after my death.

Equalizing gifts As will-makers seek to avoid probate costs by passing assets outside of their wills (by *inter vivos* gifts, joint tenancy, or by beneficiary designations) it will be increasingly common for there to be a need to equalize these gifts.

Error #9: Fancy arithmetic

Consider Helen, a widow who has two daughters, and about $200,000 in assets, including a house worth $100,000 and $30,000 in RRIFs. She gave Ida $20,000 a few years ago. She has put her house in joint tenancy with her other daughter Judith, and named Ida as the beneficiary under the RRIFs. By her reckoning, Ida is thus getting $50,000, and Judith $100,000, so she wants to include this clause, to equalize the benefits:

 My Trustees shall pay the sum of $50,000 to my daughter Ida, if my house is worth more than $100,000 on the date of my death, and to deduct from this legacy half of the amount of tax payable as a result of the inclusion of the proceeds of my RRIF in income in the year of my death.

Not only is this calculation inelegant, it is also likely to be inaccurate, since it is impossible to know what the values of any of the assets will be at the date of Helen's death.

Solution: Hotchpot I, II, III, IV

> Each beneficiary under my Will shall bring into hotchpot, upon the division of the residue of my estate, all other gifts or benefits received by him or her both during my lifetime and as a result of my death, whether under my Will or by operation of survivorship or by way of a beneficiary designation or otherwise, including the capitalized value of all other payments (such as pension and annuities) that my beneficiaries receive as a result of my death, but the value of any personal articles received by my beneficiaries shall not be brought into hotchpot.

The word "hotchpot" is derived from the term "hodgepodge" and means "the blending and mixing of property belonging to different persons, in order to divide it equally". It is a convenient way to ensure the equal distribution of residue when there have been prior gifts that the will-maker wants to take into account in the division of the residue.[125]

If you use a hotchpot provision, consider whether loans, as well as gifts are to be brought into hotchpot. If they are, they should also be forgiven, or the child to whom the loan was made will "pay" twice — once by having to repay the loan to the estate, and again by having his or her share in the estate reduced.

> I have transferred to my son, DONALD, the sum of one hundred thousand dollars ($100,000), which shall be brought into account and hotchpot without interest by my son, Donald, or by his issue, as the case may be, upon the division of the residue of my estate in accordance with Paragraph X of my Will.

> I declare that the sums, amounting to thirty thousand dollars ($30,000) that I have advanced by way of a loan to my daughter, and any other sums that I may advance to her or for her benefit after the date of this Will, or the amount of them owing to me at my death, shall not be claimed as a debt owing, but shall be brought into account with interest from my death at the rate of X% per annum, by way of hotchpot in the division of the residue of my

---

[125] Corina Weigl, "Hotchpot Clauses: A Primer" Fourth Annual Estate and Trusts Forum, LSUC, 2001; Marni M. K. Whitaker, "Hotchpot Clauses" (1992), 12 E. & T.J. 7.

> estate, by my daughter, her husband, her issue and any other person interested in her share of the residue under the trusts in Clause X.

> I direct that each child of mine shall bring into hotchpot, upon the division of the residue of my estate into the equal parts provided for in paragraph X, the value of the trusts set aside for the children of that child in paragraph Y of my Will, so that the distribution of residue to each child of mine and his or her issue as a group shall be equal.

Another (equally erroneous) instance of the "fancy arithmetic" error occurs when a client is concerned about her surviving spouse making an election under section 6 of the *Family Law Act*.[126] If the will leaves the whole estate to the spouse, of course, this is not an issue, but if the will-maker is married and wants to leave some or all of her estate to, for example, her children, you will have to consider the impact of the *Family Law Act*. Briefly, the Act gives a surviving spouse the right to elect either to take under the will, or to claim an equalization of property. While this resembles the equalization familiar to family law lawyers on separation, there are some significant differences:

1. the valuation date is the day before death,[127] so (for example) 50% of jointly held property will be included in the deceased's net family property, even though 100% will pass to the survivor by right of survivorship;

2. life insurance and pension payments passing to the surviving spouse can be set off against the equalization payment, and in fact can be claimed back by the estate if they exceed the equalization.[128]

---

[126] (1) When a spouse dies leaving a will, the surviving spouse shall elect to take under the will or to receive the entitlement under section 5. R.S.O. 1990, c. F.3, s. 6(1).

[127] "Valuation date" means the earliest of the following dates:

1. The date the spouses separate and there is no reasonable prospect that they will resume cohabitation;

2. The date a divorce is granted;

3. The date the marriage is declared a nullity;

4. The date one of the spouses commences an application based on subsection 5(3) (improvident depletion) that is subsequently granted;

5. The date before the date on which one of the spouses dies leaving the other spouse surviving. R.S.O. 1990, c. F.3, s. 4(1).

[128] Where a surviving spouse,

(a) is the beneficiary,

(continued on next page)

Sometimes, spouses in this situation will try to meet the problem by leaving a legacy to the surviving spouse:

> My Trustees shall pay to my estranged wife STELLA ESTEBAN a legacy in an amount equal to the amount of the equalization payment that, but for this clause, would have been payable to her under s. 6 of the *Family Law Act.*

The clause really accomplishes nothing, since the payment is going to be made in the same amount either way, and it will not avoid the trouble of having to go through an equalization calculation. Worse, however, is the "guestimate" clause.

> My Trustees shall pay to my estranged wife STELLA ESTEBAN if she survives me a legacy in the amount of $100,000, it being my intention that if she makes an election for an equalization payment under s. 6 of the *Family Law Act,* she shall lose this legacy.

Here, not only will the executors have to calculate the equalization payment, but in the end they may have to pay an amount that is greater than the equalization payment.

Solution: A Domestic Contract

By far the best way to preclude an equalization claim (apart from leaving all the estate to the spouse) is by a domestic contract that waives any entitlement to make such a claim. If that is not possible, then one can use life insurance and pension payments to provide disincentives to election. If it still seems possible that an election will be made against the will, however, the will-maker may want to include a clause that specifies the source of any equalization payment.

(continued from previous page)

    (i) of a policy of life insurance, as defined in the *Insurance Act,* that was taken out on the life of the deceased spouse and owned by the deceased spouse or was taken out on the lives of a group of which he or she was a member, or

    (ii) of a lump sum payment provided under a pension or similar plan on the death of the deceased spouse; and

  (b) elects or has elected to receive the entitlement under section 5, the payment under the policy or plan shall be credited against the surviving spouse's entitlement under section 5, unless a written designation by the deceased spouse provides that the surviving spouse shall receive payment under the policy or plan in addition to the entitlement under section 5. R.S.O. 1990, c. F.3, s. 6(6).

If a surviving spouse,

  (a) elects or has elected to receive the entitlement under section 5; and

  (b) receives payment under a life insurance policy or a lump sum payment provided under a pension or similar plan that is in excess of the entitlement under section 5,

and there is no written designation by the deceased spouse described in subsection (6), the deceased spouse's personal representative may recover the excess amount from the surviving spouse. R.S.O. 1990, c. F.3, s. 6(7).

If my spouse becomes entitled to receive an equalization of net family property as defined in the *Family Law Act*, my Trustees shall determine which of my properties shall be transferred to my spouse or sold for the purpose of satisfying any Judgment, Order or Settlement in favour of my spouse.

CHAPTER 8

RESIDUE

Residue

"Residue" means the estate remaining after all estate expenses, debts, and claims have been settled, and specific and general bequests have been made. Residue encompasses "all property within the general description which is not otherwise effectively disposed of by will, and carries all lapsed and void legacies".[129] Until all claims, debts and bequests have been paid, the residue does not come into existence.[130]

Error #1: No Residual Clause

An amateur will-drafter is sometimes so focused on the drafting of specific bequests that she inadvertently omits the residue clause. Even a professional will-drafter who wants to "simplify" the language, usually at the insistence of a client, may delete the term "residue". In its place, terms of a general or non-technical nature are used.

  My Trustees shall pay or transfer the whole of my money to my wife, if she survives me.

"Money", of course, is a compendious term, but might well leave assets unaccounted for.[131]

Solution: A Residue Clause

Although the courts, as a general rule, will presume against an intestacy,[132] their interpretation will be subject to the will-maker's intent.[133] The term "residue" will eliminate uncertainty.

Error #2: "Children per stirpes"

One of the most frequent errors in wills is the incorrect use of the terminology "issue" and "per stirpes". "Per stirpes" means "by the root" or "by representation". "To my issue in equal shares per stirpes" means that the gift is to go to the will-maker's children, but if any child has died before the deceased child's children are to take the child's share, and if any grandchild is also not then alive, his or her children are to take his or her share and so on. "Per stirpes", therefore, implies that a gift will not necessarily be restricted to descendants of the first degree. "Children", however, means *only* descendants of the first degree. Therefore, the term "children per stirpes" is inherently contradictory.[134]

---

[129] *Re Smith Estate*, (1904), 7 O.L.R. 619 (H.C.).

[130] *Lord Sudeley v. Attorney General*, [1897], A.C.11, 66 L.J.Q.B. 21, 75 L.T. 398, 61 L.P. 420, 45 W.R. 305, 13 T.L.R. 38.

[131] See *Perrin v. Morgan*, [1943] A.C. 399, [1943] 1 All E.R. 187 (H.L.).

[132] *Re Campbell*, [1963], 2 O.R. 633, 40 D.L.R. (2d) 681 (H.C.).

[133] A testator may intend to die intestate.

[134] Judges have, of course, struggled to find that meaning is a wonderful assortment of pairings: children per stirpes, brothers per stirpes, grandchildren per stirpes, nieces and nephews per stirpes. The fact that they are able, in a noble attempt to forestall intestacy, to find a meaning for these aberrant formulations should not lead a careful drafter to follow these treacherous paths.

My Trustees shall divide the residue of my estate among my children in equal shares per stirpes.

 My Trustees shall divide the residue of my estate among my brothers and sisters per stirpes.

 My Trustees shall divide the residue of my estate equally among Jane Smith and Mary Smith per stirpes.

Solution: "Issue Per Stirpes" A, B, C

In all of these examples, the problem is solved by recognizing that a stirpital division implies more than one generation — in short "issue". Greatest clarity is maintained when "per stirpes" is restricted to use with the word "issue".

> My Trustees shall divide the residue of my estate among my issue in equal shares per stirpes.

> My Trustees shall divide the residue of my estate among the issue of my mother and father in equal shares per stirpes.

> My Trustees shall divide the residue of my estate equally between those of my children, namely JANE and MARY, alive at my death; but if either of my children dies before me and leaves issue alive at my death, the share to which my deceased child would have been entitled if alive at my death is to be divided among that deceased child's issue in equal parts per stirpes.

Error #3: "Issue" Unqualified

"Issue" *prima facie* means all descendants. If it is not modified with "per stirpes", a gift to "my issue" will mean all of the descendants — children, grandchildren, great grandchildren and all — are to share in the gift.

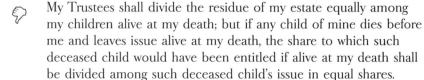 My Trustees shall divide the residue of my estate equally among my children alive at my death; but if any child of mine dies before me and leaves issue alive at my death, the share to which such deceased child would have been entitled if alive at my death shall be divided among such deceased child's issue in equal shares.

Under this clause, lacking the words "per stirpes", all descendants of a deceased child would receive an equal share — grandchildren and great-grandchildren alike.[135]

Solution: Issue Per Stirpes — A Cautionary Tale

A Cautionary Tale   The phrase commonly used in wills is "to my issue in equal shares per stirpes". Experienced estate practitioners thought they knew what it meant. A series of cases, however, has interpreted the phrase "issue per stirpes" to mean that all the living descendants of the testator were to share. In other words, these cases conflated the two terms "issue per stirpes" and "issue per capita" that in best drafting practice had been quite distinct.[136] In *Re Hamel*,[137] for example, the deceased died at age 93, leaving 5 children, 13 grandchildren, 33 great-grandchildren, and the residue of her estate "for my issue alive at my death in equal shares per stirpes ...". The court concluded, on the particular facts, that "per stirpes" should be construed to include all the issue, and divided the estate of $23,107.22 equally among the 51 descendants of the will-maker.

Solution: A General Definition of Issue Per Stirpes

Kenneth J. Webb,[138] suggests the following practice for solicitors in using the term "per stirpes":

1. It should not ordinarily be used at all where the primary beneficiaries are to be issue of the first degree. Children should be called children.

2. It should be confined to gifts over in the event of the death of a child or other beneficiary — in order to cover the possibility, real but not worth long-winded explication, that a child of a deceased beneficiary might have died survived by children. A reference to "issue per stirpes" is a convenient way of briefly incorporating all of these possibilities.

3. If it is necessary to use the phrase, then it should be defined in the will itself so as not to put either the testator or his draftsman at the mercy of a court of construction. I suggest a clause such as the following:

---

[135] As this error is common, case law has interpreted "issue" to mean "children" in certain instances. See *Sibley v. Perry*, (1802) 7 Ves. Jun. 522, 32 E.R. 211.

[136] *Re Harrington* in Ontario initiated the confusion but it was then overturned on appeal. A later case, *Re Alves*, however, reintroduced the problem in Ontario. See *Re Harrington*, unreported, Feb. 21, 1986 (Ont. C.A.), reversing (1985), 30 A.C.W.S. (2d) 125, 4 Ont. Lawyers' Weekly, No. 21, O.J. No. 1046 (H.C.); *Re Alves*, [1992] O.J. No. 3207.

[137] (1995) 9 E.T.R. (2d) 315 (B.C.S.C.).

[138] In "Some Problems in Interpretation and Drafting of Wills" in *Estates and Trusts for the General Practitioner: New Developments* (Toronto, Ont.: The Law Society of Upper Canada, 1992).

Whenever in this Will I have directed a division "per stirpes" among the issue of any person, I intend to designate the children of that person and not his or her remoter issue unless a child of that person is then deceased, in which case I intend that the share to which such deceased child would have been entitled, if living shall in turn be divided equally among his or her children and so on with each representation by a deceased individual at each level by his or her children.

Words such as "alive at my death" or "then living" should not be used in the later part of the disposition when the share is actually being divided. It may result in some confusion so that "issue per stirpes" is mistakenly interpreted to mean "issue per capita".

 My Trustees are to divide the residue of my estate in equal shares among my children alive on the Distribution Date; but if any child of mine predeceases the Distribution Date leaving issue alive on the Distribution Date, the share to which that deceased child would have been entitled if alive on the Distribution Date shall be divided among ("such issue") (or "such issue then alive") (or "my deceased child's issue who are alive on the Distribution Date") in equal parts per stirpes.[139]

In the above clause, a court could mistakenly read "such issue" to include all stock — as the previous part of the sentence sets out all "issue alive on the Distribution Date". The will-drafter, instead, should initially clarify the point in time when the division of the share is to be made and that the deceased child has in fact left issue then alive — but then in the remaining part of the sentence not identify again any particular issue.

Division on Distribution Date

 My Trustees shall divide the residue of my estate in equal shares among my children alive on the Distribution Date; but if any child of mine dies before the Distribution Date leaving issue alive on the Distribution Date, the share to which that deceased child would have been entitled if alive on the Distribution Date shall be divided among the deceased child's issue in equal parts per stirpes.

---

[139] Any of these phrases is equally open to misconstruction.

Example

 My Trustee shall divide the residue of my estate equally among my children alive at my death; but if any child of mine dies before me leaving issue *alive at my death*, the share to which that deceased child would have been entitled if alive at my death shall be divided among *such issue* in equal parts per stirpes.

This clause may be interpreted to mean that the residue is to be divided among all issue alive at the will-maker's death ("such issue"). Issue includes all children and grandchildren. To prevent such misinterpretation, "alive at my death" should be replaced with "that deceased child's issue".

 My Trustee shall divide the residue of my estate equally among my children alive at my death; but if any child of mine dies before me leaving issue *alive at my death*, the part to which that deceased child would have been entitled if alive at my death shall be divided among *that deceased child's issue* in equal shares per stirpes.

Error #4: Survivorship and Distribution Date

If a 30-day survivorship clause is included in a will, the distribution date must be amended. Otherwise, the gift of residue may fail if the spouse dies during the survivorship period.

 My Trustees shall pay or transfer the residue of my estate to my wife, MARIA, if she survives me for a period of 30 days. If MARIA dies before me my Trustees are to divide the residue of my estate equally among my children *alive at my death*; but if any child of mine dies before me leaving issue then alive, the part to which that deceased child would have been entitled if alive at my death is to be divided among that deceased child's issue in equal shares per stirpes.

This clause does not set out what will happen if Maria survives the will-maker but dies within 30 days. Also note that if a child of the will-maker also dies in the 30-day period, the share will not go to grandchildren but through the deceased child's estate to his or her beneficiary (likely his or her spouse as opposed to the grandchildren).

Solution: Distribution Date

 My Trustees shall pay or transfer the residue of my estate to my wife, MARIA, if she survives me for a period of thirty (30) days. If

> MARIA dies before me or if she survives me, but dies within a period of thirty (30) days after my death, *then on the death of the survivor of MARIA and me ("the Distribution Date")* my Trustees shall divide the residue of my estate equally among my children alive on the Distribution Date; but if any child of mine dies before the Distribution Date, leaving issue alive on the Distribution Date, my Trustees shall divide the part to which that deceased child would have been entitled if alive on the Distribution Date among that deceased child's issue in equal shares per stirpes.

Solution: General Survivorship Provision

If you find the use of a Distribution Date cumbersome, another option is to include a general survivorship clause, such as:

> Any person who fails to survive me by at least thirty (30) days shall be deemed to have died before me for all purposes.

If you are preparing mirror wills with legacies payable on the death of both spouses, do not use this general survivorship clause without amendment or there may be double legacies if the clients die within 30 days of each other.

Error #5: Anti-Lapse — No Contrary Intent and Gift Over

Gifts of residue, like gifts of realty, personal effects, and legacies, are subject to the anti-lapse provisions in the *Succession Law Reform Act*,[140] section 31.

If the anti-lapse provisions do not save the gift, then the gift or share of the residue will be distributed as if the will-maker died intestate.

> My Trustees shall pay or transfer the residue of my estate to my daughter, MAUREEN, for her own use absolutely.

Assuming that a contrary intent was not found elsewhere in the will, the residue would be divided among MAUREEN's spouse and children.[141]

---

[140] *Succession Law Reform Act*, R.S.O. 1990, c.S.26, as amended.

[141] *Dodge v. Girard* (1993), 15 O.R. (3d) 422 (Gen. Div.) held that the words "for his own use absolutely" did not express a contrary intention and section 31 applied. However, in *British Columbia (Official Administrator) v. Joseph* (1999), 30 E.T.R. (2d) 1 (B.C.S.C.) it was held that a gift to the deceased's son and daughter "in equal shares per capita for their sole use and benefit absolutely" expressed a clear intention that it was to pass jointly if a child predeceased.

Solution: "If she survives me"

The anti-lapse provisions in section 31 will yield to a contrary intention expressed in a will. The words, "if she (or he) survives me" express a contrary intention and suffice to oust the anti-lapse provisions and prevent the statutory default of gifts to spouse and children. If the gift is conditional on the beneficiary surviving, however, it will fail if the beneficiary dies before the will-maker, and there will be a partial intestacy as to that share of residue.

> My Trustees shall pay or transfer the residue of my estate to my spouse, NORMAN, if he survives me. If NORMAN dies before me the residue of my estate shall be divided among my children alive at my death in equal shares per capita.

Solution: Class Gift[142]

The anti-lapse rules do not apply to class gifts. So, if the will-maker is content to have the surviving members of a given group or class — "my children", or "my nephews" — take if one of the group predeceases, this is the answer.

Closing the Class (I)

Error #6: Failure to Close Class

In some wills, the trustee is directed to divide a gift among a class of beneficiaries "per capita". In the following example, the executor is given no direction on the face of the will as to when he is to close the class. Do the children have to be living at the testator's death; or is there some other point in time which is relevant?

> To divide the residue of my estate among my children then alive in equal shares per capita.

The class closing rules will assist the executor in identifying the beneficiaries entitled to share.[143] As a drafter, however, you can save the executor an excursion into the common law by setting out words such as "then alive" expressly.

---

[142] Sometimes, class gifts are easy to determine: e.g. "to all my children". In other instances, it may be less clear and the existence of a class will depend on the testator's intent. "Equally among my daughters A, B, and C" was held not to be a class gift in *Re Brush*, [1942] O.R. 647, [1943] 1 D.L.R. 74 (H.C.), while to my "brothers and sisters A, B, C and D" with a gift over to issue was found to be a class gift in *Re Hutton Estate*, (1982), 39 O.R. (2d) 622, 11 E.T.R. 140 (H.C.), endorsed by C.A. (1982), 39 O.R. (2d) 622.

[143] See "Class Closing Rules" in Chapter Seven, "Legacies".

Closing the Class (II)

 My Trustees shall divide the residue of my estate among my children in equal shares per capita.

Similarly, the following clause sets out that if a child dies before the will-maker, the deceased child's share is to be distributed among his issue in equal shares per stirpes. However, issue of a deceased child may continue to be born after the will-maker's death, and resort must be had to the class closing rules to clarify this ambiguity. It is preferable that clear language be set out in the will.

 My Trustee shall divide the residue of my estate equally among my children alive at my death; but if any child of mine dies before me and leaves *issue surviving,* the part to which that deceased child would have been entitled if alive at my death shall be divided among *such issue* in equal shares per stirpes.

The distinction is subtle: the word "such" identifies the issue and could be interpreted to include issue born after the will-maker.

 My Trustee shall divide the residue of my estate equally among my children alive at my death; but if any child of mine dies before me *leaving issue alive at my death,* the part to which the deceased child would have been entitled if alive at my death shall be divided among that deceased child's issue in equal shares per stirpes.

Error #7: "Considered Alive"

Although a will speaks from death, it will be read according to the circumstances at the time it is written. A will-maker will be taken to know that someone is dead, and to be making contingent arrangements only for those who die after the will is made.

 My Trustees shall divide the residue of my estate equally among my brothers living at my death, provided that if a brother of mine is then dead, survived by issue then alive, such deceased brother shall be considered alive for the purpose of making division of my estate, and his share shall be divided equally per stirpes among his issue.

Define the Class

Surprisingly, this clause does not create a gift over for the issue of a brother who was deceased at the time the will was made.[144] To be safe, when you are dealing with issue of those who are dead at the time the will is made, include a declaration of intent.

> I intend the issue of my deceased brother, SAM, to participate in the division of my estate under the foregoing provisions.

Error #8: Bad Arithmetic

A partial intestacy can occur when the residue is divided into a fixed number of shares and a beneficiary dies before the will-maker and there is no gift over. The share will be dealt with on an intestacy or in accordance with the anti-lapse rules, as is applicable. Another equally common mistake is to add the number of shares incorrectly.

> My Trustee shall divide the residue of my estate into three (3) equal shares:

> (i) One of such equal shares shall be paid or transferred to my son, JIM; and

> (ii) One of such equal shares shall be paid or transferred to my daughter, SARAH.

If Jim or Sarah dies before the will-maker, the anti-lapse provisions would apply, subject to a contrary intention set out elsewhere in the will. There would also be a partial intestacy as to the third share.

Solution: Floating Shares

In this handy drafting device, the exact number of shares is not fixed. This technique is most useful if the beneficiaries do not all belong to the same class or if the distribution is outright.

> My Trustees shall divide the residue of my estate into the requisite number of equal shares to give effect to the following distribution:
>
> (i) to pay or transfer one share to my son, JIM, if he survives me; but if JIM dies before me leaving issue alive at my death, my Trustees shall divide that share among JIM's issue in equal parts per stirpes; and

---

[144] *Sterling Estate v. Navjord*, (1989), 36, B.C.L.R. (2d) 93, 32 E.T.R. 237 (B.C.C.A.).

> (ii) to pay or transfer one share to my daughter, SARAH, if
>   she survives me; but if SARAH dies before me leaving
>   issue alive at my death, my Trustees shall divide that share
>   among SARAH's issue in equal parts per stirpes.

If Sarah dies before the will-maker, leaving no issue, all of the residue
will be paid or transferred to Jim and *vice versa*.

Error #9: Divided but not Transferred

There is a difference between the act of dividing the residue up, and
that of paying it out to the beneficiary; if the will sets up long-term trusts, the
acts can be very distant. Separating the act of dividing from the act of paying
is one way of signalling a trust, but if an immediate distribution is intended,
it is an error not to direct the estate trustees to pay the residue out immediately.

> If my spouse, ANNE, is not living on the thirtieth day following my
> death, my Trustees shall divide the residue of my estate into the
> requisite number of equal parts so that there is one part for each
> child of mine living at the death of the survivor of my spouse and
> me and one part for each child of mine not then living with issue
> then living.

No further provision is made in the will. Is one share to be transferred
to each child with a share to be divided among a deceased child's issue, or is
a share to be set aside for each child's family and divided among the child
and his issue? The clause is not clear.

Solution: Direct the Transfer

This appears to be a clause that was originally intended to preface a
long-term trust. The precedent was changed or used incorrectly, and then
circulated. This type of clause is appropriate if trusts are to be set up for
children. As a thinking drafter, you will, of course, avoid using it where an
outright distribution of the residue is intended.

Error #10: Failure of Gifts

A will should deal with the possibility that the anticipated beneficiaries
will not live to take a vested interest; a "failure of gift" clause should be
regularly included in the following situations:

1. The residue is divided among very few beneficiaries;

2. The will-maker is young and often travels with the residual beneficiaries; or

3. The will contains a life interest or long-term trust.

Wills intended to be mirror wills should not contain different failure-to-vest clauses. For example, mirror wills for a married couple often provide that the residue passes to each other, with a gift over to common issue if the spouse should predecease. If the failure clauses then differ and provide, for example, that any portion of the estate which fails to vest is to be distributed among the will-maker's siblings, the wills set up a kind of "tontine".[145]

If the mirror wills contain different provisions, the couple's objectives will not be realized. The spouse who lives longer will pass the whole of both estates to his or her side of the family. This is unlikely to be what the clients want!

Solution: Mirror Failure of Gifts

The failure of gift clauses should be the same in both wills. In this way, it will not matter which spouse survives the other as the ultimate distribution will be the same.

> If at any time after my death any portion of my estate shall not otherwise vest indefeasibly in possession of my spouse or one or more of my issue pursuant to the foregoing provisions, then on the date when it is determined that the portion of my estate will fail to vest (herein called the "Vesting Date"), I direct my Trustees to divide that portion into as many equal parts as are necessary to carry out the following provisions and to deal with the parts as follows:
>
> i. My Trustees shall divide one equal part between the following individuals who are alive on the Vesting Date, namely my wife's sister, SAMANTHA, and my wife's brother, JEFFREY, in equal shares per capita; and
>
> ii. My Trustees shall divide one equal part between the following individuals who are alive on the Vesting Date, namely my brother, SAM, and my brother, CHARLES, in equal shares per capita.

---

[145] This is a lottery, where the survivor takes all.

Error #11: Missed Opportunity

Occasionally, a client wants simply to follow the scheme for distribution on intestacy. If you want to rely on the intestacy provisions to effect the distribution in a common disaster, state that in the will; the residue passing this way will still be afforded the protection of the other provisions in the will — most notably the net family property clause — which would not apply if there is a partial intestacy.[146]

> Any property not otherwise disposed of and not ultimately vested in possession of a beneficiary by the provisions of this Will shall be paid by my Trustee to the persons who would be entitled to share in my estate if I had died intestate, without debts and unmarried, and in the proportions that those persons would share in such intestacy.

Disclaimers

Error #12: Disclaimer and Outright Distributions[147]

A beneficiary will sometimes disclaim an inheritance — usually for tax reasons. If a gift is disclaimed within a reasonable time, it is void *ab initio*. Unless there is a contrary intention set out in a will, a disclaimed legacy falls into residue; a disclaimed share of the residue passes on an intestacy.

If the gift over provision is contingent on the beneficiary dying before the will-maker, it is unclear whether the gift over will apply to a disclaimed gift. While it is unlikely that you will know in advance that a beneficiary will disclaim a share, you may specifically include a statement that if a beneficiary disclaims an interest, she will be deemed to have died before the testator, thus ensuring that any gift over will apply.

> If any child of mine disclaims any benefit under this Will, that child will be deemed to have died before me [for all of the purposes of this Will].

Since "all of the purposes" would include acting as executor of the will, the disclaimer provision would have to be revised if the intention was to allow the beneficiary to disclaim a share of the estate, but still act as executor.

---

[146] See Barry S. Corbin's "Statutory Traps in Will Drafting" in Trusts and Estates Section, *The Essential Guide for Drafting Wills* (Toronto, Ont.: Canadian Bar Association — Ontario, 1997).

[147] See "Restructuring the Will and the Testamentary Trust", Jennifer A. Pfeutzner in *Drafting Wills to Avoid Litigation*, (Toronto, Ont.: Department of Education, Law Society of Upper Canada, 2000).

CHAPTER 9

TRUSTS

While all wills technically create trusts,[148] this chapter is concerned with the drafting of on-going trusts, where the estate is not distributed as soon as the assets are realized and the debts are paid. In these wills, the estate or some part of it is to be held for a period of time in a trust.

A trust is a relationship which imposes on a trustee an obligation to deal with property over which he or she has control for the benefit of some other person or persons, called the beneficiaries. The obligation is one that the Courts of Equity will enforce, and an express trust is created to invoke this enforcement. For an express trust to exist, there must be three certainties: certainty of intention to create a trust, certainty of the subject of the trust (the property) and certainty of the objects (or beneficiaries) of the trust.

There can be as many kinds of will trusts as there are will-makers. The great strength of trusts is their wonderful flexibility. Why is it, then, that there seem to be only a few stiff precedents that find their way into wills? Too many lawyers draft trusts like Procrustes made beds![149]

Error #1: Boilerplating

There is a place for boilerplate clauses; in the general administrative clauses of a will they provide a basic "tool-kit" of powers for the executors. Boilerplate has no place, however, in the dispositive parts of a will. Not only does it fall short of the requirements in Rule 2 of the Rules of Professional Conduct for competence, but it misses the best part of doing a will — the chance to get creative in your drafting.

On the other hand, we recognize that a practice in the real world will not allow you to hand-craft every word for every client. You must get a will drafted quickly, and without investing more time than your client is willing to pay for.

While the possibilities of any given trust are endless, there are certain issues that must be addressed in every trust. The compromise between boilerplating and excessive particularity is to have a good and conveniently

---

[148] By virtue of the *Estates Administration Act* all executors are trustees:

Devolution to personal representative of deceased

2.(1) All real and personal property that is vested in a person without a right in any other person to take by survivorship, on the person's death, whether testate or intestate and despite any testamentary disposition, devolves to and becomes vested in his or her personal representative from time to time as trustee for the persons by law beneficially entitled and subject to the payment of the person's debts and so far as such property is not disposed of by deed, will, contract or other effectual disposition, it shall be administered, dealt with and distributed as if it were personal property not so disposed of. R.S.O. 1990, c. E.22, s. 2(1), as amended.

[149] Procrustes was an ancient Greek tyrant who, having overcome strangers, would force them to lie on one of his two beds. If they were too short for the long bed, he would hammer them out or stretch them on a rack. If they were too long for the short bed, he would lop them off to size.

organized set of precedents with which you are intimately familiar, and to gather the information you will need to know which precedents to use, and how they may have to be modified or combined.

Solution: A Checklist

The following is a list of the issues you will have to consider in planning the terms of any will trust:

Trust Issues Checklist

▶ Trustees

- will the executor continue as trustee?

- who should replace the trustee if he or she dies or resigns?

- should the trustee be able to add a co-trustee?

- should the trustee be paid?

- will the trustee need an advisor?

▶ Income

- who are the income beneficiaries?

- when should income be paid? during minority? at 18?

- can it be accumulated? for how long?

- should the income all be paid? or a fixed amount?

- is unused income to be capitalized or paid to someone else?

- periodicity — how often should income be paid? yearly? monthly? weekly?

- cost of living allowance — should fixed payments be adjusted for inflation?

- who will pay tax on the income? the beneficiary? the estate?

▶ Capital

- encroachment — should the trustees be able to pay lump sums of capital to the income beneficiary?

- advancement — should they be able to pay lump sums to a capital beneficiary before the trust is terminated?

- when paid — is all the capital to be paid at once, or in stages?

▶ Division Date — when does the trust terminate?

- when the beneficiary reaches a certain age?

- after a certain number of years?

- on a given event, such as the death of the income beneficiary?

- at the trustees' discretion?

- some combination of these?

▶ Gift Over

- who will take if any beneficiary dies or disclaims while the trust is still in existence?

▶ Powers in the Interim

- maintenance — can trustees use the trust for basic needs of a dependant?

- advancement — can trustees use capital to set a child up in life?

- should the will trusts have the same powers as the executors have?

The commonest situations where a will-maker needs a trust are (1) for a spouse, (2) for minor (or otherwise irresponsible) children, and (3) for disabled beneficiaries. In addition, trusts are used for tax planning and for charitable endowments. We have, therefore, provided "precedent" versions of the commonest kinds of trusts, each of which is designed to address the errors we identify. *Use these precedents only after you have adapted them to the particular needs of your client.*

1. Trusts For a Spouse

A client will consider a spouse trust either because the spouse is not well able to administer assets through inexperience or incapacity and because of the tax advantages of a spousal trust. Since any trust under a will is a testamentary trust, its income will be taxed at graduated rates. It may, then, be used to split income between the spouse and the trust or trusts, with significant tax saving. Since most couples of the middle class in Ontario will hold their property in joint tenancy, however, the benefit of tax splitting through a spousal trust must be weighed against the loss of this convenient method of passing assets and avoiding probate.

A spousal trust is a good way to meet the needs of couples in a second marriage, since it allows the assets to be made available for the surviving spouse during his or her lifetime, but ensures that they will eventually pass back to the will-maker's own children or family.

Error #2: Emptying the estate

The desire of will-makers to avoid paying probate fees (a desire that is often out of all proportion to the size of the fees themselves) has made devices for passing assets outside of the will popular: joint tenancy, registered plans, life insurance, and *inter vivos* trusts proliferate. While it is not exactly a drafting error, it is surely the most arid of exercises to create beautifully drafted testamentary trusts for someone who will have almost no assets to put into them.

 You must review your client's assets as part of the will-drafting exercise. Use a form to gather information from your client in advance of a first meeting. Not only will this reduce the time you must spend, but it will allow you to have pointed questions ready. Use a checklist to remind you and your clients about assets that may have been overlooked. See Chapter Thirteen, "Practice Matters", for a sample checklist.

A spousal trust simply cannot be constituted from an estate consisting of assets held jointly with right of survivorship with the spouse!

We have actually heard lawyers opine that if they do not inquire about assets, but simply draft the will the client tells them to, they cannot be held responsible for the result. Apart from reducing the lawyer to little more than a scribe taking dictation, this is not only irresponsible but wrong in law. Consider *Earl v. Wilhelm*,[150] where the lawyer was held liable when he drafted a will purporting to deal with assets that legally belonged to the will-maker's corporation.

 Ask clients to bring in copies of deeds and investment statements to confirm the legal ownership of their assets.

---

[150] *Earl v. Wilhelm* (2000), 183 D.L.R. (4th) 45, [2000] 4 W.W.R. 363, 216 W.A.C. 71, 189 Sask. R. 71, 31 E.T.R. (2d) 193, 1 C.C.L.T. (3d) 215 (C.A.), leave to appeal to S.C.C. refused 191 D.L.R. (4th) vi.

Where the parties are setting up a spousal trust, you may prepare deeds changing ownership from joint tenancy to tenancy in common and change investment assets to remove any right of survivorship as part of the estate planning process. Real estate agents, investment counsellors, accountants and (sometimes) even lawyers are so inured to married couples holding as joint tenants, however, that the scheme may be undone if the couple moves and the new property is registered in joint tenancy, or if they restructure their investments.

☞   **When you have set up spousal trusts for couples in a second marriage, include a reminder that they should hold their assets as tenants in common in your reporting letter.**

Error #3: Tainted Spousal Trust

In order for the spousal trust to qualify for a deferral of capital gains under the *Income Tax Act*, it must be set up according to the strictures in the Act. Section 70(6) of the Act defines a spousal trust as:

> "a trust, created by the taxpayer's will, that was resident in Canada immediately after the time the property vested indefeasibly in the trust and under which
>
> (i)   the taxpayer's spouse or common-law partner is entitled to receive all of the income of the trust that arises before the spouse's or common-law partner's death, and
>
> (ii) no person except the spouse or common-law partner may, before the spouse's or common-law partner's death, receive or otherwise obtain the use of any of the income or capital of the trust".[151]

If the terms of the trust allow someone other than the spouse to benefit, the trust will not qualify under the *Income Tax Act* as a spousal trust. The trap for the unwary drafter is that the powers granted to the trustee in the standard administrative provisions of the will may defeat the will-maker's intention. If, for example, the will contains a power for the trustee to loan assets interest free to a beneficiary, or to allow a beneficiary to live in real property belonging to the trust, the trust will be disqualified as allowing someone other than the spouse to benefit.

---

[151] *Income Tax Act*, R.S.C. 1985, Chapter 1 (5th Supp.), s. 70(6).

Solution: Restrict the Trust Powers

You can review every trust power in the will for the possibility that someone other than the spouse may benefit, or you can use the following clause:

> Notwithstanding anything in my Will, the administrative powers contained in it do not authorize my Trustees to act, during the lifetime of my spouse, in any way that may disqualify the trust fund established in paragraph X of my Will as an exclusive spousal trust under paragraph 70(6)(*b*) of the *Income Tax Act*. In particular, my Trustees are prohibited from any act or omission that may permit anyone other than my spouse to obtain the use of any of the income or capital of the trust fund during my spouse's lifetime.[152]

Error #4: Monolithic Trusts

Where the will-maker has assets that may have capital gains, it is well worth having a spousal trust that meets the requirements of the *Income Tax Act* for a spousal trust. The terms of such a trust may, however, be too narrow for the purposes of the will-maker. If the income is significant, it may be neither necessary nor tax efficient to have it all paid to the spouse, rather than sprinkling it among the family.

Solution: Dual Trusts

The following clause allows trustees to separate the assets of the estate, and hold those with appreciated capital gains in a qualifying spousal trust, and some or all of the other assets in a more general family trust with a large number of potential beneficiaries.

> If my spouse, DOREEN, survives me, my Trustees shall divide the residue of my estate into two (2) parts, each part being made up of one (1) dollar and those other assets from the residue of my estate that my Trustees in their absolute discretion shall determine. In allocating assets to the two (2) parts, my Trustees shall consider allocating to the Spouse's Trust (as defined below) those assets having accrued taxable capital gains or recapture. My Trustees' decision regarding allocation of assets shall be determinative for all purposes.

---

[152] See Chapter Ten, "Administrative Clauses", for a simpler version of this clause.

1. My Trustees shall hold one of the parts (the "Spouse's Trust") in trust during the lifetime of my spouse, DOREEN. My Trustees shall pay the net income from the Spouse's Trust to DOREEN, and may pay to or use for the support, maintenance or benefit of DOREEN those amounts out of the capital of the Spouse's Trust that my Trustees in the exercise of their absolute discretion consider appropriate from time to time. My Trustees shall not be required to exercise an even hand in the exercise of their discretion, but may favour the income beneficiary over capital beneficiaries.

2. (a) My Trustees shall hold the other part (the "Family Trust") in trust, and until the death of DOREEN my Trustees may pay to or for the support, maintenance, education or benefit of DOREEN or any one or more of my children, their spouses or other issue of mine and, to the exclusion of any one or more of them, those amounts out of the net income or out of the capital of the Family Trust that my Trustees in their absolute discretion consider appropriate. My Trustees shall not be required, in exercising their discretion under this clause, to maintain an even hand between the beneficiaries, but may prefer one beneficiary over another, and may prefer one class of beneficiary over another.

   (b) Any net income that is not paid out in any year may be accumulated and added to the capital of the Family Trust, except that after twenty-one (21) years from my death, all of the net income shall be paid to, or for the benefit of or to the exclusion of one or more of DOREEN, my children, their spouses or other issue of mine in the proportion and manner that my Trustees deem advisable.

3. Upon the death of the survivor of DOREEN and me (the "Distribution Date"), my Trustees shall add together the Spouse's Trust and the Family Trust or the amounts of them then remaining to form the residue of my estate and, if I have issue living on the Distribution Date, they shall divide the residue among my issue in equal shares per stirpes.

Like trusts for the disabled, family trusts under a dual trust arrangement are often intended to favour one of several beneficiaries. Make sure that the "even hand" principle is excluded, so that the trustees are not forced to treat the children equally with the spouse.[153]

2. Trusts for Children

Will-makers often set up trusts for children who are either minors or children younger than the will-maker thinks can handle assets. If the reason for setting up a trust is that the parent lacks confidence in the children, the trust is usually held to whatever age the will-maker thinks will produce the requisite level of sagacity. While will-makers do set up trusts to hold money until their children are age 65, such an arrangement seems bound to produce bitterness, if not actual litigation. On the other hand, like a spousal trust, a trust for children may be set up for the tax benefits of income splitting. Such trusts are usually for life, but with liberal discretion that will allow them to be collapsed earlier if the trustees choose.

 1. If my spouse, COLIN, is not alive on the thirtieth (30th) day following my death, then at the death of the survivor of my spouse and me (the "Date of Distribution") my Trustees shall divide the residue of my estate into as many equal shares as are necessary to carry out the following provisions, and shall deal with those shares as follows:

    (a) one (1) equal share shall be paid or transferred to each child of mine alive at the Date of Distribution who has attained the age of thirty-five (35) years;

    (b) one (1) equal share shall be set aside for each child of mine alive at the Date of Distribution who has not attained the age of thirty-five (35) years; and

    (c) one (1) equal share shall be set aside for each child of mine who has died before the Date of Distribution leaving issue then alive.

2. My Trustees shall deal with the shares set aside as follows:

---

[153] See the discussion of the even-hand principle, and the precedent for excluding it in the section on pure discretionary clauses, below at p.20.

(a) (i) Each share set aside for a child alive at the Date of Distribution shall be kept invested. Until the child for whom the share is held attains the age of thirty-five (35) years, my Trustees shall pay to or apply for the general benefit of that child so much of the income and capital of the share as my Trustees in their absolute discretion consider appropriate from time to time. Any surplus income shall be accumulated and added to the capital of share, but after twenty-one (21) years from my death all the net income shall be paid to the child for whom the share is held.

(ii) If at the Date of Distribution a child of mine has attained the age of twenty-five (25) years or when a child of mine attains the age of twenty-five (25) years, my Trustees shall pay one-third of the capital and accumulated income of that child's share then remaining to that child for his or her own use absolutely.

(iii) If at the Date of Distribution a child of mine has attained the age of thirty (30) years or when a child of mine attains the age of thirty (30) years, my Trustees shall pay one-half of the capital and accumulated income of that child's share then remaining to that child for his or her own use absolutely.

(iv) When that child attains the age of thirty-five (35) years, my Trustees shall transfer the balance of that child's share to that child for his or her own use absolutely.

(v) If my child dies before attaining the age of thirty-five (35) years, leaving issue then alive, my Trustees shall divide that child's share or the amount of it not yet received by that child, among the issue of that child in equal parts per stirpes. If that child leaves no issue surviving him or her, and I have issue alive, the share shall be divided among my issue in equal parts per stirpes.

(vi) If, however, an interest passes to a child of mine for whom a share of my estate is already being held in trust under my will, that interest shall be added to that child's trust and administered in the same manner.

(b) One share for the issue of each child of mine who has died before the Date of Distribution, leaving issue then alive, shall be divided among the issue of the deceased child in equal parts per stirpes, and my Trustees shall hold those parts in trust for any issue under the age of thirty-five (35) years on the same terms, with the necessary modifications, as are provided for the shares held for children of mine.

Error #5: No Gift Over (*Saunders v. Vautier*)

The rule in *Saunders v. Vautier*[154] states that the beneficiary of a trust, whose interest is (1) fully vested and (2) represents the whole of the beneficial interest, and (3) who is legally competent, can require the trustee to distribute the trust assets immediately. While the principle is not hard to grasp, it has a nasty way of cropping up in trusts anywhere property is to be held for someone past the age of majority.

In the event that my wife, SANDRA, dies before me or survives me but dies within a period of thirty (30) days of my death, my Trustees shall hold and keep invested the residue of my estate for the benefit of my daughter, EMILY, and until she attains the age of thirty-five (35) years, pay to or apply for her benefit the whole or that part of the net income and that part or parts of the capital of the residue that my Trustees in their absolute discretion deem advisable. Any portion of the net income not paid to or applied for the benefit of EMILY shall be accumulated by my Trustees and added to the capital of my estate, but after the twenty-one (21) years have passed since my death, my Trustees shall pay to or apply for the benefit of EMILY the whole of the net income. Upon EMILY attaining the age of thirty-five (35) years, the remainder of the residue of my estate shall be paid or transferred to her.

In this clause, Emily has all of the interest in the trust, both in the income and the capital. There is no possibility that she will lose it, since it is not conditional nor is it subject to any divestment. Thus, Emily's interest is vested, and only the enjoyment or possession of it is delayed. As a result, once Emily is of age (18 in Ontario) she can demand that the trustees turn the property over to her, since it is hers by right. This is not a matter of making an application to court, but a rule of law — the Rule in *Saunder v. Vautier.*

The simplest way to prevent the operation of the rule, and to ensure that the trustees can hold the funds until Emily is 35, is to make the gift conditional on her attaining that age.

If my daughter EMILY dies before attaining the age of thirty-five (35) years leaving issue alive at her death, the residue of my estate or the amount of it then remaining shall be divided among the issue of EMILY in equal shares per stirpes. My Trustees shall hold

---

[154] (1841), 4 Beav. 115, 49 E.R. 282, affirmed (1841), 1 Cr. & Ph. 240, 41 E.R. 482, [1935-42] All E.R. Rep. 58. The facts in the original case are not that familiar, although the principle in the case is well known. The testator in the case left £2500 in stock for his great-nephew when he attained the age of 25. At 21, the nephew applied to court to have the stock turned over to him and succeeded.

> these shares in trust upon the same terms, with the necessary modifications, as are provided with respect to the residue directed to be held in trust for EMILY.

It is not sufficient to make a gift over to another known person, since even if the trust is vested in several persons, if they are all of age and agree they can "bust the trust".

 If my daughter EMILY should die before attaining the age of 35 years, the residue of my estate or the amount of it then remaining shall be held for my son EDGAR in trust upon the same terms as are provided with respect to the residue directed to be held in trust for my daughter EMILY.

Error #6: Ascertainable Beneficiaries

The principle of *Saunders v. Vautier* can be expanded to apply to any situation where all of the beneficial interests are identifiable and vested. Watch for a place where the contingent gift is to the issue alive at the will-maker's death.

 (1) During the lifetime of my wife, NIGELLA, my Trustees shall keep invested the residue of my estate and shall pay the net income to or for my wife, NIGELLA. My Trustees may at any time pay to or for the benefit of my wife, NIGELLA or to or for the maintenance, education or benefit of my children or any of them those amounts out of the capital of the residue that my Trustees in their absolute discretion consider advisable.

(2) Upon the death of the survivor of my wife, NIGELLA, and me, my Trustees shall divide the residue of my estate then remaining into as many equal shares as there are children of mine *alive at my death*, and children of mine who do not survive me but leave issue *who survive me*.

The problem here is that the gift over after the spouse's life interest is to beneficiaries who can be identified with certainty from the time of the will-maker's death. The widow and children together own all of the vested beneficial interest in the trust, and collectively can invoke the rule in *Saunders v. Vautier* to terminate the trust.

Solution: Class Closed at Distribution

 (1) During the lifetime of my wife, NIGELLA, my Trustees shall keep invested the residue of my estate and shall pay the net income

> to or for NIGELLA. My Trustees may at any time pay to or for the benefit of NIGELLA or to or for the maintenance, education or benefit of my children or any of them those amounts out of the capital of the residue that my Trustees in their absolute discretion consider advisable.
>
> (2) Upon the death of the survivor of NIGELLA and me (the "Division Date"), my Trustees shall divide the residue of my estate then remaining into as many equal shares as there are children of mine alive *on the Division Date* and children of mine not then alive but who have issue alive *on the Division Date.*

Error #7: Narrow Terms

A trustee who holds money in trust for children should have the necessary powers to distribute funds when they are required. Most will-makers think of the need for money for education, but what about a serious illness? What about paying for a wedding, or a house, or setting up in practice as a professional?[155]

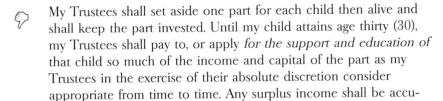

My Trustees shall set aside one part for each child then alive and shall keep the part invested. Until my child attains age thirty (30), my Trustees shall pay to, or apply *for the support and education of* that child so much of the income and capital of the part as my Trustees in the exercise of their absolute discretion consider appropriate from time to time. Any surplus income shall be accumulated and added to the part.

The problem here is that the phrase "support and education" may not cover all of the contingencies. Other phrases, such as "maintenance and advancement" or "proper support and maintenance" or "maintenance and education" are common, but equally narrow. "Maintenance", properly speaking, is a payment from income to support the beneficiary at a subsistence level (food, shelter, clothing, and medical care).[156] It is generally restricted to minors. "Advancement" is a payment from capital, but for

---

[155] Marni M.K. Whitaker "Drafting Payment Terms in Children's Trusts" in Second Annual Estates and Trusts Forum (Toronto: Dept. of Continuing Legal Education, Law Society of Upper Canada, 1999).

[156] See *Cook v. Noble* (1886), 12 O.R. 812 (H.C.). K. Thomas Grozinger, "The Ontario Law of Advancement on an Intestacy" (1993) 12 Est. & Tr. J. 396-404.

limited purposes, to set up a beneficiary in life.[157] If the intention is to give the trustees a broad power to help the child in whatever way the need arises, then the discretion must be more broadly worded.[158]

> My Trustees shall set aside one part for each child alive at the Distribution Date and shall keep the part invested. Until my child attains the age of thirty (30) years, my Trustees shall pay to, or apply *for the support, education, and general benefit* of that child so much of the income and capital of that child's part as my Trustees in the exercise of their absolute discretion consider appropriate from time to time. Any surplus income shall be accumulated and added to that child's part.

Error #8: Gift Over to Siblings

A trust for children will sometimes pass a share to the "brothers and sisters" of a beneficiary who dies before receiving her full share. Remember that "brothers and sisters" will not necessarily exclude half-sisters and half-brothers.[159]

> If any grandchild of mine dies before attaining the age of 30 years, my Trustees shall divide the part or the amount not yet received by that grandchild among the issue of that grandchild in equal shares per stirpes. If that grandchild leaves no issue surviving him or her, the part shall be divided among that grandchild's brothers and sisters who survive him or her in equal shares per capita.

In this example, the gift could end up passing to children who are no blood relation of the will-maker. Consider if Wanda, the will-maker, has a daughter Dottie, who has a son Sam. Dottie divorces, and Sam's father remarries and has sons who are Sam's step-brothers, but not Dottie's children or Wanda's grandchildren. These are the beneficiaries under Wanda's will, if Sam dies before reaching 30.

---

[157] See the Ontario Law Reform Commission's Report on the Law of Trusts (Ontario: Ministry of the Attorney General, 1984). The Ontario Law Reform Commission defined the power of advancement as "the authority to pay capital to, or for the benefit of a minor so that he may take advantage of some opportunity that will further him in life" (pp. 317-318). For example, an advancement might pay a substantial debt for a youth who had gambled heavily, or purchase a business or a partnership for him to begin a career.

[158] *Ibid.*, at p. 334.

[159] The terms "sibling" and "brother or sister" are not defined in the *Succession Law Reform Act*, although the sections on intestacy somewhat ambiguously include "kindred of the half-blood". Of course, in a will, the intention of the will-maker is what matters, and where that cannot be determined, extrinsic evidence may be adduced. If it is simply a matter the client has not considered, however, this is no help. See A. H. Oosterhoff, *Oosterhoff on Wills and Succession: Text, Commentary and Cases*, 5th ed. (Scarborough, Ont.: The Carswell Company, 1998), pp. 80-81.

Solution: Specify the Relationship

If any grandchild of mine dies before attaining the age of thirty (30) years, leaving issue then alive, my Trustees shall divide the part or the amount of it then remaining among the issue of that grandchild in equal shares per stirpes. If that grandchild leaves no issue surviving him or her, the part shall be divided among that grandchild's brothers and sisters *who are also grandchildren of mine* who survive him or her in equal shares per capita.

If any grandchild of mine dies before attaining the age of thirty (30) years leaving issue then alive, my Trustees shall divide the part or the amount of it then remaining among the issue of that grandchild in equal shares per stirpes. If that grandchild leaves no issue surviving him or her, the part shall be divided among the *issue of the parent* of that grandchild *who is also a child of mine* in equal shares per stirpes.

Note that the clauses above will work with either floating shares or fixed shares, but if floating shares are used, the phrase "leaving issue then alive" may be omitted, since if there is no issue alive at the deceased beneficiary's death, the share will collapse.

Error #9: Confusing Alternative Gifts

There are two instances where you will have to provide an alternative gift: (1) where the beneficiary dies before the will-maker, and (2) where assets are held in a trust, and the beneficiary dies before the termination of the trust. Do not confuse them. The commonest error is to suppose that if you have made provisions for the one event, you have also covered the other.

My Trustees shall divide the residue of my estate so that there is one part for each of my children, MICKIS, UGIS and ARVIL, and pay one part to each child who has attained the age of twenty-five (25) years, but if any of my children is under the age of twenty-five (25) years at my death, my Trustees shall hold his part invested, and until that child attains age twenty-five (25), my Trustees shall pay to that child or apply for the general benefit of that child so much of the net income and capital of the part as my Trustees in the exercise of their absolute discretion consider appropriate from time to time. Any surplus income shall be accumulated and added to the part. When my child attains age twenty-five (25), my

Trustees shall transfer the balance of the part to my child for his
or her own use absolutely. If any child of mine dies before
attaining the age of twenty-five (25) leaving issue who survive me,
his or her share shall be divided among his or her issue in equal
shares per stirpes.

The problem here is that if a child dies before the testator, there is no
provision for what happens to his share. The drafter has dealt with the
Saunders v. Vautier problem in the final sentence, but that is not sufficient
to deal with the share of a predeceasing child.

Solution: Two Contingent Gifts

(a) My Trustees shall divide the residue of my estate so that there is
one part for each of my children, MICKIS, UGIS and ARVIL, but if
a child of mine dies before me leaving issue who survive me, his
part shall be divided among his issue in equal shares per stirpes.

(b) My Trustees shall pay one part to each child who has
attained the age of twenty-five (25) years, but if any of my children
is under the age of twenty-five (25) years at my death, my Trustees
shall hold his part invested, and until that child attains age twenty-
five (25), my Trustees shall pay to that child or apply for the general
benefit of that child so much of the income and capital of the part
as my Trustees in the exercise of their absolute discretion consider
appropriate from time to time. Any surplus income shall be accumulated and added to the part.

(c) When my child attains the age of twenty-five (25) years, my
Trustees shall transfer the balance of the part to that child for his or
her own use absolutely. If any child of mine dies before attaining
the age of twenty-five (25) years leaving issue alive at his death, his
or her part shall be divided among his or her issue in equal shares
per stirpes.

3. Trusts For a Disabled Beneficiary

Special care is needed when drafting trusts for a beneficiary, usually a child,
who is or may be entitled to benefits under the *Ontario Disability Support
Plan Act.* [160] Since the ODSPA regulations disqualify anyone with "liquid
assets" of more than $5,000 from benefits, a legacy to someone who is or
may be in receipt of benefits should be in trust. The regulations allow up to

---

[160] *Ontario Disability Support Plan Act*, 1997, S.O. 1997, C.25.

$100,000 to be held in a trust, if the funds are derived from an inheritance or life insurance. Most practitioners prefer, however, to make use of a "Henson" trust, named after the case in which the Divisional Court confirmed that such a trust could not be used by the Ministry as a reason to terminate benefits under the predecessor to the ODSPA.[161]

 Since the regulations allow only $100,000 to be held in trust, any bequest to an actual or potential recipient of benefits should be held in a Henson trust. In addition to concerns about the size of the trust, we recognize that the regulations can be (and have been) changed by Ministry fiat.

Henson or Pure Discretionary Trusts Leaving money outright to a person who receives or may be entitled to receive *ODSPA* benefits can be a serious error. Merely holding the funds in trust, however, is not sufficient.

 My Trustees shall divide the residue of my estate in equal shares per stirpes among my issue alive at my death, but the share of my son MAX shall be set aside and kept invested and the net income derived therefrom shall be paid to or for the benefit of my son MAX, in the manner and proportions that my Trustees in their absolute discretion deem advisable. On the death of my son, his share shall be divided in equal shares per stirpes among the issue of my son as shall survive him.

In order to avoid the impact of the ODSPA regulations, the trust must provide that no part of the income or capital vests in the beneficiary. It must be purely discretionary. The clause above could disentitle the beneficiary to benefits because it directs that the income is to be paid to him, even though the Trustees can determine the manner and proportion.

Solution: A Discretionary Trust

 If my son, MAX, survives me, my Trustees shall set aside one half of the residue of my estate upon trust (the "Special Trust"), and

---

[161] *Ontario (Min. Of Community and Social Services) v. Henson* (1989), 36 E.T.R. 192 (Ont. C.A.). See also Mary Louise Dickson, Rod Walsh and Orville Endicott, *The Wills Book: Benefits, Wills, Trusts and Personal Decisions Involving People with Disabilities in Ontario*, rev. ed. (North York, Ont.: Ontario Association for Community Living, 1999), Mary Louise Dickson, "Trust Blitz: Persons with Disabilities" in *A Practitioner's Guide to Using Trusts Effectively* (Toronto: Dept. of Continuing Education, Law Society of Upper Canada, 1999), Mary Louise Dickson, "Special Issues Surrounding Trusts for Persons with a Disability" in *Creative Uses of Trusts in Estate Planning* (Toronto: Insight Press, 1997), Mary Louise Dickson and Hilary Laidlaw, "Henson-type Trusts: To Use, or Not to Use" in *Advising People with Disabilities and Their Families* (Toronto: Dept. of Education, Law Society of Upper Canada, 2001).

during the lifetime of MAX, my Trustees shall pay to or for the
benefit of MAX as much of the income and capital of the Special
Trust as my Trustees in their absolute discretion deem appropriate
[Note A]. Any income not paid out in any year shall be accumulated and added to the capital of the Special Trust, but after
twenty-one (21) years from my death, any income not paid to or for
the benefit of MAX shall be divided among (charities or other
beneficiaries) in the proportion and to the exclusionof any one or
more of them, as my Trustees in their absolute discretion deem
appropriate [Note B]. It is my wish that my Trustees in exercising
their discretion consider primarily the comfort and welfare of MAX.
I expressly declare that my Trustees shall not be required to maintain an even hand when investing and administering the Special
Trust, but may in their discretion favour one beneficiary over
another or one class of beneficiary over the other [Note C]. No
interest in the Special Trust shall vest in MAX unless actually paid
to or for him. Upon the death of MAX, my Trustees shall pay the
expenses of his last illness and his funeral, to the extent that these
are not paid from other sources, from the Special Trust, and if
MAX has issue then alive, my Trustees shall divide the Special
Trust or the amount of it then remaining among the issue of MAX
in equal shares per stirpes, but if he leaves no issue then alive
among my issue in equal shares per stirpes.

☞   **Some precedents include a specific reference to preserving
entitlement to government benefits, such as: "When
exercising their discretion, my Trustees shall also consider
and, insofar as they consider advisable, take steps to
maximize, other sources of income and government
assistance available to my son MAX, if payments from the
Special Trust were not made". The phrase adds nothing to
the Trustee's powers, and may flag the trust for unwonted
attention by the Ministry.**

Error #10: Non-Discretionary Payments

Sometime nervous will-makers will want to see the Trustee obligated to
make payments to the principal beneficiary. They are uneasy with the
breadth of discretion granted to the Trustees. Even if the obligation extends
only to payments allowed in the current regulations, however, the fact that
the beneficiary has any enforceable interest may disqualify him.

Solution: A Letter of Wishes (Note A)

There is a long tradition of trustees being given memoranda or letters of wishes to guide them in the exercise of their discretion.[162] While not binding, they do allow will-makers the comfort of setting out in some detail the way they would like to see the discretion exercised, including medical personnel and helpful advisors. For the worried parent of a helpless child this can be very important. Since the letter is not a public document, it should not be referred to in the will. While trustees are not legally bound to follow a letter of wishes, they are bound to consider factors relevant to the exercise of their discretion.[163]

> My Trustees shall pay to or for the benefit of my son, MAX, so much of the income and capital of the Special Trust as my Trustees in their absolute discretion deem appropriate.

Solution: An Advisor (For a Corporate Trustee)

Where the trustee is to be a trust company, one of the problems is that those administering the funds may have little direct knowledge of the daily needs of the principal beneficiary. One answer is to appoint someone to keep them apprised of the beneficiary's situation, and to make requests for distributions as needed. Such an advisor can also help to allay fears about the abuse of the Trustee's discretion. Be careful, however, not to give the advisor power to do more than advise, or you may have made him a trustee, or undermined the discretion of the trustees. The following are two clauses to be added to a trust when the trustee is a trust company under a separate trust:

> Without in any way restricting the exercise by my Special Trustees of the discretion given to them, and without imposing a legal obligation on them, I declare that it is my wish that in making decisions concerning payments to or expenditures on behalf of my son, FRANCIS, they consult with and be guided by the advice of my children (other than FRANCIS) who are living in the city of Hamilton from time to time and by the advice of (organization) or any other organization that my Special Trustees consider appropriate

---

[162] See the discussion of memoranda in Chapter Five, "Personal Property".

[163] *Edell v. Sitzer.* (2001), 55 O.R. (3d) 198 (Sup. Ct. Just.). See also Maurice C. Cullity, "Judicial Control of Trustees' Discretions" (1975) 25 U. of T. Law J. 99, and Maurice Cullity, "Exercise of Discretionary Powers" in *Recent Developments in Estate Planning and Administration: Special Lectures of the Law Society of Upper Canada* (Toronto: Richard de Boo, 1980), at p. 13.

> from time to time with respect to the arrangements to be made for the care of FRANCIS.

Powers for Special Trustee

> My Special Trustees shall have the same powers and shall be entitled to exercise the same discretion when administering and investing the Special Trust as are given in my will to my Trustees with respect to the administration and investment of my general estate.

Error #11: Partial Intestacy

The *Accumulations Act*[164] will not allow interest to be accumulated for longer than 21 years. If the trust is to last for that long, you must designate a beneficiary for the interest that will be paid out after the accumulation period. If no beneficiary is named, it passes on intestacy (if the gift is a gift of residue), and thus may vest in the beneficiary. Not to provide for income after 21 years is an error in any trust, but the problem is particularly critical in a trust for a recipient of social benefits, because the fact that the interest may vest in the beneficiary may disqualify her from benefits from the start.

Solution: A Gift Over of Income after 21 Years (Note B)

> ... but after twenty-one (21) years from my death, any income not paid to or for the benefit of my son, MAX, shall be divided among (charities or other beneficiaries) in the proportion that my Trustees in their absolute discretion deem appropriate.

Many Henson trusts include a clause that empowers the trustees to make payment varying in amount and frequency. Once the even hand is ousted (see below) this is probably unnecessary, but the clause can be inserted as a reminder to the trustee. Arguably, if payments were made on a regular basis the beneficiary could be found to have an enforceable interest.

Varied Payment

> I specifically authorize my Trustees to make payments varying in amount and at the time or times that my Trustees in the exercise of

---

[164] *Accumulations Act,* R.S.O. 1990 , c. A-5., as amended.

their discretion consider advisable, keeping in mind that the comfort and welfare of my son, MAX, is my first consideration.

Error #12: Even Hand Not Excluded

The so-called "even hand" rule requires a trustee to treat all beneficiaries equally, in the absence of an indication otherwise. Many discretionary trusts will allow the trustee the power to favour one beneficiary over another, but the absence of such a power is a particularly serious error in a trust for an ODSPA beneficiary. The will-maker wants to have the principal beneficiary treated better than other beneficiaries, who are merely there to ensure that the trust does not vest in interest. Without an exclusion of the "even hand" rule, it can be argued that the trustee is obliged to pay a determinable portion of the trust income to the favoured beneficiary. If that beneficiary has an enforceable interest under the trust, it may result in a loss of ODSPA benefits.

Solution: Oust the Even Hand (Note C)

I expressly declare that my Trustees shall not be required to maintain an even hand when investing and administering the Special Trust, but may in their discretion favour one beneficiary over another or one class of beneficiary over the other.

Discretionary trusts, of course, are set up for other beneficiaries as well. A clause that relieves the trustee of the obligation of even-handedness is important in any trust where the expectation is that one of the beneficiaries will be given preferential treatment. In dual trusts, for example, where the family trust allows for payment to any of the spouse, children, or other issue, the trust may still be intended principally to benefit the spouse, and the Trustee must be relieved of the even hand obligation if she is not to be in breach of the trust when, for example, she pays all of the income to the spouse. A general instruction for the trustees to ignore the even hand rule, and excusing them from liability if they do, can be used in any will with a discretionary trust.

Protection from Liability

My Trustees shall be fully protected in exercising any discretion granted to them in this Will, and shall not be liable to the beneficiaries or their heirs or personal representatives by reason of the exercise of their discretion. My Trustees shall exercise the powers

> and discretion given to them in what they deem to be the best interests, whether monetary or otherwise, of the beneficiaries, even if that exercise favours one beneficiary over another or would not be an impartial exercise of their duties or not even-handed among the beneficiaries and the exercise of their powers and discretion shall be binding upon all of the beneficiaries and shall not be subject to any review, by anyone.

4. Family Trusts

Sometimes, the children of a will-maker already have their income taxed at the top marginal rate. In these cases, the will-maker may set up trusts for the children to allow them to split income between the trust (which as a testamentary trust will have graduated rates of tax on income) and the child. When one purpose of a trust for the family is income-splitting, it will generally last for life, but have a clause that allows the Trustees to collapse it. There are many matters to consider in setting up such a trust, not least of which is the desire of will-makers to treat all of their children equally, but to recognize their differences. We give one basic precedent for a Trust of this type.

> On the death of the survivor of my spouse, JANET, and me (the "Division Date") my Trustees shall divide the residue of my estate into as many equal shares as are required to make one share for each child of mine alive at my death and one share for each child of mine who dies before me leaving issue alive at my death. My Trustees shall pay and transfer one of these equal shares to each of the appropriate Special Trustees (as defined below), to be held by them in trust ("the Trust") upon the following terms:
>
> (i) The Special Trustees shall have all the same powers and discretions that my Trustees have under my Will.
>
> (ii) For the purposes of this clause X of my Will, the term "spouse" means a person of the opposite sex to whom a child of mine is married or with whom a child of mine has cohabited in a conjugal relationship for a period of three (3) years immediately before the relevant time and with whom the child is cohabiting and not separated at the relevant time and shall also include that person who was the spouse of my child, at the time of my child's death

until that person remarries or commences to cohabit with another person in a conjugal relationship.

(iii)   Shares for a Surviving Child

1. The Special Trustees of each Trust for a surviving child shall be the child for whom the share is set aside and that child's spouse, or if either my child or his or her spouse is unable or unwilling to act, any other person or persons that my Trustees shall appoint.

2. The Distribution Day of each Special Trust shall be the earlier of (a) the date of death of my surviving child to whom the trust relates and (b) any earlier date that the Special Trustees select.

3. Until the Distribution Day, the Special Trustees may pay to any one or more of that child, his or her spouse, and his or her children, and to the exclusion of any one or more of them for their general benefit, those amounts out of the net income and capital of the Trust that the Special Trustees in their absolute discretion consider appropriate from time to time.

4. After twenty-one (21) years have passed since the Division Date, the Special Trustees shall divide the net income derived from the Trust among any one or more of my child, his or her Spouse, and his or her children, and to the exclusion of any one or more of them, as the Special Trustees in their absolute discretion consider appropriate from time to time.

5. If the Special Trustees have selected as the Distribution Day a date prior to the death of my child, the Special Trustees shall pay and transfer the Trust or the part of it then remaining to my child, for his or her own use absolutely.

6. If the Distribution Day is the date of death of my child, the Special Trustees shall dispose of the Trust as that child may by will appoint. In default of appointment, or to the extent that it does not take effect, the Special Trustees shall divide the Trust or any amount of it then remaining among the issue of that child, in equal shares per stirpes, subject to paragraph X (dealing with shares of grandchildren). If that child leaves no issue alive on the

Distribution Day, the Special Trustees shall divide the Trust or the amount of it then remaining among my issue in equal shares per stirpes, subject to paragraph X (dealing with shares of grandchildren). Any share passing to another child of mine for whom a share is already being held under this clause shall be added to his or her share to be held on the same terms.

(iv) Shares for a Predeceased Child

1. The Special Trustees of each share set aside for a child who dies before me shall be that child's spouse (if any) and any other person or persons that my Trustees shall appoint.

2. The Special Trustees shall hold the share for the issue of my predeceased child in equal shares per stirpes, subject to paragraph X (dealing with shares of grandchildren).

The precedent above refers to a clause dealing with the shares of grandchildren. Any time there is a gift to children, outright or in trust, with a gift over in the event that the child either predeceases or dies before reaching the requisite age, consider including a clause along these lines.

Solution: Grandchildren's Trusts

If a grandchild or other issue of mine (a "Beneficiary") becomes entitled to receive any portion of the residue of my estate before attaining the age of thirty-five (35) years, that portion (the "Portion") shall be held and invested by my Trustees upon the following terms:

(a) Until the Beneficiary attains the age of thirty-five (35) years, my Trustees shall pay to or apply for the benefit of that Beneficiary as much of the income and capital of the Portion as my Trustees in their absolute discretion consider appropriate from time to time. Any income not so paid shall be accumulated and added to the Portion. After the maximum period permitted by law for the accumulation of income, my Trustees shall pay the net income derived from the Portion to or for the benefit of that Beneficiary.

(b) When that Beneficiary attains the age of thirty-five (35) years, my Trustees shall transfer the balance of the Portion to him or her.

(c) If that Beneficiary dies before attaining the age of thirty-five (35) years, my Trustees shall divide the Portion or the amount not yet received by that Beneficiary, among:

(1) the issue of the Beneficiary, in equal shares per stirpes, or if the Beneficiary has no issue then alive,

(2) the issue of the parent of the Beneficiary who is a blood relation of mine, in equal shares per stirpes, or if that parent has no issue then alive,

(3) my other issue, in equal shares per stirpes; and each share shall be treated as a Portion and each issue as a Beneficiary under this clause X of my Will.

(d) Any Portion held in trust shall vest absolutely in the Beneficiary, on the earlier of the following two dates:

(1) the date upon which the Beneficiary is entitled absolutely to the Portion, or

(2) the last day of the period which is the longest period under which vesting may be lawfully postponed.

5. Charitable Trusts   + p. 191

Sometimes a will-maker (usually one with no close family that she wants to benefit) decides to leave the residue of the estate to charity. If the gift is to an existing charity the issues are similar to those that arise when a legacy is left to charity.[165] If the will-maker intends, however, to have the trustees administer the gift, the will itself will set up the charitable trust.

☞ **The Public Guardian and Trustee's Charitable Property Program publishes a list of pre-approved wording for objects of charitable corporations. While the pre-approved wording may not match exactly what your client has in mind, the PGT's list is a very useful starting place for drafting purposes in a charitable trust.[166]**

---

[165] For a discussion of these issues, see Chapter Seven "Legacies".

[166] The list is available on the PGT's website http://www.attorneygeneral.jus.gov.on.ca.

> I direct my Trustees to hold the residue of my estate upon trust in a fund ("the Fund") to be invested and reinvested by them and to apply the annual net income derived from the Fund for the following purposes:
>
> 1. [Insert the purposes for which the trust is set up.]
>
> 2. I authorize my Trustees, if at any time they consider it advisable, to pay or transfer the Fund to a charitable institution to be held by the proper officers of that institution upon the trusts and conditions herein set forth. I declare that the receipt of the person who professes to be the Treasurer or other proper officer for the time being of the charitable institution and his undertaking to carry out the above trusts shall be a complete release to my Trustees. If, in the opinion of my Trustees, it becomes impossible, inadvisable, or impractical to use the Fund for the purposes set out above, or if my Trustees are of the opinion that the whole or part of the Fund is not required for those purposes, my Trustees shall use the Fund or any part of it in the manner that they in their absolute discretion consider advisable for purposes that they consider at any time and from time to time to be consistent with the spirit and intention of this gift.

It is possible to leave the choice of particular charities or purposes up to the executors. At one time, a tax receipt would not be given in these circumstances, but the Ministry of Finance has now accepted the Trustee's choice as sufficient, and will issue receipts.[167]

Successor Trustee

Error #13: No Successor Trustees

If a trust is to be endowed in perpetuity, it will outlast the executor of the will, unless the executor is a corporation. For this reason, a client setting up a trust for charitable purposes should talk to a trust company about having it

---

[167] See Technical Interpretations 2000-0055825 and 2001-0090205.

act as trustee. If a corporate trustee is objectionable, the will must provide for the replacement of trustees.[168]

 (1) My Trustees, at any time that they in their absolute discretion consider appropriate, may appoint one or more additional Trustees to act with them.

(2) Any Trustee may resign on thirty (30) days' written notice to the other Trustees and to the adult and competent beneficiaries of my estate, but there shall at all times be at least two Trustees. A resigning Trustee shall not be required to pass accounts unless required by the other Trustees or by the adult and competent beneficiaries to do so.

Perpetuities Clause

Error #14: Perpetuities

The rule that prohibits vesting at a remote point in time and the rule against perpetual tenure are generally lumped together as "The Rule Against Perpetuities". While the latter applies only to non-charitable trusts, the former applies to any trust, including a charitable trust.

To avoid an egregious error in this area, run a perpetuities "test," based on the common law rule:

Any interest that is not certain to vest before the perpetuities period is void. The perpetuities period is 21 years beyond the last death of any person connected with the trust alive at the time of the will-maker's death.

Suppose Winifred, who has no family other than one daughter Drusilla, makes a gift to "my grandchildren who reach the age of 50 years, but if none does, to ABC Charity". If Winifred had grandchildren living at her death, the gift would be sure to vest within their lifetimes. If there are no grandchildren at her death, however, it is possible that Drusilla will die childless. Even if she has children after Winifred's death, they are not lives-in-being. Drusilla is the measuring life, but if Drusilla has a child, and then dies immediately, that is the end of the life-in-being. Since the grandchild would have to be 50 before the gift vested, and that would happen more than 21 years after Drusilla's death, the gift is void under the common law rule. Note that the gift is void from the start, even though we do not know how long Drusilla will live, or whether she will have children at the time of Winifred's death. Any possi-

---

[168] The *Trustee Act* does include some terms for replacing trustees, but only if there have been two to begin with, and the method of replacement (at the choice of the remaining trustee) may not be desirable.

bility that the gift will not vest within 21 years of Drusilla's death invalidates the gift from the point of Winifred's death. Note that this is the common law rule, which has been modified by statute to allow trustees to "wait and see" whether the gift will vest before declaring it void.

If you will not be certain exactly who is to take a share of the estate until 21 years after all the people who are alive when the will speaks are dead, you risk having the gift declared void. Consider the use of a general clause that vests these interests automatically before the expiry of the perpetuities period.[169]

> Notwithstanding anything in my Will, any interest in my estate held in trust shall vest absolutely in the person or institution entitled to receive the income of that interest or in another person or institution that my Trustees, in their absolute discretion appoint, on the earlier of the following two dates: (a) the date upon which the person or institution is entitled absolutely to the interest, or (b) the last day of the period of twenty-one (21) years from the death of the last to survive me, my spouse and my issue alive at my death.

---

[169] To illustrate how remoteness of vesting might affect a charitable trust, consider *Re Schjaastad* [1920] 1 W.W.R. 327, 50 D.L.R. 445 13 Sask. L.R. 114 (C.A.). The will made a gift "to the first Norwegian Lutheran Orphans' Home built in Saskatchewan or Alberta". There was no such home at the time of the will, or at the time of the will-maker's death, or when the matter came before the court, nor was it likely there ever would be. The gift was found to be in violation of the rule against remoteness of vesting, and the gift reverted to the estate.

CHAPTER 10

EXECUTORS AND TRUSTEES
POWERS AND RIGHTS

The Common Law

The administrative powers and duties included in a will to expedite the administration of the estate must be examined against the fundamental duties that spring from the executor's status as a fiduciary. These fundamental duties are:[170]

(1) To discharge her duties personally;

(2) Not to let personal interests conflict with the estate; and

(3) Not to favour one beneficiary over another.

These fundamental duties are subject to an overarching duty to act honestly, vigilantly and with prudence. Duties may be varied by the terms set out in the will. For example, trustees cannot be excused from liability for acts of gross negligence.[171] However, the degree to which these fundamental duties can be varied is not always clear. One key issue to revisit continually when drafting the administrative powers and duties is:

Why is a trust power or obligation to be included; and if a lower standard is to be introduced — why?

Fundamental duties and obligations are designed for the protection of beneficiaries who are often minor, elderly or otherwise vulnerable. Although a standard clause is useful, you must consider each fact situation and the will-maker's intentions before its automatic inclusion.

---

[170] Donovan Waters, in *Wills Drafting*, April 29, 1987 (Toronto Dept. of Education, The Law Society of Upper Canada, 1987), at pp. c-3 and c-4. Law Society of Upper Canada.

[171] Jordan M. Atin, "Protection of Trustees" in *Drafting Wills to Avoid Litigation* (Toronto: Dept. of Education, Law Society of Upper Canada, 2000).

Error #3: No Trust Power Provisions

The Trustee Act

In an effort to keep the will document short and simple, some wills do not include any administrative provisions. If the will is silent, the executors and trustees must rely on the powers conferred on them by statute or common law. Initially, trust powers were conferred by statute to make certain that trustees were given the minimum requisite powers to administer the average estate. Many of the authorized powers in the *Trustee Act* arose out of the administrative provisions regularly included by solicitors in the trust documents at the time.[172] The legislature wanted to ensure that the inadvertent exclusion of a power would not impede the administration of an estate. These statutory powers, however, are quite limited in number and scope and it is necessary to broaden them to deal with modern estates.

If the will is silent, trustees have the following powers:

1. The Power to Sell

The *Trustee Act* does not confer on the trustees a power of sale. Although the *Trustee Act* does contain provision on the mode of sale, it only applies if a power of sale otherwise exists.[173] There is an implied power to pay debts and to sell assets to satisfy payment of legacies if there is no provision in the will which transfers the assets of the estate to the executor. If a power of sale cannot be implied, recourse must be had to section 17(1) of the *Estate Administration Act.*[174]

2. Power to Apply to the Court for an Opinion[175]

3. Power to Pay Funds into Court[176]

---

[172] Frederic William Maitland, *Equity: a Course of Lectures*, by F.W. Maitland, edited by A.H. Chaytor and W.J. Whittaker, 2nd ed. Rev. (Cambridge University Press, 1936: reprinted 1969).

[173] Ontario Law Reform Commission, p. 238.

[174] Trustee Act, s. 17(1) Powers of executors and administrators as to selling and conveying real estate — The powers of sale conferred by this Act on a personal representative may be exercised for the purpose not only of paying debts but also of distributing or dividing the estate among the persons beneficially entitled, whether there are or are not debts, and in no case is it necessary that the persons beneficially entitled concur in any such sale except where it is made for the purpose of distribution only.

[175] Trustee Act, section 60.(1) Trustee, etc., may apply for advice in management of trust property — A trustee, guardian or personal representative may, without the institution of an action, apply to the Superior Court of Justice for the opinion, advice or direction of the court on any question respecting the management of administration of the trust property or the assets of a ward or a testator or intestate.

[176] Trustee Act, s. 36(1) Payment into court by trustees of trust funds or securities by order of court — Where any money belonging to a trust is in the hands or under the control of or is vested in a sole trustee or several trustees and it is the desire of the trustee, or of the majority of the trustees, to pay the money into court, the Superior Court of Justice may order the payment into court to be made by the sole trustee, or by the majority of the trustees, without the concurrence of the other or others if the concurrence cannot be obtained. R.S.O. 1990, c. T.23, s. 36 (1); 2000, c. 26, Sched. A, s. 15 (2).

4.   Power to Obtain Passing of Accounts[177]

5.   Power to Issue Receipts[178]

6.   Power to Compromise Claims[179]

Although it is preferable to have the benefit of a court order in settling a claim, the *Trustee Act* does confer on the trustee this power.

7.   Limited Power to Employ Agents[180]

Section 20(1) authorizes the trustee to appoint agents in a limited set of circumstances. The common law also allows the trustee to delegate powers if the task would be regarded in business as reasonable.

8.   Power to Invest In Prudent Investments and Delegate Investment Decision Making

9.   Power to Renew a Lease

---

[177] Trustee Act, section 23 When Trustee May File Accounts — A trustee desiring to pass the accounts of dealings with the trust estate may file the accounts in the office of the Superior Court of Justice, and the proceedings and practice upon the passing of such accounts shall be the same and have the like effect as the passing of executors' or administrators' accounts in the court. R.S.O. 1990, c. T.23, s. 23 (1); 2000, c. 26, Sched. A, s. 15 (2).

[178] Trustee Act, section 24 Receipts of trustees to be effectual discharges — The payment of any money to and the receipt thereof by any person to whom the same is payable upon any trust, or for any limited purpose, and such payment to and receipt by the survivors of two or more mortgagees or holders or the executors or administrators of such survivors or their assigns, effectually discharges the person paying the same from seeing to the application or being answerable for the misapplication thereof. R.S.O. 1990, c. T.23, s. 24.

[179] Trustee Act, section 48.(1) Payment of debts — A personal representative may pay or allow any debt or claim on any evidence that the representative thinks sufficient.

[180] Trustee Act, s. 20(1) Power to authorize receipt of money — By solicitor — A trustee may appoint a solicitor as agent to receive and give a discharge for any money or valuable consideration or property receivable by the trustee under the trust. By banker — (2) A trustee may appoint a manager or a branch manager of a bank listed in Schedule I or II to the *Bank Act* (Canada) or a solicitor to be the trustee's agent to receive and give a discharge for any money payable to the trustee under or by virtue of a policy of assurance or otherwise. Appointment not a breach of trust — (3) A trustee shall not be charged with a breach of trust by reason only of having made or concurred in making any such appointment. Liability of trustee, in certain cases, not affected — (4) Nothing in this section exempts a trustee from any liability that would have been incurred if this Act had not been passed, in case the trustee permits any money, valuable consideration, or property to remain in the hands or under the control of the banker or solicitor for a period longer than is reasonably necessary to enable the banker or solicitor to pay or transfer the same to the trustee. R.S.O. 1990, c. T.23, s. 20.

A trustee has power to renew a lease although not to enter into a new one.[181]

10.   Power to Insure[182]

The trustee may insure a building, unless he is bound to convey the building to a beneficiary on request. There is a current restriction that the level of insurance not exceed 75% of the value of the building.

11.   Power to Dedicate for Highway Purposes[183]

12.   Limited Power to Borrow Money[184]

Include the Necessary Powers

The *Trustee Act* sets out that nothing in the Act authorizes a trustee to do anything that the trustee is in express terms forbidden to do, or to omit to do anything that the trustee is in express terms directed to do by the

---

[181] Trustee Act, 22. (1) Power of trustees of renewable leaseholds to renew — A trustee of any leaseholds for lives or years that are renewable from time to time may, if the trustee thinks fit, and shall, if required by any person having any beneficial interest, present or future or contingent, in the leaseholds, use the trustee's best endeavors to obtain from time to time a renewed lease of the same land on reasonable terms, and for that purpose may from time to time make or concur in making a surrender of the lease for the time being subsisting, and do all such other acts as are requisite; but where, by the terms of the settlement or will, the person in possession for life or other limited interest is entitled to enjoy the same without any obligation to renew or to contribute to the expense of renewal, this section does not apply unless the consent in writing of that person is obtained to the renewal on the part of the trustee.

[182] Trustee Act 21.(1) Power to insure buildings — A trustee may insure against loss or damage by fire, tempest or other casualty, any building or other insurable property to any amount, including the amount of any insurance already on foot, not exceeding three-fourths of the value of such building or property, and pay the premiums for such insurance out of the income thereof or out of the income of any other property subject to the same trusts, without obtaining the consent of any person who may be entitled wholly or partly to such income. Exception (2) This section does not apply to any building or property that a trustee is bound forthwith to convey absolutely to any beneficiary upon being requested to do so. R.S.O. 1990, c. T.23, s. 21.

[183] Trustee Act 19 Dedication or sale of land by trustee for municipal highway — With the approval of the Ontario Municipal Board or of a judge of the Superior Court of Justice, a person who holds land or a charge or claim against it or has control of the legal title, upon any trust or for a specified or particular purpose, may, to the extent of the estate or interest, dedicate or sell, or join in dedicating or selling, to the corporation of the municipality within which it is situate, any portion of the land required by the corporation for the work of establishing extending, widening or diverting a street, and the Board or the judge may approve thereof if it appears that it will not have the effect of defeating or seriously affecting the substantial objects or intent of the trust or purpose but the approval is not necessary if such dedication or sale is otherwise within such person's powers. R.S.O. 1990, c. T.23, s. 19; 2000, c. 26, Sched. A, s. 15 (2).

[184] Trustee Act, s. 44(1) Power to raise money by sale or mortgage to satisfy charges — Where by any will coming into operation after the 18th day of September, 1865, a testator charges land, or any specific part thereof, with the payment of debts or with the payment of any legacy or other specific sum of money, and devises the land so charged to executors or to a trustee without any express provision for the raising of such debt, legacy or sum of money out of such land, the devisee may raise such debt, legacy or money by a sale of such land or any part thereof, or by a mortgage of the same.

instrument creating the trust.[185] Trustee powers can be broadened in the trust instrument. Without a set of appropriate powers, there may be additional delay and expense.

Powers to Include for the Average Estate

Based on the variety of wills we have encountered, there does not appear to be agreement on the fundamental powers which should be regularly included in the average will. However, it makes sense to include the following powers in order to ensure an orderly administration of the estate unless the will-maker or the nature of the will plan specifically requires that they be removed.[186]

1. The Power to Pay Debts

2. The Power to Sell

3. The Power to Postpone Conversion

4. Power to Hold for Minors and Make Payments to Guardians

5. Investment Powers

6. The Power to Distribute Assets in Specie

7. The Power to Repair, Partition, Lease and generally deal with Real Estate

8. The Power to Make Elections

9. The Power to Borrow

10. The Power to Appoint Agents

Power to Pay Debts

A creditor's right to be paid out of the assets of an estate is determined by the law. It cannot in any manner be controlled by the terms of the will. The assets of an estate devolve to the personal representatives and subject to the payment of debts, are to be distributed to beneficiaries in accordance with

---

[185] Trustee Act 68 — Nothing in this Act authorizes a trustee to do anything that the trustee is in express terms forbidden to do, or to omit to do anything that the trustee is in express terms directed to do by the instrument creating the trust. R.S.O. 1990, c. T.23, s. 68.

[186] The following samples are not meant to replace the many good books which set out a comprehensive selection of precedents. Instead, they are included for illustrative purposes only.

the terms of the will.[187] The trustee is under a duty to pay these debts as soon as possible.

Funeral expenses are a first charge on the assets, followed by the cost and expense of administering the estate including executors' compensation.[188] As to the remaining debts of the will-maker, there is no priority among different creditors[189] — except for those whose debts are secured. In solvent estates, debts are to be paid in full.

Subject to a contrary intention in the will, the order in which assets are applied to debts seems to be as follows:[190]

The general personal estate not bequeathed at all

Real property not bequeathed at all

The real and personal property comprised in the residuary bequest

Real property devised in trust to pay debts

Real or personal property charged with the payment of debts and devised or bequeathed subject to the charge

General legacies, including annuities and demonstrative legacies that have become general

Specific legacies (including demonstrative legacies that have not become general) and specific devises to contribute *pro rata*

Real and personal property in respect of which the deceased had a general power of appointment which he or she exercised

Paraphernalia of the deceased's spouse

---

[187] Estate Administration Act, section 2(1) — Devolution to the personal representative of the deceased — All real and personal property that is vested in a person without a right in any other person to take by survivorship, on the person's death, whether testate or intestate and despite any testamentary disposition, devolves to and becomes vested in his or her personal representative from time to time as trustee for the person's by law beneficially entitled, and subject to the payment of the persons debts and so far as such property is not disposed of by deed, will, contract or other effectual disposition, it shall be administered, dealt with and distributed as if it were personal property not so disposed of.

[188] *Re Shields Estate* (1994), 6 E.T.R. (2d) 25.

[189] There may be priority for certain family law claims.

[190] As set out in Oosterhoff, A.H. *Text, Commentary and cases on Will and Succession*, p. 39 and *Widdifield, on Executors Accounts*, op. cit. note 7 at p. 86.

If there are insufficient assets in an estate to satisfy all debts, the creditors share in equal proportions.[191] The following is a standard payment of debts clause:

> My Trustees shall pay out of and charge to the capital of my general estate my just debts and funeral and testamentary expenses and I hereby authorize my Trustees to defer, commute or prepay any of these debts, funeral, or testamentary expenses.

You should make certain to consider any obligations owing by a testator. A separation agreement or domestic contract may require the estate to provide continuing support to a former spouse or children. It may be appropriate to include a clause in the will to address this situation.

The debts clause does not imply that any mortgage should be discharged by the estate. If the estate is to discharge a mortgage, it must be set out in the will.[192] Finally, if there are multiple wills with respect to either foreign property or domestic assets, the debts clause should set out how the payment of tax is to be divided among the multiple estates.[193]

Power to Sell and Postpone Conversion

In almost all situations, the executor will want broad powers to sell set out in the will. If the power to postpone is not conferred in a will, the executor is expected to sell the assets within the executor's year. To force a sale immediately may not be prudent depending on the circumstances. As a result, the power to postpone is often included with the power to sell.

---

[191] Trustee Act, section 50(1) — In case of deficiency of assets, debts to rank proportionately — On the administration of the estate of a deceased person, in the case of a deficiency of assets, debts due to the Crown and to the personal representative of the deceased person, and debts to others, including herein debts by judgment or order, and other debts of record, debts by specialty, simple contract debts and such claims for damages as are payable in like order of administration as simple contract debts shall be paid proportionately and without any preference or priority of debts of one rank or nature over those of another but nothing herein prejudices any lien existing during the lifetime of the debtor on any of the debtor's property.

[192] See Chapter Six "Real Estate" for statutory sections and precedents.

[193] See Chapter 12, "Multiple Wills".

> My Trustees shall use their discretion in the realization of my estate with power to sell any part of my estate at any time and on any terms, and either for cash or credit or for part cash and part credit as they, in their absolute discretion, decide. I further authorize my Trustees to postpone the conversion of any part or parts of my estate for whatever length of time they in their absolute discretion determine. My Trustees shall have a separate power to retain any of my investments or assets in the form existing at my death at their absolute discretion without responsibility for loss and whether or not it is an investment or asset in which a trustee may by law invest.

Power to Hold for Minors and Make Payment to Guardians

> (a) If any person becomes entitled to receive a share of my estate while under the age of majority, my Trustees shall keep that share invested and, until that person attains the age of majority, my Trustees shall pay or apply for the benefit of that person as much of the income and capital as my Trustees in the exercise of an absolute discretion consider advisable.
>
> (b) I authorize my Trustees to make any payments for a person under the age of majority to a parent or guardian or other person standing *in loco parentis* to that person, or to make any payment directly to the person that my Trustees in their absolute discretion consider appropriate. Any evidence that my Trustees have made a payment shall discharge my Trustees with regard to that payment.

Investment Powers

Prior to July 1, 1999, Trustee Act investments were restricted to those listed in the then sections 26 and 27 of the Act (i.e. the legal list). The list has been eliminated and a trustee is now directed to exercise the care a prudent investor would exercise in making investments.

Subject to the terms of the will,[194] the trustee must diversify investments and consider the following criteria:

1. general economic conditions;

2. the effect of inflation or deflation;

---

[194] Notwithstanding the above provisions, section 27(9) sets out the trustee is not required to act in a manner which is inconsistent with the terms of the trust.

3. the tax consequences of investment strategies;

4. the role of each investment in terms of the overall portfolio;

5. expected return from income and appreciation of capital;

6. need for liquidity, regularity of income and preservation or appreciation of capital; and

7. the asset's special nature or value to the purposes of the trust to any beneficiary.

It is prudent for a trustee to consult with an investment advisor and obtain an investment plan speaking to the criteria in the Act to protect himself from liability. If trustees are investing funds directly, they are permitted to invest in mutual funds. Trustees can also now delegate investment decision making to an investment advisor provided that there is compliance with section 27 of the *Act.*

Trustees' Discretion

> My Trustees when making investments for my estate shall not be limited to investments authorized by law for trustees but may make any investments they in their absolute discretion consider prudent and to be in the best interests of my estate.

Prudent Investor Standard

> My Trustees when making investments for my estate shall be limited to investments authorized by law for trustees.

> **If a large asset, investment or an operating company may continue to be held by the estate, the will should explicitly release the trustees from any liability by reason of so doing. Otherwise, the trustees may be questioned for failing to diversify and perhaps acting imprudently. The Trustee Act specifically sets out that the special nature of the asset should be considered and the investment provisions are subject to the terms of the trust instrument.**

No Criteria or Diversification

The following clause should be used only for relatively small estates, to assist unsophisticated trustees.

> My Trustees, when making investments for my estate, shall not be subject to the criteria in planning for, or the requirement to diversify investments of, trust property prescribed by law for trustees.

Power to Distribute Assets in Kind

If the will is silent, the trustees can only distribute trust property in specie if all of the beneficiaries agree,[195] so an "in specie clause" should be included in a will to expedite the administration of the estate.

> My Trustees may divide, distribute or allocate any asset of my estate in kind and at the valuation to be determined by my Trustees in their absolute discretion. In determining the valuation, my Trustees may consider future expectations for the asset as my Trustees in their absolute discretion consider appropriate, including any tax liability or credit. Any decision made by my Trustees in this regard shall be binding on all persons concerned.

Real Estate

If there is a remote possibility that the will-maker will own real property at her death, a real estate clause must be included. There is no statutory authority to exchange, partition,[196] lease, maintain, or repair real estate.[197]

---

[195] Ontario Law Reform Commission, Report on the Law of Trusts, p. 248.

[196] The power to partition would be subject to the provisions of the *Planning Act.*

[197] Ontario Law Reform Commission, p. 240.

If any real or leasehold property forms part of my estate, my Trustees may, in their absolute discretion:

1. exchange, partition, or otherwise dispose of the whole or any part of the property either for cash or credit or for part cash and part credit as my Trustees consider appropriate;

2. lease property for any term or terms and subject to any conditions and covenants;

3. accept surrenders of leases and tenancies;

4. pay money out of the income and capital of my general estate for repairs or improvements and generally manage and maintain the property;

5. give options; and

6. give or renew any mortgage or borrow any money upon any mortgage or pay off any mortgage at any time after my death.

A clause such as this one should be reviewed with a will-maker and modified to reflect his intent.

Power to Make Elections

The will-maker should confer this power on the trustees in the will.

My Trustees may make, or choose not to make, any allocations, elections, determinations, designations, and applications as my Trustees in their absolute discretion consider to be in the best interests of my Estate, and specifically any allocations and elections necessary under the *Income Tax Act* (Canada) or any similar legislation of any province or other jurisdiction in force from time to time.

Power to Borrow

Section 44 of the *Trustee Act* provides a limited power to borrow money:

44. Where by any will coming into operation after the 18th day of September, 1865, a testator charges land, or any specific part thereof, with the payment of debts or with the payment of any legacy or other specific sum of money, and devises the land so charged to executors or to a trustee

without any express provision for the raising of such debt, legacy or sum of money out of such land, the devisee may raise such debt, legacy or money by a sale of such land or any part thereof, or by a mortgage of the same.

A broader power should be conferred on the trustee, however, since there are many possible reasons why a trustee may need to borrow. Lack of liquidity and need of funds to pay taxes could be one situation in which the trustee would need to borrow.

> My Trustees may borrow on behalf of my estate such amount or amounts and on such terms and conditions as they in their absolute discretion deem advisable, and, for the repayment of any amount borrowed, may mortgage, charge, pledge, hypothecate or otherwise encumber any of the assets of my estate.

Appointment of Agents

Historically, trustees have been permitted to delegate their powers when the particular task would have been regarded in business as reasonable to delegate.[198] The potential complexities in the administration of an estate, and the fact that people are busy and move around mean that express authorization to appoint agents should be included in a will as a precaution. This ability does not derogate from the trustees duty to supervise appointed agents properly.

> I authorize my Trustees at any time to engage the services of any trust company, lawyer, accountant, bookkeeper, investment advisor or other professional advisor or organization to assist them in the management and administration of my estate, and my Trustees shall pay for any of these services out of the income or the capital of my estate as they in their absolute discretion determine.

Other Powers To Be Considered

Consider the inclusion of the following powers, depending on the beneficiaries, the nature of the assets, and the dispositive provisions in the will.

---

[198] *Speight v. Gaunt* (1883), 9 A.C. 1.

If the Will Contains On-going Trusts

Annuities

Holding small trusts may cost more than it's worth. The will-maker may want the trustees to have the option to purchase an annuity and wind up an estate, but without the inclusion of this power, the trustees may be improperly delegating their discretion.

> I authorize my Trustees to purchase an annuity for life or a term of years for any beneficiary where the cost of the administration of any trust fund is disproportionate to the value of the share as determined by my Trustees in their absolute discretion. I expressly authorize my Trustees to purchase an annuity notwithstanding that a contingent or remainder beneficiary may no longer be entitled to any potential contingent or remainder interest.

Early Vesting

Like the Annuity Clause, this clause permits the trustee to pay the balance of the fund to a beneficiary or a parent or legal guardian in circumstances where the administrative cost of holding it in trust outweighs the benefits of the trust.

> Notwithstanding anything else in this Will and any Codicil, if my Trustees are holding any share of my estate in trust for any beneficiary and my Trustees in their absolute discretion determine that the cost of administering the fund is disproportionate to the value of the share, I authorize my Trustees to pay the remainder of that share to the beneficiary or to the parent or legal guardian of the beneficiary as they in their absolute discretion determine.

Without this power, the court could find that the trustees exercised an improper delegation of discretion.

Accumulation of Income

The *Accumulations Act* sets out that income cannot accumulate for more than 21 years. In other words, after 21 years from the death of the will-maker, income can no longer be added to the capital of a trust: it must be disbursed.[199] The following clause directs that if a share is being held for a

---

[199] No disposition of any real or personal property shall direct the income thereof to be wholly or partially accumulated for any longer than one of the following terms:

(continued on next page)

child, any income not used shall be accumulated by the trustee and added to the capital, but if income can no longer be accumulated, it is to be paid out to the child.

> If in any year that my Trustee hold the share or any part of it, any portion of the net income is not paid or applied for the benefit of the child, such portion shall be accumulated by my Trustee and added in the following year to the capital of such share to be dealt with as part of it, provided that after the expiration of the maximum period for which income may be accumulated under the laws governing my estate, if my Trustee is then holding the share or any part of it, my Trustee shall thereafter pay to or apply for the child the whole of the net income of the share.

Co-mingling of Trusts

At common law, a trustee is unable to co-mingle trust funds.[200] However, a will-maker may want to specifically authorize the trustee to co-mingle trust funds in certain instances. If the trustee is holding several trusts for beneficiaries on similar terms, the will-maker may want to allow the trustee to co-mingle them. This power may be especially useful if the trustee is a professional and charges a minimum fee for the administration of each testamentary trust. If an insurance trust and a testamentary trust are being held for the same beneficiary on similar terms, the will-maker may again want to allow the trustee to co-mingle them to reduce the administrative cost.

> My Trustees may in their absolute discretion co-mingle assets comprising my estate, or insurance proceeds held in a separate testamentary trust, with other moneys or assets held by my Trustees either in trust for any one or more of my beneficiaries of my estate or under trusteeship of my Trustees outside of my estate.

(continued from previous page)
1. The life of the grantor.
2. Twenty-one years from the date of making an *inter vivos* disposition.
3. The duration of the minority or respective minorities of any person or persons living or conceived but not born at the date of making an *inter vivos* disposition.
4. Twenty-one years from the death of the grantor, settlor or testator.
5. The duration of the minority or respective minorities of any person or persons living or conceived but not born at the death of the grantor, settlor or testator.
6. The duration of the minority or respective minorities of any person or persons who, under the instrument directing the accumulations, would, for the time being, if of full age, be entitled to the income directed to be accumulated.

[200] *Re Smullen Estate* (1995), 6 E.T.R. (2d) 299 (Ont. Gen. Div.).

The Power to Lend

A power to lend may be required, especially if a long-term trust may be administered.

> I authorize my Trustees from time to time to lend money from my estate on such terms and conditions and for such length of time as my Trustees in the absolute discretion determine. I also declare that my Trustees may lend money for the express purpose of earning income for my estate or for such other purposes connected with my estate as my Trustees in their discretion from time to time may deem advisable. [*My Trustees may lend out of my estate to any person or corporation notwithstanding that the person or corporation may be a member of my family or a beneficiary.*] My Trustees shall not be liable for any loss that may happen to my estate in connection with any such loan made by them in good faith.

 It may not always be appropriate to authorize the lending of money to a family business because of the potential conflict of interest.

No Even Hand

If a life interest is created in a will, the will-maker may want to relieve the trustees of the duty to maintain an even hand between the life tenant and the remainder.

> In exercising their discretion with regard to the investment, retention, or selling of any particular asset held by my estate, my Trustees shall not be required to maintain an even hand between the life tenants and the residuary beneficiaries of my estate, provided that all of these decisions made by my Trustees are made prudently and in good faith.

Qualifying Spousal Trust

Several standard trust powers, such as the power to lend, may inadvertently taint a spousal trust. The following clause may be included to prevent it.

 Notwithstanding anything contained in this Will, my Trustees shall not have any power to do anything which will disqualify the "spousal trust" provided in this my Will from being a spousal trust within the meaning of the *Income Tax Act* or any successor legislation.

Note that this clause in a will would prevent a tainting — even if the trustee pragmatically wanted to taint the trust for tax purposes.

Charitable Receipts and Gifting Powers

If the will-maker intends to make charitable bequests, a receipts clause should be included in all instances.

 The receipt of the person professing to be the Treasurer or other proper Officer for the time being of each organization receiving a benefit under the terms of this Will shall be a sufficient discharge to my Trustees, who shall have no further responsibility in connection with it.

Transactions with Trustees

Unless it is otherwise provided in the will, a trustee cannot purchase an asset from the estate without court approval because a trustee cannot self-deal.[201] If a trustee is a family member and the will-maker wants to confer the power on a trustee to purchase an asset without court approval, include the following power:

 In my Trustees' personal capacity, my Trustees may purchase any assets from my estate if the purchase price and other terms are unanimously approved by my Trustees and by the adult beneficiaries of my estate. My Trustees shall not be required to obtain approval of any Court for that purchase.

---

[201] Widdifield, op. cit., page 277.

Settlement of Claims

Trustees are given a power to pay debts and to compromise, compound, abandon, submit to arbitration or otherwise settle any debt under the *Trustee Act.* This provision can be expanded in the will, although a trustee would likely want the court to approve any settlement in a potentially litigious estate or where the assets include a business.

> Without the consent of any person interested under my Will, my Trustees may compromise, settle, contest or waive any claim at any time due to or by my estate and may make any agreement with any person, government or corporation which shall be binding upon all persons interested in my estate.

Power to Carry On Business

No express statutory provision enables a trustee to continue to carry on a business.[202] It could be argued that a general power to postpone the conversion of an asset of the estate may permit the trustees to postpone the sale of a business for the benefit of a life tenant.[203] The trustee could also attempt to argue that the business constitutes an investment to be carried on under the powers of investment. However, even assuming these arguments could be made, operating a business which is a going concern may not be regarded as prudent. Accordingly, if there are business interests, a power to carry on the business should be specifically included in the will.

> I authorize my Trustees without being liable for any loss occasioned thereby to retain as an investment of my estate any business or company which I may own or in which I may have a controlling or proprietary interest at the time of my death ("the Business"), to continue and carry on or to participate in the carrying on of the Business, to reorganize, incorporate, wind up, or dispose of the Business, to advance capital to the Business out of my general estate, and generally to do all things in connection with the Business that I myself could do if living.

Securities

The *Trustee Act* does not directly give the trustees the ability to exercise the rights and powers attendant upon the ownership of shares of a corporation. It could be argued that since the shares are vested in the trustees, they

---

[202] Ontario Law Reform Commission Report, p. 243.

[203] *Re Crowther, Midgely v. Crowther,* [1895] 2 Ch. 56.

should be entitled to exercise the powers of the shareholder. However, it is not clear whether this is the case.[204]

> My Trustees shall have the power to deal with any shares or other interests which I may have in a company at my death to the same extent as if I were alive. My Trustees shall have the power to take up new or further shares, join in any reorganization, exchange shares or interests, and give, accept or exercise options. My Trustees may pay any money out of the income or capital of my estate as determined by my Trustees which may be necessary for any of these purposes.

Jurisdictional Issues

1. Proper Law

> This Will shall be governed by the laws of the Province of Ontario.

2. Change of Law

> This Will shall be governed by the laws of the Province of Ontario. My Trustees, in their absolute discretion, may transfer the situs of any trust created under this Will to any jurisdiction selected by my Trustees from time to time. After any change of situs, my Trustees may by instrument in writing resolve that the Trust Fund be administered exclusively under the laws of (and subject, as required, to supervision of the courts of) the jurisdiction to which it has been transferred.

3. Administration Bond

In Ontario, the court is not legally bound by a will-maker's request to waive the requirement of a bond for a non-Commonwealth executor, but this clause may be persuasive.

---

[204] Ontario Law Reform Commission Report, p. 244.

> My Trustees wherever resident or domiciled are to be relieved from giving any bond or security with respect to the administration of my estate in any jurisdiction unless such bond or security is mandatory by law.

4.   Foreign Agent Clause

> My Trustees may, in their absolute discretion, appoint a representative of my estate in one or more of the U.S.A. or in any other country, and I authorize my Trustees to choose any person or corporation in their absolute discretion and to take the necessary steps to have such person or corporation appointed.

Corporate Trustee

If a corporate trustee is appointed, a comprehensive list of trust powers conferred on the trustees will be needed. In addition to the powers already described, the following will be required:

1.   Registration of Assets

The following clause enables the registration of the assets in the street name of the Trustee for convenience.

> If my Trustees in their absolute discretion deem it advisable, any assets forming part of my estate may be held or registered in the name of such nominee or nominees (or both) as my Trustees in their absolute discretion may select.

2.   Power to Invest in Bank affiliated with Corporate Trustee

Due to a potential conflict of interest, a Corporate Trustee may not invest in its own assets or in an affiliated bank without a clause which allows it to do so.

> I authorize my Trustees to retain or purchase securities, shares, obligations or interests in the Bank or its related group of companies.

3.   Expansion of Powers

Finally, consider augmenting your list of administrative trustee powers with a general expansive statement such as this:

(a) Until the final distribution of my estate and until the trusts set out in this Will have been fully performed, my Trustees have the power to perform, without court authorization, every act which a prudent person would perform for the purposes of the trusts under my Will.

(b) My Trustees may do all supplementary or ancilliary acts or things and execute all instruments to enable them to carry out the intent and purpose of the powers here set out.

CHAPTER 11

GUARDIANSHIP OF MINORS, FUNERAL DIRECTIONS, CODICILS AND MEMORANDA, FAMILY DEFINITIONS, AND OTHER WILL-RELATED MATTERS

This chapter groups together a number of issues that are usually dealt with at the end of the will. Other than the fact that they are somewhat peripheral to the will, they do not have a great deal in common.

Will-like provisions such as funeral arrangements and guardianship clauses will not have any impact on probate, nor are they likely to require a probated will. Therefore, where the clients make double wills, it is immaterial in which of the two wills they are included. If the majority of the liquid assets are covered by one will, the funeral directions should probably go there, since the most immediately available funds are most likely to be used for funeral costs. On the other hand, guardianship clauses should go in the will that is likely to be used to administer the trusts for the children.

Error #1: Full Funeral Directions

Legally, it is not an error to include funeral directions in a will; the executor has custody of the deceased's remains and has the legal authority to determine their disposition.[205] The instructions in the will are not, however, binding on the executor.[206] In any case, there is the practical problem that the will may well not be consulted until after the funeral when it is not only too late, but when it may cause real anguish to family members who have done something different from what the will sets out.

Funeral homes promote pre-planned and pre-paid funerals, but the executor and the family will have to know about the arrangements for them to be effective. We encourage clients to talk about the funeral with family, but many are reticent. At the very least, you must let clients know that, while you can include the funeral directions in a will, there is a real risk that this means of conveying their instructions may be ineffective.

Error #2: "Scatter my ashes"

If clients do leave funeral instructions, they should be expressed as wishes, rather that as mandatory requirements. The executor will not only not be legally obliged to follow them (although most will try their best), but he may actually be prohibited. Never underestimate the ingenuity of willmakers. They will want to be buried standing up, with the remains of their (already buried) child,[207] to have their ashes mixed with their spouse's or their pet's, to have ashes scattered over every conceivable venue, to have their body preserved by cryogenics, and a thousand other unconventional ends. When the *Funeral, Burial and Cremation Services Act, 2002*[208] comes into force, many favourite sendoffs (such as being scattered on the shores of your beloved lake) may actually be prohibited.

Scattering remains

(4) No person shall scatter cremated human remains at a place other than at a scattering ground operated by a person

---

[205] *Hunter v. Hunter* (1930), 65 O.L.R. 586, [1930] 4 D.L.R. 255 (H.C.); *Edmonds v. Armstrong Funeral Homes Ltd.,* [1931] 1 D.L.R. 676, [1930] 3 W.W.R. 649, 25 Alta. L.R. 173 (C.A.).

[206] *Schara Tzedeck v. Royal Trust Co.* (1952), [1953] 1 S.C.R. 31, [1952] 4 D.L.R. 529.

[207] *Sopinka (Litigation guardian of) v. Sopinka,* (2001) 55 O.R. (3d) 529, 42 E.T.R. (2d) 105 (Ont. S.C.J.).

[208] *Funeral, Burial and Cremations Services Act, 2002,* S.O. 2002, c. 33.

licensed under subsection (1) unless the person is permitted by regulation to scatter cremated human remains in such circumstances, at such a place or in such a manner as may be prescribed.

We suspect that unlicensed scattering will continue, especially on private property, but will-makers must recognize that any instruction that would compel a breach of the law will be void.

It is my wish that my remains be cremated. I am deeply attached to my cottage on Lake Huron, having spent some of the happiest times of my life there, and I therefore desire that my ashes be scattered over the waters of Lake Huron near my cottage. I trust that my Trustees will make their best efforts to honour this wish, so far as they are able.

Organ Donation

Organ and tissue donation are governed by the *Trillium Gift of Life Network Act*.[209] The Network co-ordinates the collection and distribution of organs and tissue for transplant. Although the executrix under a will has custody of the body for the purposes of funerals, burial or cremation, she is not authorized by the Act to give a consent for organ transplants.[210] On the other hand, an attorney under a Power of Attorney for Personal Care can give medical consents, including consents for very invasive procedures, but since the Power is spent with the life of the donor, the Attorney cannot give a prospective consent to transplants after death. The consents of both the deceased and the family are necessary.[211]

As with directions for a funeral, the will-maker cannot rely on consents contained in a will being read until well after the critical point (which in the case of transplants is right at the time of death). Donor cards are helpful, and discussions with the family who will likely be called on to make transplant and donation decisions are critical.[212] Sometimes the will-maker wants to

---

[209] *Trillium Gift of Life Network Act*, R.S.O. 1990, c. H.

[210] The list of those who can give consent for use of body after death includes: "the person's spouse or same-sex partner; or. . .the person's children; or. . . the person's parents; or. . . the person's brothers or sisters; or. . . the person's next of kin; or. . . the person lawfully in possession of the body". R.S.O. 1990, c. H.20, s. 29 (2). The executor may be "lawfully in possession of the body" in some regards, but it is not clear that the intention is to give a personal representative the power to consent.

[211] If the deceased, while still living, consented to a donation, medical authorities will still want the family's permission, since the Act requires that the consent not have been withdrawn. While the family can consent to a donation after death, they can do so only if the deceased had not objected while alive.

[212] Donor cards can be printed from the website: www.giftoflife.on.ca.

indicate a preference for disposition of the body. Medical research is less urgent in the requirement for consent, and these provisions may effectively be included in a will.

 The will may be too late for putting consents to organ and tissue donation, but clients who are preparing a Power of Attorney for Personal Care or a Living Will should be encouraged to include a statement consenting to donation.

 Upon my death, I request that my body be made available to the Department of Anatomy of the University of Eastern Ontario (or to the nearest Medical School), to be used for medical education and research.

 It is my wish that my remains be cremated, and that any service be simple and dignified.

Guardians for Minors

While a will allows the will-maker to dispose of property, that may not be the biggest concern that your client has. Typically, parents and those who are care-givers for vulnerable adults are as concerned about making appropriate arrangements for their dependants as they are about avoiding probate. Children are not property, but the *Children's Law Reform Act*[213] does allow for temporary arrangements for the care of minor children to be made in a will.

Testamentary Custody and Guardianship

61. (1) A person entitled to custody of a child may appoint by will one or more persons to have custody of the child after the death of the appointor.

(2) A guardian of the property of a child may appoint by will one or more persons to be guardians of the property of the child after the death of the appointor.

(3) An unmarried parent who is a minor may make an appointment mentioned in subsection (1) or (2) by a written appointment signed by the parent.

---

[213] *Children's Law Reform Act*, R.S.O. 1990, c. C.12, as amended.

(4) An appointment under subsection (1), (2) or (3) is effective only

    (a) if the appointor is the only person entitled to custody of the child or who is the guardian of the property of the child, as the case requires, on the day immediately before the appointment is to take effect; or

    (b) if the appointor and any other person entitled to custody of the child or who is the guardian of the property of the child, as the case requires, die at the same time or in circumstances that render it uncertain which survived the other.

(5) Where two or more persons are appointed to have custody of or to be guardians of the property of a child by appointors who die as mentioned in clause (4)(b), only the appointments of the persons appointed by both or all of the appointors are effective.

(6) No appointment under subsection (1), (2) or (3) is effective without the consent of the person appointed.

(7) An appointment under subsection (1), (2) or (3) for custody of a child or guardianship of the property of a child expires 90 days after the appointment becomes effective or, where the appointee applies under this Part for custody of the child or guardianship of the property of the child within the 90-day period, when the application is disposed of.

(8) An appointment under this section does not apply to prevent an application for or the making of an order under section 21 or 47.

(9) This section applies in respect of,

    (a) any will made on or after the 1st day of October, 1982; and

    (b) any will made before the 1st day of October, 1982, if the testator is living on that day.

Error #3: No Power to Appoint

Section 61 of the CLRA does not apply to every will-maker. Only those entitled to custody can make an appointment of a guardian by will. Therefore, a parent who does not have custody, but only a right to access visits, for example, cannot appoint a guardian for her children. A client who has joint custody with primary care and control of the children who reside with her may assume that she is entitled to name a guardian, but she is not. Where two people have custody, they must agree — and this may not be possible. Fortunately, such parents are unlikely to travel together, so the chances of them dying "at the same time or in circumstances that render it uncertain which survived the other" are slim.[214]

Solution: Harmony: Agreed Guardian

Practically, you should encourage your client to agree with the ex- (or current) spouse, but if agreement is improbable, appoint the client's choice, and make it clear that it may not govern.

> If my wife VALERIE dies before me, and if at my death any child of mine is under the age of majority, I appoint by sister BHAVANA PATEL to be the guardian to have care of any of my minor children during their minorities, and to the extent that I am capable so of doing, to be guardian of the property of each minor child, but if she is or becomes unable or unwilling to act, I appoint my sister-in-law DEBORAH MICKFORD to be the guardian of care and property in her place.

Where a client has serious concerns about a former spouse or other family member having guardianship of minors, she should make a detailed memorandum to accompany the appointment in her will. The memorandum should be witnessed, so that it can then be presented in evidence as to her wishes at any hearing as to custody of the child.

---

[214] There are, of course, cases where family relations have degenerated into violence, and murder and suicide result. While this in not an event that you are likely to plan for, consider the irony that while the surviving parent (the murderer in the murder-suicide scenario) would be precluded by the common law from inheriting from his victim-spouse, he would still have the last say in who had custody of the children — at least for ninety days — if no other person or agency intervened.

Error #4: Appointing a Guardian of Property

> If my wife, SOPHIE, dies before me, I appoint my friend GORDON MOLNAR to have custody of each of my minor children and to act as the guardian of the property of that child.

The power to appoint a guardian of property by will rests with the existing guardian. Although parents may assume that they are their children's guardians of property, they are not, unless and until they are appointed by the court. The clause above would, therefore, be ineffective unless the will-maker actually was the guardian of property.

> If my wife, SOPHIE dies before me and if at my death any child of mine is under the age of majority, I appoint my friend GORDON MOLNAR to have custody of each of my minor children, and, to the extent that I am capable so of doing, I appoint my friend GORDON MOLNAR to be the guardian of the property of each minor child.

Since an appointment by will lasts for only 90 days, the court will have to make a determination, according to the best interests of the child, about custody. A parent's thoughtful choice of guardian will be given some weight, but is not determinative. Since the appointed guardians must apply to court to make the arrangement permanent, some clauses include the following provision:

> If the guardian(s) here appointed consent to have custody of any minor child of mine it is my wish that, within ninety (90) days from my death, he or she may apply to court to have custody of my child and to act as the guardian of the property of my child pursuant to the *Children's Law Reform Act.* The costs of the application, if any, shall be paid from the residue of my estate.

Subsection 55(1) of the CLRA requires a guardian of property to post a bond. The wording of the statute appears to be mandatory, but since the amount of the bond is in the discretion of the court, will-makers who do not want to have their child's guardian bonded can include a statement to that effect:

> It is my wish that any person acting as a guardian for a child of mine not be required to furnish an administration bond in respect of the appointment.

Error #5: No Money for Guardians

If your clients have not considered it, you must raise with them the question of how the upbringing of their children is to be financed, if the clients die while their children are young. Parents may overlook the financial burden that will be placed on the guardians who undertake to raise one or more children. If they expect the quality of their children's lives to be close to what it might have been (and the guardians not to be resentful of the obligation they have assumed), they must make funds available to the guardian from the estate or other sources, such as an insurance trust.

Solution: Liberal Payments

> I do not wish that a person who undertakes the care of a child of mine should suffer financial hardship as a result. My Trustees are, therefore, authorized to make payments from the income and capital of any share of my estate being held for a child of mine who is under the age of majority, to any person who has custody of that child, including a person acting as Trustee of this Will (referred to as the "Guardian") for any expenses that in the opinion of my Trustees are reasonably incurred by the Guardian in providing a home for a child of mine. My Trustees may advance funds for expenses such as additional daily living costs, reasonable payments for enlarging the Guardian's home or acquiring a new home, or the cost of a new automobile. Funds may be loaned to the Guardian on such terms and conditions as my Trustees in their discretion consider reasonable, or may be given outright to the Guardian. In exercising their discretion, I express my wish that my Trustees bear in mind the best interests of my child or children and my desire to provide for them as happy a home life as possible.

The clause above is very liberal. Some clients may want to narrow its scope, depending on their own financial resources and those of the guardian they anticipate caring for the children.

Error #6: Guardians as a Couple

The CLRA allows for more than one person to be appointed as guardian, and many will-makers will think of naming a couple as guardians. But what if the sister and her husband do not stay together? or what if the sister dies? Do they still want the brother-in-law looking after their children? Given the short duration of the statutory guardianship, it may not matter, but if there is really only one of the couple they are attached to, they should name only that one person, and save confusion.

Codicils

Codicils were once used regularly to incorporate minor amendments and in the days of quill pens, or even typewriters, people often made two or more codicils, rather than pay to have a whole new will written out. Clients continue, from a false economy we suppose, to think that it is easier and cheaper just to make a codicil than a whole new will.

Making a codicil, however, is full of opportunities for error. What happens if, for example, the codicil is lost or separated from the will? What if the codicil inadvertently revokes the will? Each paragraph in the will that must be referred to in the codicil is a new chance for an error.

There are three instances when we believe it is better to make a codicil, and some where you should never undertake it.

Make a codicil when:

1.   You are confirming a previous will — for example when the client is marrying and does not want to revoke his will.

> This is a Codicil to the Will of me, GARY GROOM, of the City of Mississauga, which Will is dated the 5th day of March, 1997.
>
> > 1. The following clause shall be inserted immediately following the first sentence of my Will:
> >
> > > "This will is made in contemplation of my marriage to BRIDGET BRIDE, of the City of Belleville, which is planned for the 4th day of July 2003."
> >
> > 2. In all other respects I confirm my Will.

2.   It really is just one simple change to be made in the will.

> This is a Codicil to the Will of me, IVOR WYNTERS, of the City of London, and Province of Ontario, which Will is dated the 8th day of May, 1999.
>
> > 1.   I revoke Clause 2 of my Will. I declare that the following clause numbered 2 shall be inserted in its place, and shall have the same effect as if it had been originally inserted therein.

> "2. (a) I appoint my son BENJAMIN to be the Executor and Trustee of my Will. If my son BENJAMIN does not survive me or is or becomes unwilling or unable to act as my Executor and Trustee before all the trusts set out in my Will have been fully performed, I appoint my daughter JANE to be the Executor and Trustee of my Will.
>
> (b) In my Will, I refer to the Executor and Trustee or Executors and Trustees, original or substituted or surviving, as my 'Trustees'."
>
> 2. In all other respects I confirm my Will.

3. Finally, a codicil may be prepared where there is doubt about the capacity of the will-maker, since making a codicil will not revoke the existing will, which will continue to be safeguarded.

Error #7: Faulty References

The largest single source of error with codicils is incorrect reference to the will — getting the date of the underlying will wrong, or citing the wrong paragraph or sub-paragraph number to be changed.

Solution: Proofread

See the four-eyes principle in the "Practice Matters" Chapter.

Error #8: No Will

Do not undertake to prepare a codicil to a will when you do not have the original. If you have a copy, chances are that the original will is no longer in existence, and you are creating not a codicil, but a highly defective will.

Solution: Get the Original

Locate the original, or make a new will.

Error #9: Revoking the Will

If you start from a will precedent, rather than a precedent for a codicil, you may include a revocation clause, and undo the will you are meant to be building on.

    This is a Codicil to the Will of me, HARVEY HUNTER, of the City of Thunder Bay, and Province of Ontario, which Will is dated the 25th day of July, 1998. I REVOKE all former wills and other testamentary dispositions made by me.

1. I declare that the following clause numbered 3(d) shall be inserted in my Will after the clause numbered 3(c), and shall have the same effect as if it had been originally inserted therein. "3(d) My Trustees shall pay the sum of $10,000 to my son GRANT, if he survives me, but if he does not survive me to his daughter GRETTA if she survives me."

2. In all other respects I confirm my Will.

Family Definitions

When the *Children's Law Reform Act* did away with any legal distinction between children born in and outside of wedlock, it created new work for executors who, if the will simply referred to "issue" or "children" had to consider the possibility (especially with a male will-maker) that there were unknown children that had not been identified, and would have to be sought out. As a result it became common practice to include in a will an "exclusion of illegitimates" clause. Unfortunately, as common-law relationships abound, these clauses may unintentionally exclude children that the will-maker wants to include.

Error #10: Exclusion of Illegitimates

ANY REFERENCE in this Will or in any Codicil to it to a person in terms of a relationship to another person determined by blood or marriage shall not include a person born outside marriage nor a person who comes within the description traced through another person who was born outside marriage, except that any person who has been legally adopted shall be regarded as having been born in lawful wedlock to his or her adopting parent and any person who is born outside marriage and whose natural parents subsequently marry shall be regarded as having been born in lawful wedlock.

It is possible to relieve the Trustees of fruitless searches without excluding children of a stable common-law relationship.

Solution: Definition of Relationships

Any reference in my Will to a person in terms of a relationship to another person determined by blood or marriage shall not include a person born outside marriage or a person who comes within the description traced through another person who was born outside marriage, except that:

1. any person who has been legally adopted shall be included as the child of his or her adopting parent,

2. any person who is born outside marriage, and whose natural parents subsequently marry, shall be included as the child of his or her natural parent, and

3. any person who is born outside marriage, but whose parent who is related to me by blood has, in my Trustees' opinion, shown a settled intention to treat that child as their own, shall be included as the child of that parent.

Definition of Spouse

 For greater certainty, and for the purposes of this Will, the term "spouse" shall mean a person of the opposite (or of either) sex to whom a beneficiary is married at the relevant time, and with whom the beneficiary is cohabiting (and not separated) and shall also include that person who shall have been the spouse of my beneficiary at the time of the beneficiary's death until that person remarries or commences to cohabit with another person of either sex in a conjugal relationship.

Family Law Orders and Agreements

The *Family Law Act* definition of property in subsection 4(2) excludes property acquired by inheritance after the date of marriage from net family property. Income on the property, however, is excluded only if the will expressly states that it is excluded.

Divorce judgments and separation agreements will often result in a willmaker having an obligation to provide for dependants in his will.

 The provisions made for a child or children of mine under this paragraph X of my Will are made, in part, for the purpose of satisfying any obligation my estate may have pursuant to a separation agreement, court order or otherwise to pay support to a parent of or for the benefit of my children. Those payments shall not be made in addition to amounts otherwise payable by my estate pursuant to a separation agreement, court order or otherwise, but shall be on account of those amounts that my estate is legally obligated to make.

You should review any domestic agreements and court orders, to see what obligations your client has to support a former spouse or children. Including a provision to meet obligations of this kind can help to defend a will against support claims under Part V of the SLRA, and against claims for equalization of property under the *Family Law Act*.

Payments for Minors

Unless there is no chance that a minor will be entitled to receive an interest in an estate, minority clauses should always be included in a will. Without provision to hold money and use money for the benefit of minors, the trustee will have to pay the funds into court. To access the funds, resort would have to be made to the Court.

Error #11: Incomplete Clauses

Some wills do not contain any minority clauses. Other wills confer on the trustees the authority to use the funds for the minor but not to pay it out to a parent, guardian, or person standing *in loco parentis*.

Solution: Minority Clause

> (a) If any person becomes entitled to receive a share of my estate while under the age of majority, my Trustees shall keep that share invested and, until that person attains the age of majority, my Trustees shall pay or apply for the benefit of that person as much of the income and capital as my Trustees in the exercise of an absolute discretion consider advisable.
>
> (b) I authorize my Trustees to make any payments for a person under the age of majority to a parent or guardian or other person standing *in loco parentis* to that person, or to make any such payment directly to the person that my Trustees in their absolute discretion consider appropriate. Any evidence that my Trustees have made a payment shall be a sufficient discharge to my Trustees.

Error #12: 21 years of Age is No Longer the Age of Majority

Many minority clauses continue to refer to 21 years of age as the age of majority. If the will-maker wants the funds to be held until a minor attains an older age, trust provisions must be set out elsewhere in the will.[215] If an older age is simply specified in these provisions with no gift over, the minor will be able to demand the funds at 18 years of age.[216]

Some lawyers include a comprehensive minority clause which postpones vesting of an interest for all beneficiaries until attaining a certain age with the appropriate gifts over. Because of the potential perpetuity issues, we prefer the trust provisions to be set out in specially drafted dispositive provisions, so that these sorts of factors can be considered.

---

[215] See Chapter Eight, "Trusts".

[216] For a discussion of *Saunders v. Vautier*, please see Chapter Eight on Trusts.

CHAPTER 12

MULTIPLE WILLS

A will may cover some but not all of the testator's property. The law has long recognized the possibility of bifurcating an estate, but until recently, the device of multiple wills was used most commonly by those who had property in another jurisdiction. Essentially, one will includes assets which will require probate, while a separate will is prepared for the assets which may not require probate. The benefit of this strategy is that it shelters assets from estate administration tax.

Section 1 of the *Estate Administration Tax Act* defines "value of the estate":

> 1. the value which is required to be disclosed under section 32 of the *Estates Act* (or a predecessor thereof) of all the property that belonged to the deceased person at the time of his or her death less the actual value of any encumbrance on real property that is included in the property of the deceased person.

In turn, subsection 32(3) of the *Estates Act* sets out as follows:

211

Evaluation of limited grant

32(3) Where the application or grant is limited to part only of the property of the deceased, it is sufficient to set forth in the statement of value only the property and value thereof intended to be affected by such application or grant.

The *Granovsky*[217] case approved the use of multiple wills as a means of probate planning. Justice Greer held that there is no legislative prohibition against a limited grant of a primary will, nor any requirement that the estate trustees submit the secondary will for probate and pay estate administration tax on the value of assets governed by it. The Ontario government appealed the decision, but the appeal was never perfected. As a result, the judgment stands as good law and the strategy has now become common in Ontario for clients who own significant assets which may not require probate.[218]

The following is a list of assets commonly dealt with in a will not intended to be submitted for probate:

- Land registered under the *Registry Act*

- Land registered under the *Land Titles Act* if the transmission application following death will be the first transaction involving the land after conversion to the Land Titles System

- Land registered under the *Land Titles Act* which is worth less than $75,000

- Shares of private corporations

- Shares of public corporations with low values

- Personal effects

- Canada savings bonds within certain dollar limits

- Unsecured loans

Solicitors are now working through the challenges which will inevitably be faced when administering assets under a will which has not been granted probate.[219]

---

[217] *Granovsky Estate v. Ontario*, (1998) 21 E.T.R. (2d) 25, 53 O.T.C. 375, 156 D.L.R. (4th) 557 (Ont. Gen. Div.).

[218] Nova Scotia amended its *Probate Act* October 1, 2001. The new legislation sets out that probate tax imposed on assets which pass by will(s). . . It effectively ousts the use of the muliple strategy. See *Probate Act*, S.N.S. 2000, c. 31, amended by S.N.S. 2001, c.5 and S.N.S. 2002, c. 5.

[219] For a more detailed discussion of the practical difficulties in administering an estate governed by two or more wills, please see Marni M.K. Whitaker, "Practical Difficulties in the Administration of an Estate Governed by Two or More Wills" in *Estates and Trusts Forum, Fifth Annual Estates and Trusts Forum* (Toronto, Ont.: Continuing Legal Education, Law Society of Upper Canada, 2002).

As well, certain executors may insist on probate, notwithstanding that the asset may not require it, because of liability concerns. An application under Part V of the *Succession Law Reform Act* may not be made after six months from the grant of letters probate. Although the court can allow an application after this six-month period, it would be restricted to the undistributed portion of the estate.[220]

Accordingly, if no certificate was obtained, the six-month period would not begin to run and there is a concern that all assets would be subject to a claim — even those assets distributed. In *Gilles v. Althouse et al*,[221] the Supreme Court of Canada held that a valid order could be made, notwithstanding that the estate had already been distributed. Therefore, failure to obtain probate could extend the risk of the executor and as such, full releases should be obtained against all possible dependants.

Another concern is that an executor who is not a beneficiary does not have the protection afforded by section 47 of the *Trustee Act*. It provides for the revocation of erroneous grants.[222]

> **Expenses** (2) The person acting under the revoked probate or appointment may retain out of any part of the estate remaining undistributed the proper costs and expenses incurred in the administration.

> **Fraud** (3) Nothing in this section protects any person acting as personal representative where the person has been party or privy to any fraud whereby the grant or appointment has been obtained, or after becoming aware of any fact by reason of which revocation thereof is ordered unless, in the latter case, the person acts under a contract for valuable consideration before the person becomes aware of the fact.

---

[220] Limitation period — 61(1) Subject to subsection (2), no application for an order under section 58 may be made after six months from the grant of letters probate of the will or of letters of administration.

Exception — (2) The court, if it considers it proper, may allow an application to be made at any time as to any portion of the estate remaining undistributed at the date of the application.

[221] *Gilles v. Gilles Estate* (sub nom. *Gilles v. Althouse*) (1975), 53 DLR (3d) 410, [1976] 1 S.C.R. 353, (1975) 4 N.R. 36, [1975] 5 W.W.R. 547, (1975) 20 R.F.L. 41.

[222] 47. (1) Where a court of competent jurisdiction has admitted a will to probate, or has appointed an administrator, even though the grant of probate or the appointment may be subsequently revoked as having been erroneously made, all acts done under the authority of the probate or appointment, including all payments made in good faith to or by the personal representative, are as valid and effectual as if the same had been rightly granted or made, but upon revocation of the probate or appointment, in cases of an erroneous presumption of death, the supposed decedent, and in other cases the new personal representative may, subject to subsections (2) and (3), recover from the person who acted under the revoked grant or appointment any part of the estate remaining in the person's hands undistributed and, subject to the *Limitations Act*, from any person who erroneously received any part of the estate as a devisee, legatee or one of the next of kin, or as a husband or wife of the decedent or supposed decedent, the part so received or the value thereof.

Section 47 may be an issue for executors such as trust companies or other third parties. Again, the executor might be prepared to accept indemnities from the beneficiaries.

Notwithstanding these concerns, the dual will strategy remains viable in certain instances as there is very little down side. In a worst case scenario, the will has to be submitted for probate and the estate and its beneficiaries are in the same position that they would have been in if only one will had been prepared. However, the will-drafter should be cognizant and anticipate these potential issues when discussing the will plan with clients.

There are several variations on the ways in which two wills are identified:

- Ontario Will and Foreign Property Will

- Limited Property Will and General Will

- Corporate Properties Will and General Will

- Primary Will and Secondary Will

- Public Will and Private Will

As long as the identification of the two wills is consistent, it doesn't matter what you call them. We like "Primary and Secondary Will", because it helps remind us of the order in which the wills have to be executed. The two wills must be drafted so as to mesh with each other seamlessly. The most frequent errors occur when the wills fail to do so.

Error #1: No Introductory Clause

The introductory clause should set out a general description of the will and what assets it will cover.

Solution: Introductory Clause

PRIMARY WILL

> This is the Last Will of me, CLAUDE CLIENT, of the City of Ottawa in the County of Carleton, Province of Ontario with respect to all of my property except my Secondary Estate (as hereinafter defined), made this 1st day of March, 2003. I refer to this will as my "Primary Will".

> SECONDARY WILL
>
> This is the Last Will of me, CLAUDE CLIENT, of the City of Ottawa in the County of Carleton, Province of Ontario with respect to my Secondary Estate (as hereinafter defined), made this 1st day of March, 2003. I refer to this will as my "Secondary Will".

Error #2: Revoking One of the Double Wills

SECONDARY WILL

I REVOKE all former wills and other testamentary dispositions made by me.

The above clause will inadvertently revoke the Primary Will.

Solution: No Revocation in Secondary Will

> PRIMARY WILL
>
> Revocation
>
> I revoke all former wills and codicils made by me.
>
> SECONDARY WILL
>
> I have an existing Will executed on the 4th day of March, 2003, which deals with all of my property except for my Secondary Estate, which I do not intend to revoke.

> **If one will revokes all prior wills, and the other revokes only those wills dealing with the special property, the order in which the wills are executed matters. Make sure that you or your assistant sets up the execution so that the wills are signed in the right order.**

Error #3: Warring Executors

The appointment of different executors in the wills could create substantial practical difficulties and liability issues.[223] If the executors are not the same on both wills, they must be able to work together. Often the multiple

---

[223] In *Carmichael v. Carmichael Estate* (sub nom. *Carmichael v. Sharpley*) (2000), 46 O.R. (3d) 630, 184 D.L.R. (4th) 175, 31 E.T.R. (2d) 33, [2000] O.T.C. 718 (Sup. Ct. Just.), the court held that an application for the removal of the executors could proceed without probate.

wills are not specific and leave much to the discretion of the executors. Agreement must be had on which executor is to file income tax returns and pay taxes. As well, there may be ongoing administrative issues.

From a drafting perspective, the executor and trustee appointment remains standard. However, if additional statements which deal with compensation or burden of administration issues[224] are going to be included, the drafter should be certain to make the necessary modifications.

> I appoint my wife, ANNE, and my lawyer, CAMERON, to be the Executors and Trustees of this Will and I hereinafter refer to them as "my Trustees". I direct that my lawyer, CAMERON, shall assume the burden of administration of my Secondary Estate and shall have charge of all accounts and shall keep in her possession all the assets of my Secondary Estate. I declare that my lawyer, CAMERON, shall be entitled to receive and shall be paid out of my Secondary Estate, as compensation for her acting as one of my executors and trustees under my Secondary Estate, the reimbursement and other compensation provided for in the *Compensation Agreement* between CAMERON and me signed on the 3rd day of April, 2003, and I declare that the terms of the *Compensation Agreement* shall be valid and binding in all respects to fix the compensation payable to CAMERON as though the *Compensation Agreement* was expressly embodied in this Will.

Error #4: Failure to Define the Assets

It is best to be as specific as possible. In some instances, a will-drafter also includes a blanket clause to include any further assets which the willmaker owns at his death which will not require probate.

Solution: Definition of Estates

> 1. Primary Estate: The term "my Primary Estate" shall mean all my worldwide and personal property other than my Secondary Estate.
>
> 2. Secondary Estate:(a) My Secondary Estate shall mean all my worldwide real and personal property that is in fact disposed of by my Secondary Will. My Secondary Estate shall comprise the following:

---

[224] The court held in *Re Silver Estate* (1999), 31 E.T.R. No. 5026(2d) 256 (Ont. Sup. Ct. Just.) that it had the jurisdiction to pass accounts in instances where the will was not probated.

> any shares or indebtedness of (*) Limited, or any successor corporation, or any shares or securities received in exchange or substitution of such shares or indebtedness; and
>
> all of my personal, domestic or household or garden use property or ornament which I shall own at my death; and
>
> any interest I shall have in the real property municipally known as 123 River Street, Toronto, Ontario, at my death.

Error #5: Tainting the Unprobated Will

Be clear about which will is to be submitted for probate, and keep the assets dealt with in the probated will to a minimum. Beware of tainting the unprobated will. If one of the assets covered in the secondary or special will cannot be transferred without a Certificate of Appointment as Estate Trustee, you may be compelled to probate the secondary will, thus defeating the purpose of the double wills. Consider using a "disclaimer" clause, to allow the trustees of the special will to disclaim any property that might compel an application for probate.

Solution: Disclaimer

> I authorize my Trustees to disclaim entitlement to receive any property listed in the definition of my Secondary Estate, and any property so disclaimed by my Trustees (within sixty (60) days following the date of my death) shall not form part of my Secondary Estate, but shall be part of my Primary Estate to be dealt with under my Primary Will. My Trustees may disclaim property for any reason that they in their absolute discretion consider appropriate including, without derogating from the scope of that discretion, securing the result that my Secondary Will does not have to be submitted to the Court for the granting of Letters Probate or a Certificate of Appointment as Estate Trustee.

In some circumstances (e.g. polluted property that carries liability under the *Environmental Protection Act*; real estate where the probate status is unclear because it is in an area being converted from *Registry Act* to Land Titles), you may make a third or tertiary will.

☞   **Put designations in the Probate Will. Since life insurance and registered plans will pass outside of the estate, they will not be subject to the Estate Administration Tax (EAT) or Probate anyway. Since some financial institutions require a probated will before releasing funds, however,[225] it is prudent to put the designations in the will that will be probated.**

☞   **Put "extra testamentary" material in the right Will (see Chapter Eleven, Funeral Directions, Guardianship, and other extra-testamentary provisions).**

Error #6: Transfer to Trustees

For clarity, the clause should be appropriately modified.

> PRIMARY WILL
>
> > I give my Primary Estate to my Trustees upon the following Trusts:
>
> SECONDARY WILL
>
> > I give my Secondary Estate to my Trustees upon the following Trusts:

Error #7: Don't Pay the Same Debts Twice

The wills must clearly delineate the estate and assets which will be responsible for the payment of taxes. This issue is especially critical if the beneficiaries in the Primary and Secondary Wills differ.

Solution: Discretion of the Trustee

The following clause is problematic if the beneficiaries differ in each of the wills.

---

[225] *Rozon v. Transamerica Life Insurance Co. of Canada* (1999) O.J. No. 4538 (Ont. C.A.) held that a probated will could not be required by a life insurer before it released funds when the funds were payable to the estate. Whether this will carry over to all situations is unclear. Moreover, do you really want to have to go to the Court of Appeal before your client's widow gets the insurance?

PRIMARY WILL

> My Trustees shall pay out of the capital of my general Primary Estate my debts and funeral and testamentary expenses, and I hereby authorize my Trustees to prepay any taxes. I have made a similar provision for the payment of debts, expenses and taxes in my Secondary Will and I direct my Trustees along with the Executors and Trustees of my Secondary Will to determine a reasonable allocation of the debts, expenses and taxes between my Primary Estate and my Secondary Estate.

[SECONDARY WILL]

> My Trustees shall pay out of the capital of my general Secondary Estate my debts and funeral and testamentary expenses and I hereby authorize my Trustees to prepay any taxes. I have made a similar provision for the payment of debts, expenses and taxes in my Primary Will and I direct my Trustees along with the Executors and Trustees of my Primary Will to determine a reasonable allocation of such debts, expenses and taxes between my Primary Estate and my Secondary Estate.

Solution: Include the Debts Clause in Only One of the Wills

Error #8: Double Legacies

Finally, if the same legacy is set out in both wills it would be paid out twice.[226]

Error #9: Insufficient Assets in Primary Estate

If legacies are included, the solicitor must determine which estate will pay the legacies. As well, the will-maker must contemplate what she wants done if the assets in one estate are insufficient to fund the legacies.

Solution: Incorporation

SECONDARY WILL

> To the extent that those assets of my Primary Estate, governed by the provisions of my Primary Will, executed on

---

[226] If a legacy is to be left in lieu of compensation, the issue of it being paid out twice must be considered. See Chapter six, "Legacies" for a discussion of double legacies.

> the 4th day of June, 2003, which Primary Will was exe-
> cuted prior to my Secondary Will, are insufficient to satisfy
> the debts, expenses, duties and taxes as provided for in
> Paragraph X of my Primary Will and/or the legacies set
> out in Pararaph Y of my Primary Will, I direct the Trustees
> of my Secondary Estate to satisfy any such deficiencies
> with the assets held by my Trustees under my Secondary
> Will and to the extent I incorporate by reference the
> provisions of Paragraphs X and Y of my Primary Will into
> my Secondary Will with the necessary modifications.

Error #10: Failure to Differentiate Between Primary and Secondary Estate

Will-drafters sometimes fail to amend their administrative and general clauses. These clauses continue to generically refer to "my estate". When crafting the terms of multiple wills, it is better that the terms "Secondary Estate" and "Primary Estate" be used for clarity.

> SECONDARY WILL
>
> Investments Clause
>
> I hereby declare that my Trustees when making invest-
> ments for my *Secondary Estate* shall not be limited to
> investments authorized by law for trustees but may make
> any investments which they consider prudent and in the
> best interests of my *Secondary Estate.*

CHAPTER 13

PRACTICE MATTERS

We know that will drafting is only one part of the whole picture of a practice. This chapter is about the context of will drafting — all the things that intertwine with your decisions about how you draft, from the discussions you have with your client to the paper on which you print the will.

1. Intake Forms

You want to keep the time you spend on any will to a minimum. Forms and checklists streamline the process of gathering information before you actually begin to draft. There are two approaches to information gathering: you can take the time to go over the checklist with your clients, or you can have them or their advisor (if that is your first contact) fill in some of the information. Remember, however, that more is going on here than just gathering information. To have capacity to make a will, a client must know: (1) the nature and extent of her assets; (2) the natural objects of her bounty; and (3) the nature of the will-making act.[227] There is no substitute for a careful interview, in which the will-maker is asked about these very things. You must, however, use your judgment — not every client will require a full interview, nor will an efficient practice allow for you to spend a couple of hours with every client before you even begin to draft. We suggest that where capacity is a concern, you invest the time in a personal interview; but where it is not an issue, you use an information gathering form, sent out in advance or filled in while the client waits to meet you for a short, initial interview (that confirms the information and prepares the estate plan).

There are a number of versions of an intake form. The following is a short Personal Information Form, suitable for clients to complete while they wait for an interview:

---

[227] The classic test is articulated in *Banks v. Goodfellow* (1870), L.R. 5 Q.B. 549. See also the application of the test in Ontario in *Murphy v. Lamphier* (1914), 31 O.L.R. 287. (Ch.), aff'd 32 O.L.R. 19, 20 D.L.R. 906 (Div. Ct.). Recently in *Hall v. Bennett Estate*, [2003], O.J. No. 1827 (C.A.), Charron J.A. defined capacity as follows:

> "... It has often been repeated that a testator must have 'a sound disposing mind' to make a valid will. The following requirements can be extricated from the case law. In order to have a sound disposing mind, a testator: .. must understand the nature and effect of a will;
>
> .. must recollect the nature and extent of his or her property;
>
> .. must understand the extent of what he or she is giving under the will;
>
> .. must remember the persons that he or she might be expected to benefit under his or her will; and
>
> .. where applicable, must understand the nature of the claims that may be made by persons he or she is excluding from the will.
>
> [15] It is also clear from the jurisprudence that the test to be met to prove testamentary capacity is a high one and the onus falls on the propounder of the will. The jurisprudence abounds with statements that it is not sufficient simply to show that a testator had the capacity to communicate his or her testamentary wishes. Those wishes must be shown to be the product of a sound and disposing mind as described above." She continues with a review of the most relevant case law in Ontario.

WILL INTAKE — PERSONAL INFORMATION - Client A

Name (in full):	
Other Names Used:	
Address:	
Telephone Number:	Occupation:
Date of Birth:	Place of Birth:
Citizenship:	S.I.N.:
Other Residence:	
Marital Status ☐ M ☐ C/L ☐ S ☐ W ☐ Engaged — Name of Fiance(e):	
Divorce/Separation/Marriage Agreement: ☐ No ☐ Yes — Date of Agreement/Order:	

Client B's Information (If Applicable)

Spouse's Name (in full):	
Other Names Used:	
Address:	
Telephone Number:	Occupation:
Date of Birth:	Place of Birth:
Citizenship:	S.I.N.:
Other Residence:	
Divorce/Separation/Marriage Agreement: ☐ No ☐ Yes — Date of Agreement/Order:	

Existing Wills? ☐ No ☐ Yes — Prepared by:	Date:

Children and Grandchildren
— Use the back of this sheet if your require more room

Name, Address, Telephone	Step	Date of Birth	Marital Status
Child #1			
		Notes:	
Grandchildren:			
Child #2			
		Notes:	
Grandchildren:			
Child #3			
		Notes:	
Grandchildren:			

Other Dependants:
Other Advisors:

2. Information to Bring

It is useful to have a list of information a new client should bring to the first interview. Some solicitors also include an Asset Summary Statement — a sample of which we have also included. Not all clients like this homework, but a certain type of person enjoys the process because it makes him get organized. If a client is going to find the Asset Summary Statement overwhelming or if it will impede the process, put it on a clipboard (along with the Personal Information Sheet) to be completed in reception just prior to your meeting. Those who don't want to complete the statement on their own can wait to complete it in the meeting. Having the clients complete the form is a defensive practice, however, since lawyers are not renowned for neat and legible note-taking.

LIST OF MATERIAL TO BRING

Dear Client,

Being prepared for the interview with [Larry Lawyer] will help to make the best use of time for both of you. Here is a list of material you should bring, and information you should have ready when you come to discuss your will:

— your full name, including any former names and nicknames and any different combinations of names you have used

— your address and telephone number for all your residences (cottage, winter residences, etc.) and your workplace

— your date and place of birth, your citizenship and social insurance number;

— full names, addresses, and dates of birth for your potential beneficiaries (spouses, children, grandchildren, etc.)

— names, addresses and telephone numbers for your professional advisors (accountant, financial planner, family doctor)

— copies of any domestic contracts (separation agreements, marriage contracts, etc.)

— copies of any business partnership agreements or shareholder agreements to which you are a party

— recent statements for your investments

— the names of the beneficiaries under your life insurance plans and registered plans (RRSPs and RRIFs)

— the title to any real estate (bring a copy of the Deed if it is available).

ASSET SUMMARY

Assets — Include assets belonging to you or your spouse, with the date and cost on acquisition and current value.

1. Real Estate	
(a) Location:	(b) Location:
Value:	Value:
Original cost:	Original cost:
In whose name:	In whose name:
Mortgages	
(a) Amount owing:	(b) Amount owing:
Name of mortgagee:	Name of mortgagee:

2. Bank Accounts	
(a) Name of bank:	(b) Name of bank:
Address:	Address:
Account number:	Account number:
In whose name:	In whose name:
Average balance:	Average balance:

3. Household goods and contents:	

4. Automobiles and Boats	
(a) Value:	(b) Value:
In whose name:	In whose name:

5. Life Insurance	
(a) Name of company:	(b) Name of company:
Policy number:	Policy number:
Type of plan:	Type of plan:
Beneficiary:	Beneficiary:
Value of benefit:	Value of benefit:
Owned by:	Owned by:

6. Investments *(use an additional sheet if necessary)*	
RRSPs, Pensions, Annuities	
(a) Name:	(b) Name:
Contract number:	Contract number:
Beneficiary:	Beneficiary:
Anticipated value:	Anticipated value:
Stocks, bonds, and mutual funds (with original costs and estimated market values)	
Other investments (GICs, Term Deposits, etc.)	
Loans to Others:	
Location of Valuable Documents (safe deposit box):	

7. Liabilities	
(a) Amount owing:	(b) Amount owing:
Name of creditor:	Name of creditor:

3. Critical Path

At the first interview with a will client, you should establish what must be done, who will do it, and when. Make a chart, have the clients initial it, and give them a copy to keep. This will help prevent unreasonable expectations, and it will also keep the matter of getting the will signed immediate for both you and your client. Here is a sample of such a chart.

Estate Planning Steps for: WILFRED AND JENNIFER WATSON			
Task	**Responsible**	**Due**	**Done**
Initial Meeting	All	Sept. 19, 2003	√
Discuss cottage with son	Jennifer	Sept. 27, 2003	
Bring deed to cottage	Wilfred	Sept. 29, 2003	
Research title to cottage	Lawyer	Oct. 1, 2003	
Review life insurance with agent	Wilfred	Oct. 1, 2003	
Planning letter	Lawyer	Oct. 2, 2003	
Discuss plan with children	Jennifer and Wilfred	Oct. 8, 2003	
Approval/amendment of plan	Jennifer and Wilfred	Oct. 15, 2003	
Draft wills sent out	Lawyer	Oct. 22, 2003	
Comments and amendments	Jennifer and Wilfred	Nov. 5, 2003	
Meeting to execute wills	All	Nov. 9, 2003	
Initialled: JW WW LL			

A simpler process involves gathering information, drafting, and executing the wills. The stages would be:

initial contact, usually by telephone	assistant	the client is given the list of material to bring to the interview, and quoted the usual base fee with proviso about higher rates for more complex work — an appointment is set
first interview	lawyer	information is gathered and the plan developed — retainer and critical path (if necessary) are signed
drafting	assistant/lawyer	all drafts should be read by two people

drafts mailed to client	assistant	the covering letter includes the anticipated date for execution and the expected fee
revisions	assistant or lawyer	clients are asked to telephone or e-mail with revisions in advance of the execution date
execution	assistant and lawyer	immediately after execution, the client is given copies of documents to take with him, and a draft account — payment is deposited to trust until the final bill
processing	assistant	affidavits of execution are prepared and sworn, the wills stored and entered in the document register, and the final account is prepared
reporting letter	assistant and lawyer	the reporting letter is mailed with the final account

4. U.S. Tax Calculation

Planning for Canadian resident citizens. who hold significant U.S. assets is a large topic, beyond the scope of this book. There are many Canadian resident citizens, however, who have U.S. assets, but fall below the level at which they must be concerned about U.S. estate tax. You do not have to send your clients off to a cross-border expert the minute you hear they have a Florida condominium. Here is a quick reference that should allow you to determine when a client should be concerned about U.S. estate tax.

U.S. situs assets include: real estate in the U.S.; cash in U.S. currency or U.S. accounts (there are some exceptions, including personal U.S. bank deposits) business or trade assets in the U.S.; shares in U.S. corporations (even in an account in Canada); if the client owns U.S. situs securities directly, even in a discretionary managed account, they will count; bonds, debentures, and other debt obligations of U.S. corporations and governments; tangible personal property situated in the U.S. (i.e. cars, art, etc.); U.S. pension plans (including IRAs and 401(k) plans); and U.S. shares held in a Canadian RRSP or RRIF also count.

Calculate the total value (in US$) of worldwide assets. Life insurance death benefits are included if the client owns the policy. Jointly-owned assets are included. The following thresholds are 2003 values.

A. $60,000 — If U.S. situs assets are less than US$60,000 on death there is no U.S. Estate Tax.

B. $1,000,000 — If worldwide assets are less than US$1,000,000 on death there is no U.S. Estate Tax.

C. $1,200,000 — (a) If worldwide assets are less than US$1,200,000 upon death *and* there is no U.S. real estate then there is no U.S. estate tax payable.

(b) If worldwide assets are less than US$1,200,000 and more than US$1,000,000 on death *and* there is U.S. real estate, U.S. estate tax applies to the value of the U.S. real estate at death.

(c) If worldwide assets are more than US$1,200,000 on death, U.S. estate tax applies on all U.S. situs assets.

Note: If your client may be subject to U.S. estate tax, consider referring your client to a practitioner who is familiar with the U.S. system, or at least getting some assistance in developing the plan. In addition to federal estate tax, many states also levy their own estate tax.[228]

5. Working with Third Parties

Lawyers are accustomed to a confidential relationship with their clients, and are sometimes unsure of how to respond when it comes to estate planning. Remember that, whoever gives you the referral — whether it's your golf buddy or the best business client you ever dealt with — you *must* take your instructions from the will-maker. He or she alone is your client. At least once in the process, you should spend enough time alone with the client to satisfy yourself about his commitment to the instructions so that he feels comfortable telling you if he has reservations about any part of the plan.[229] Nevertheless, it is often required to co-operate with a number of other parties, family and professional, and the lawyer who insists on working alone not only misses the opportunity to learn from other players, but risks missing the

---

[228] U.S. Estate Tax rate of 55% will gradually decrease to 0% in 2010. In 2011, it returns to its previous high.

[229] See *Re Worrell*, [1970] 1 O.R. 184, 8 D.L.R. (3d) 36 (Surr. Ct.) for a judicial view of the solicitor's obligation when taking instructions.

nuances of family relationships that should inform good drafting.

Trust companies often refer clients to lawyers to have wills drafted in which the trust company will be executor. As potential executor, the trust company wants to see clauses in the will that give it the powers needed to deal with any possible problems, so you may have to put more administrative clauses in a trust company will than you usually do. If you do a significant amount of drafting for trust companies, make up a set of "standard" clauses to suit their particular requirements, and insert it as a whole in each will.[230]

☞ **Trust companies often take instructions from clients they are referring and forward the clients to the drafting lawyer. You should contact the client directly to confirm the instructions and your retainer and fee. A telephone call may suffice, but make sure you probe enough to be sure the instructions are accurate and complete.**

Trust companies are in business and they put a high priority on having a will done speedily — so should you.[231] Trust companies will also typically want to review drafts of the will and keep the original wills in their vault. Some practitioners are hesitant about this involvement, but if the clients approve (presumably they will), the review by a will consultant at a trust company is very helpful. Will consultants read a lot of wills, and usually have a lot of experience and a lot of precedents. Having them review your wills is a rare opportunity to talk about how you draft, and having an in-house consultant review the will is an easy way of meeting the "four eyes" principle (see below).

Family members are often called in to consult in the planning process. Children are also frequently the initiators of the planning process for a parent who has been dilatory. On the theory that a plan in which the children have at least been consulted is less likely to meet with resistance when the will comes to be probated, we generally welcome family participation, with some caveats:

a. Family members are often protective of a will-maker who is losing capacity, and will jump in with answers to questions. If your interview alone with the will-maker leaves you in doubt, get an outside

---

[230] See Chapter Ten, "Administrative Trust Powers" for a list of the clauses that trust companies will probably require, and some precedents.

[231] See Chapter One "Introduction" for a review of some cases where solicitors have been found negligent for failing to have a will prepared and executed expeditiously. See also, Martyn Frost, *With the Best Will in the World: Negligence in Will Preparation* (London: Legalease, 2000).

assessor to confirm capacity. Clients are usually willing to participate if they understand the assessment as protecting the will from attack.

b. Be cautious when one member of the family is leading the process, especially if that one is the biggest beneficiary under the new will, or has unique provisions for himself.

c. Be sure that you confirm with the client that you are authorized to speak to family members.

d. Finally, ensure that any instructions that come through the family are confirmed with the will-maker in a private meeting.

Accountants, financial planners, gift planners, and bankers are also often the ones to initiate a will-making process. They are not only good sources of referrals for a wills practitioner, but helpful sources of information. Especially if the estate is large and the tax implications are complex, having an accountant to assist in the plan is a great benefit. Financial planners and bankers often have relationships of long duration with the client, and are familiar both with their assets and with their family and business structure. As always, you must be careful to take your instruction from the client.

6. Fees

General practices used to run on the assumption that the real money was to be made on administering the estate, and the will could be done for relatively little. Since the risk was low — until recently the client was the only one who could sue a lawyer for negligence, and she was usually dead before the problem arose — the will was treated as a loss leader. Lawyers are sensitive to the general public belief that they are overpaid, and many clients expect to get a will at the same price that their parents paid.

If you are going to give complex drafting the time it requires, you must be willing to charge enough to make it profitable. If your clients are resistant to hourly charges, however, make an estimate of the average time required to prepare wills and quote a "package" fee. Clients like the certainty, and you will like not having to docket your time. Will drafting, unlike litigation, is a relatively predictable process, and you will usually be adequately compensated if you quote a fixed fee.

One way to minimize the resistance clients may have to paying your fee is to quote it early in the process; we suggest that you publish a fee brochure, and we also like to put the fee into the covering letter that goes out with drafts in a simple procedure. Clients who will be billed at an hourly rate should also sign a retainer, with the hourly rate quoted. Finally, resist mightily the temptation to cut your fees in response to "Larry Lawyer down the street can do the will for $250". Remember that even what seems at first to be a simple drafting matter can rapidly become complex if you have two clients who are not doing mirror wills, or an unusual disposition.

7. Drafting Help

As you draft, you will, we hope, keep this book close at hand, but you may find a complex or novel problem to send you searching, whether to research the law or to find new precedents. Appendix C is a bibliography of published sources and websites for the will-drafter that we rely on, and on which, in part, this book is built.

The list of websites is by no means exhaustive. It is trite to say that information available on the web is vast and ever expanding and changing. The practical implication is that you must check the sites periodically, to see what is new, and bookmark some of the ones of greatest interest. You will soon find that you have a few favourites, to which you return regularly.

While the marketing of your practice is not a subject for this book either, you might consider the benefits of having a good website of your own to which your colleagues and clients can turn on a regular basis.[232]

8. Powers of Attorney

Powers of Attorney deserve a book all to themselves. Nevertheless, since they are frequently made at the same time as a will, any discussion of practice matters should consider how they are handled in the context of will drafting.

Consider that the work of the will can be completely undone by the careless use of a power of attorney — for example, if all assets are moved out of the estate into joint tenancy or a trust by the attorney. It is important to the integrity of an estate plan, therefore, that the attorneys be "on side".

The attorney for property is obliged and entitled, under the *Substitute Decisions Act*, to review the will.[233] The name of the attorney should, there-

---

[232] See "Consumer Research Decima — Milt Zwicker's Estate Tools and Marketing Guide" in *The Essential Guide for Drafting Wills* (Toronto, Ont.: Canadian Bar Association — Ontario, Trusts and Estates Section, 1997).

[233] Section 33.1 A guardian of property shall make reasonable efforts to determine,

(a) whether the incapable person has a will; and

(continued on next page)

fore, be recorded on the list of those who may review the will (see authority to release, authority to view, below).

Since Powers of Attorney for Personal Care are often needed on short notice, and are not effective unless and until the donor becomes incapable, at the signing meeting, we give the client original copies to make available to the appointed attorney.

Powers of Attorney for Property that are restricted on their face — with terms such as "this power of attorney is to be used only in the event that I am incapable of managing property" — are less than fully useful, since the attorney must establish to the third party with whom she is dealing that the condition has been met. This is true even if the condition is just that the first appointed attorney is unwilling or unable to act. Sometimes the form includes a statement that the written assurance of the attorney that the condition has been met is sufficient, but that seems to vitiate the point of having the condition in the first place. We prefer to make a separate document for each person who is appointed, and to control the release of the documents with a letter of direction.

9. Joint Retainers

It seems clear that if you act for a couple to prepare their wills, you have a joint retainer.[234]

The following circumstances would indicate a joint retainer:

(continued from previous page)

    (b) if the incapable person has a will, what the provisions of the will are. 1996, c. 2, s. 21.

Property in another person's control

33.2 (1) A person who has custody or control of property belonging to an incapable person shall,

    (a) provide the incapable person's guardian of property with any information requested by the guardian that concerns the property and that is known to the person who has custody or control of the property; and

    (b) deliver the property to the incapable person's guardian of property when required by the guardian. 1996, c. 2, s. 21.

Property includes will

(2) For the purposes of subsection (1), the property belonging to a person includes the person's will. 1996, c. 2, s. 21.

Copies of documents

(3) A person who has custody or control of any document relating to an incapable person's property that was signed by or given to the incapable person shall, on request, provide the incapable person's guardian of property with a copy of the document. *Substitute Decisions Act*, S.O. 1992, as amended 1996, c. 2, s. 21.

[234] The Law Society's Committee on the issues of joint retainers in the preparation of spousal wills reported to Convocation on September 5th 2002. See Professional Regulation Committee, Law Society of Upper Canada, *Report to Convocation, September 5, 2002* (Toronto, Ont.: Policy Secretariat, Law Society of Upper Canada, 2002).

- ▶ the parties attend at the lawyer's office at the same time;

- ▶ the parties meet with the lawyer together;

- ▶ the parties appear to have a common goal, and instruct the lawyer together on achieving that goal;

- ▶ the wills are executed at the same time;

- ▶ one account is rendered to both clients;

- ▶ a single reporting letter is usually prepared for both clients.

Where there is a joint retainer to prepare a will, the Rules of Professional Conduct will soon require the lawyer to inform the clients that information will be shared, and that he or she cannot prepare different wills later without the other partner's agreement.[235]

---

[235] The proposed addition to Rule 2.04(6) reads:

"A lawyer who receives instructions from spouses or partners as defined in the *Substitute Decisions Act*, 1992 S.O. 1992 c. 30 to prepare one or more wills for them based on their shared understanding of what is to be in each will should treat the matter as a joint retainer and comply with subrule (6). At the outset of this retainer, the lawyer should advise the spouses or partners that if one of them were later to contact the lawyer with different instructions, for example with instructions to change or revoke a will without informing the other spouse or partner, the lawyer has a duty to inform forthwith the other spouse or partner of the contact and to decline to act unless both spouses or partners agree. After advising the spouses or partners in the manner described above, the lawyer should obtain their consent to act in accordance with subrule (8)." *Report to Convocation*, op. cit., note 12, at p. 36.

The following is a form of written retainer that should help you comply with the requirements of the proposed amendment:

Retainer

To: Will Lawyer

From: Clara and Claude Client

We retain you to act on our behalf in connection with our estate planning/the preparation of our Wills (and Powers of Attorney). We authorize you to employ such agents or others and to delegate tasks as you may deem proper.

The goal of our estate planning is to achieve the common objectives of both of us while preserving positive family relations. We acknowledge that now or in the future, however, our interests may be in conflict with one another, but we consent to having you act for both of us. We acknowledge that if one of us were later to contact you with different instructions, for example with instructions to change or revoke a Will without informing the other one, you have a duty to inform forthwith the other one of us of the contact and to decline to act unless we both agree. Finally, we both understand that Wills and Powers of Attorney may be revoked or amended at any time without the knowledge or consent of the other spouse or you.

We acknowledge that you may receive information, confidential or otherwise, from one or both of us, and from other professionals and family members. We acknowledge that no information supplied to you by one of us can be kept from the other. We request and authorize you to disclose the information you receive to either one or both of us. We release the firm from any liability for damages resulting from such disclosure.

Payment for your services is normally based on a fixed fee, as set out in your Fee Brochure, a copy of which has been provided to us, but the complexity, difficulty and importance of the matter, and special circumstances such as urgency may result in the matter being billed on the basis of the time involved, calculated at your current hourly rate of $XXX per hour.

DATED AT KINGSTON, this Friday, May 30th, 2003.

Signed (Client #1)

Signed (Client #2)   Witness

10. The Physical Document

Paper — Use good quality paper, since a will may have to last a long time. Ordinary office paper may be high in acid, which will cause the paper to deteriorate and crumble. Look at a newspaper that has been out in the sun for a few days, and you will get an idea of what awaits a will printed on cheap paper. Legal stationers carry "will paper" which is acid neutral, and ruled along the margins, but any good quality, acid neutral paper will do. Do not waste the money you spend on good paper by storing the will in an acid rich envelope. Acid neutral envelopes are available from stationers who supply libraries and archives, and are easier to obtain than they used to be.

Wills are best stored flat, since folding and unfolding them to put them into a small envelope may wear away the type and weaken the paper. Laser printers, in particular, may produce type that is easily lifted, either by repeated folding, or by plastic covers (which should be avoided in any case). Rather than print the will with a laser printer, print the copy to be "trued up" for the clients, and then photocopy it onto the will paper.

Only one original will should ever be prepared, so there is no confusion about which is the will, or whether it has been revoked. It is common to provide clients with a copy of the will that is "trued up" at the time of execution, to show that it was signed. A trued up copy is one in which the signatures have been written in, to indicate that they were executed. It gives the client all the information he needs, it can be handed over immediately following execution, and it will not be confused with an original as a good photocopy may be.

If your clients are elderly, consider printing the will in a larger type — like 14 point. Even one point higher makes a difference to the legibility of the will for those whose vision is slightly impaired. Leaving 1 $^1/_2$ or double spaces between lines, extra space between paragraphs, and using lots of headings will also help your client to understand the structure and detail of the document. It may take a few more pages, but few investments will give you as good a return in client satisfaction.

11. Signing the Will

Usually, clients sign the will in front of witnesses in your office. Sending the will out for execution is a risky practice, since you have no control over its proper execution, and even if you give very clear instructions, they may not be followed. If the client cannot come to the office, it is better for you to go to her than to send the wills out. If necessary, send your assistant, but avoid sending the will alone. Consider the words of an English judge, finding a solicitor who had sent a will out for execution negligent when only one witness signed the will:

> ". . . a prudent solicitor regards it as his duty to take reasonable steps to assist his client in and about the execution of his will, rather than merely to inform the client how it is to be signed and attested. This means that once the client has approved the draft of a will a prudent solicitor will either invite the client to his office so that the will can be executed there or visit him with a member of his staff to execute the will at the client's house . . . any testator is entitled to expect reasonable assistance without having to ask expressly for it. It is in my judgment not enough just to leave written instructions with the testator. In ordinary circumstances, just to leave written instructions and to do no more will not only be contrary to good practice but also in my opinion negligent."[236]

Make sure that the witnesses remain in the room throughout the execution. This may seem a small point, but they will have to swear that they saw the will executed and that it was done in the presence of both witnesses.[237]

Affidavits of execution should be prepared immediately after the will is signed, and stored with the will. The affidavit should be taken by a commissioner for oaths who was not also a witness to the will. If the circumstances of the signing are unusual, both the attestation clause and the affidavit of execution may have to be amended:

a. For a person who does not speak English (or has limited comprehension) the attestation clause should be amended to read:

☞ **"Signed by the Testator, WLADISLAW WILLMAKER, who does not understand English, as his Will, after the Will had first been translated by XY and read over in Polish to the Testator in our presence and it appeared to be understood and approved by him, in the presence of us, both present at the same time, who at his request, in his presence, and in the presence of each other, have subscribed our names as witnesses."**

---

[236] Longmore J. in *Esterhuizen v. Allied Dunbar*, [1998] 2 F.L.R. 668, [1998] Fam. Law 527. Other cases have relieved a solicitor from negligence where the will was sent out and the two witnesses were not present at the same time, because the client was relatively sophisticated.

[237] See *Re Gray*, an unreported judgment of June 24, 1997, of Lloyd J., Chancery Division, where the will was not admitted for probate because the two witnesses were not present at the same time. The solicitor was sued for negligence.

The affidavit of execution should include the following statement:

☞ **"Before its execution, the document was translated into Polish for the will-maker, who does not speak English, by XY. The document was read over to the will-maker in Polish and the will-maker appeared to understand the contents."**

There should be a separate affidavit for the translator, which lists her credentials, and states that she faithfully translated the will.

b. For a person who is physically unable to sign (as the result of a stroke, for example) the attestion clause will need to be amended to read:

☞ **"Signed in the presence of the Testator, WALLACE WILLMAKER and on his instructions by Steven Secretary, with the name of the Testator, Wallace Willmaker, who is unable to sign, as the Will of the Testator, after the Will had first been read over to the Testator in the presence of us both, and it appeared to be understood and approved by him, in the presence of us, both present at the same time, who at his request, in his presence, and in the presence of each other, have subscribed our names as witnesses".**

The affidavit of execution should include the following statement:

☞ **"Before its execution, the document was read over to the Testator, who appeared to understand and approve the contents. The document was executed in the presence of both witnesses and in the presence of the Testator and on his instructions by Steven Secretary with the name of Wallace Willmaker".**

c. For a will-maker who is blind or illiterate, the attestation clause should read:

"Signed by the Testator, Wallace Willmaker, [by his mark] [or] [who is blind], as his Will, after the Will had first been read over to the Testator in our presence and it appeared to be understood and approved by him in the presence of us, both present at the same time, who at his request, in his presence, and in the presence of each other, have subscribed our names as witnesses".

The affidavit of execution should include:

"Before its execution, the document was read over to the Testator, who (was blind/signed by making his/her mark). The Testator appeared to understand the contents".

d. Where there have been changes marked in the will, the affidavit of execution should read:

"The following alterations, erasures, obliterations or interlineations that have not been attested appear in the document:

\<list alteration\>

The document is now in the same condition as when it was executed."

12. Storing the Will

Wills should be stored flat, preferably in fire and flood resistant places. If you prepare wills for trust companies, they will usually store the original will. Any lawyer in the business of preparing wills must have adequate facilities for storage. If you are concerned about the amount of space, you might consider using the court storage facilities. Wills can be placed on deposit with the court, and stored for a modest fee, which can be billed as a disbursement to the client.

One option we discourage is giving the original will to the client to store. If the will is in the safe deposit box, the document the executor needs to get access to the box is locked away. There are other problems: if the client has custody of the will, it can easily fall into the hands of beneficiaries, who may not be relied upon to resist the temptation to make it "disappear" if they do not like the contents. Moreover, if the will cannot be found, you will be faced with the presumption that the will-maker revoked it, and a resulting intestacy.

13. Acknowledgement of Release, Authority to Release, Authority to View

If you have custody of the will, you will need a log book to record where it is at any given time and an alphabetical list of all wills, for ease in finding them. If the will is removed, because the will-maker or her attorney has removed it, or because a new will has replaced it, or because the client has died, that should be recorded in the log. Keep a simple log with the will itself, to record the ins and outs. We like to stamp onto the will envelope a chart, which will list the documents it contains, the names of those authorized to review them, and the dates a document is checked in or out.

Client: Tracy Healthy

Persons Authorized to Review: client, spouse Steve, daughter Donna (alternate POA)

Date Deposited	Document	Out	Signature	In
Feb. 3, 2001	Primary Will			
"	Secondary Will			
"	CPOA (spouse)	Monday, March 3, 2003	"Steve Healthy"	
"	CPOA (daughter)			
"	PPOA			

14. Reporting Letters

Defensive practice requires that you put down in writing what you did (and did not do) for the client in a reporting letter. The following is a basic form of such a letter, which can be adapted to the circumstances of each file.

Dear Client(s):

Re: Will(s) and Powers of Attorney/Estate Planning

I am pleased to report that we have now completed affidavits of execution, and placed your original Wills and Powers of Attorney in our storage for safe keeping [OR forwarded your original Wills and Powers of Attorney to Ontario Trust Co. for safe-keeping].

[Optional] As part of your estate planning, you have also made the following changes to your assets:

RRSPs/Life Insurance: Your Will changes the beneficiaries of your RRSPs/Life Insurance Policies [with . . . Account/Policy No. . . .] to . . .

You must write/We have written to the financial institution to inform them of the change in beneficiary.

Please note that if you make a new Will, or if your Will is revoked by any other means, the life insurance designation is also revoked.

Real Estate: You have transferred your real property at [address].

Your Will governs the disposition of these properties only as long as they are held as tenants in common. If you hold property in joint tenancy, your Will cannot determine how it will pass on your death.

Investments: You have transferred [insert data].

Your Will cannot control these accounts if they are changed to give your spouse or anyone else a right of survivorship.

You should review your Will and your estate plan periodically. I recommend that you read over your Will at least every three years, to ensure that it still meets your requirements. If changes occur in your personal and financial affairs, you may need changes to your Will and other documents sooner.

For Married Couples: Since I have acted for you both in this matter, I would have to inform you both if one of you requests changes, and require the consent of you both to make changes to either Will.

For Single Clients: Marriage revokes a Will, so if you plan to marry, please contact me to discuss the steps necessary to confirm or change your Will.

Changes in legislation and court cases can also affect your estate plan. If you become aware of new legislation or hear or read about court cases or rulings that appear to affect your plan, please call me. Finally, please keep me advised of changes in your address and/or telephone numbers.

I take this opportunity of submitting to you our account for services rendered. I trust you will find it satisfactory. If you have any questions or comments, please let me know.

Yours very truly,

15. Four Eyes

In a perfect world, no document would ever have a misprint, a typographical error, a spelling mistake, a missing word or line, or a misnumbered paragraph. In the real world all of these things happen, and so every document should be read by at least two people (the "Four Eyes" principle). And one of those people *must* be a lawyer. You can delegate the preparation of an initial draft to an assistant, but the preparation of a will is not, or should not be, a "routine task" that can be done wholly by a non-lawyer.

Some lawyers create a "Will Summary" or a "Will Map". Not only can this be helpful in assisting a client to understand a very complex will, but it can help the drafter to lay out a plan of the estate disposition, and see where there may be gaps that would, in the contingency not provided for, create an intestacy. Two words of warning, however: (1) be careful that the will map and the will are actually parallel; and (2) give the will map to the client only after they have reviewed the drafts; if it is sent out with the drafts, there is a good chance the client will not really read the drafts, but will rely instead on the "Will Map".

A Little Digression on Paralegals and the Drafting of Wills

On May 31, 2000, the Honourable Peter Cory delivered to the Attorney General for Ontario a report entitled "A Framework for Regulating Paralegal Practice in Ontario" setting out a framework for regulating paralegal practice in Ontario. It included the recommendation that unsupervised paralegals could:

> "draw a simple will in the following circumstances:
>
> — where the assets consist of no more than the matrimonial home, bank accounts, life insurance policies, RRSPs, annuities and personal chattels; and
>
> — where the distribution of those assets is straightforward, for example, all to a spouse and if the spouse should predecease the testator, or if there is no

spouse, to be divided in equal shares per stirpes among the children [*sic*]."

We would like to quote the Law Society's response:

"A will, whether simple or complex, can only be produced as an end product of a comprehensive client interview. Proper advice requires a thorough knowledge of at least 12 statutes.[238] The person giving advice should also be familiar with the common law concepts of testamentary capacity, undue influence, duress, abatement, incorporation by reference, voidance for uncertainty or public policy, conflicts of laws and the legal principles set out in *Saunders v. Vautier.*

The assessment of issues of capacity, undue influence and suspicious circumstances is key to the creation of a valid will and makes the potential risk to the consumer greater than some people may recognize. Incompetent practice in this area can harm not only the testator, but also innocent third parties such as beneficiaries. It is remarkably easy to err in drafting a will, as many do-it-yourself wills and wills drafted by non-lawyers have amply demonstrated.

There is no consensus about whether will-drafting is an appropriate area for paralegal practice. Some propose allowing paralegals to do 'simple' wills. It has been argued that paralegals could receive adequate training through available college courses. Others argue that without a working knowledge of the statutory and case law in the area of wills interpretation, family law, dependants' relief, etc., a will-drafter will not be able to properly assess whether the contemplated will is in fact 'simple'. Thus, will-drafting can be quite routine, or highly specialized, depending on the testator's specific circumstances. However, the determination can only be made after a thorough legal assessment of all the circumstances.

Any service requiring judgments respecting issues such as capacity and the relevance of other areas of law (for example, family, income tax and insurance law) raises sufficient potential risk to conclude that only lawyers should provide this service.

---

[238] *Succession Law Reform Act, the Family Law Act, Substitute Decisions Act, Estate Administration Tax Act, Income Tax Act, Children's Law Reform Act, Insurance Act, Accumulations Act, Perpetuities Act, Registry Act, Land Titles Act and the Estate Administration Act.* Please see Law Society of Upper Canada, *An Analysis of 'A Framework for Regulating Paralegal Practice in Ontario'* (Toronto, Ont.: Law Society of Upper Canada, July 24, 2000), at pp. 38-40.

Having just written a book replete with the errors that bedevil even the most knowledgeable and experienced lawyers when they draft, we could not agree more.

The Last Word

Wills are dual-natured documents. Just as people have a physical presence and a spirit, the will addresses the material possessions of the will-maker and it contains the last words that she may leave for those who love her. Sometimes clients want to put spiteful or angry messages in their wills. We discourage this for compassionate and practical reasons, as such a will is more likely to be challenged. Let the will-maker speak gently through the documents you draft. Be alert to your role, not only in transmitting the property of your client but in assisting a fellow mortal in his attempt to face his own death, and in putting on paper the words that may resonate profoundly with the family who read it.[239]

A well-drafted and well-rounded will serves your clients' interests by letting them feel that they have 'put [their] house in order'.[240] It is also, in our experience, one of the most fulfilling aspects of a legal practice. Most lawyers like doing wills — not because they are easy (we hope that at this point in the book you no longer believe that), but because they are challenging. They demand all the skill and professionalism that can be mustered to confront the most basic issues of our lives in the service of a social and personal good. Few things in practice, or in life, are as satisfying.

---

[239] In his book *On Being a Christian and a Lawyer* (Utah: Brigham Young University Press, 1981), Thomas Shaffer, who practices what he calls 'the law of the dead' begins with a classic problem : 'A middle-aged, wealthy woman says to you, "I want to give all that I have to the Christian Anti-Communist Crusade, and nothing to my husband and children".' He uses the problem to open a discussion not only of what you can do in drafting wills, but of what you will do and how you see your role in relation to your client's. Shaffer's book is of particular interest in exploring a range of ethical issues in the context of 'the law of the dead'.

[240] There is a movement that encourages people to write 'ethical' wills, to pass on not only their wealth, but their values as well. Whether you pursue this approach to drafting or not, the growth of this movement may say something about the failure of the legal wills we draft to address the real needs of our clients. See Scott C. Fithian, *Values Based Estate Planning* (John Wiley & Sons, 2000); Barry K. Baines, *Ethical Wills: Putting Your Values on Paper* (Harper Collins, 2001), and Jack Reimer and Nathaniel Stampfer, *So That Your Values Live On: Ethical Wills and How to Prepare Them* (Jewish Lights Publishing, 2002).

A P P E N D I X **A**

→ p 253

erased away

Outright Distribution Will

This is the Last Will of me, ANNE AMAZING, also known as ANNE CLIENT, of the City of Kingston in the County of Frontenac, Province of Ontario.

Revocation

1. I revoke all former wills and codicils made by me.

Executor and Trustee

2. a. I appoint my friend, CLAUDE CLIENT ("CLAUDE"), to be the Estate Trustee, Executor, and Trustee of my Will, but if CLAUDE dies before me or is or becomes unwilling or unable to act as my Estate Trustee, Executor and Trustee before the trusts set out in my Will have been fully performed, then I appoint my sister, CHARLOTTE SIMPKINS ("CHARLOTTE"), and my friend, DAVID DINO ("DAVID"), to be the Estate Trustees, Executors, and Trustees of my Will in the place of CLAUDE.

   b. I refer to my Estate Trustee, Executor and Trustee or Estate Trustees, Executors and Trustees, original, substituted or surviving, as "my Trustees".

Transfers To Trustees

3. I give all my property to my Trustees upon the following trusts.

Personal Property

    a. To deliver my antique gold watch that I received from my grandfather, and that has been in the family for seven generations, to my beloved son, ROBERT AMAZING, or if he dies before me, to my son STEPHEN AMAZING, if he survives me.

    b. To dispose of all remaining articles of personal, domestic and household use or ornament belonging to me at my death, including consumable stores, and all automobiles and accessories then owned by me among my children alive at my death, as my Trustees in their absolute discretion deem advisable. Without in any way limiting the discretion of my Trustees hereunder, it is my wish that in disposing of these articles, they give effect to my wishes as expressed in any memorandum which I may leave with my Will.

Debts and Death Taxes

    c. To pay out of and charge to the capital of my general estate my just debts and funeral and testamentary expenses and I hereby authorize my Trustees to defer, commute or prepay any of these debts, funeral or testamentary expenses.

Conversion of My Assets

    d. To use their discretion in the realization of my estate with power to sell any part of my estate at any time and on any terms, and either for cash or credit or for part cash and part credit as they in their absolute discretion decide. I further authorize my Trustees to postpone the conversion of any part or parts of my estate for whatever length of time they in their absolute discretion determine. My Trustees shall have a separate power to retain any of my investments or assets in the form existing at my death at their absolute discretion without responsibility for loss and whether or not it is an investment or asset in which a Trustee may by law invest.

Residue

    e. To divide the residue of my estate equally among my children alive at my death; but if any child of mine dies before me leaving issue alive at my death, the part which that deceased child would have been entitled if alive at my death shall be divided among that deceased child's issue in equal shares per stirpes, subject to the trust provisions set out in paragraph 3(f) of my Will.

Trust Provisions For Issue

f. If a grandchild or other issue of mine (a "Beneficiary") becomes entitled to receive any portion of the residue of my estate before attaining the age of twenty-five (25) years, that portion ("the Portion") shall be held and invested by my Trustees upon the following terms:

  i. Until the Beneficiary attains the age of twenty-five (25) years, my Trustees shall pay to or apply for the benefit of that Beneficiary as much of the income and capital of the Portion as my Trustees in their absolute discretion consider appropriate from time to time. Any net income not so paid shall be accumulated and added to the Portion. After the maximum period permitted by law for the accumulation of income, my Trustees shall pay the net income derived from the Portion to or for the benefit of that Beneficiary.

  ii. When that Beneficiary attains the age of twenty-five (25) years, my Trustees shall transfer the balance of the Portion to him or her.

  iii. If that Beneficiary dies before attaining the age of 25 years leaving issue then alive, my Trustees shall divided the Portion or the amount of it then remaining among the issue of that Beneficiary, in equal shares per stirpes.

Failure of Gifts

g. If at any time after my death any portion of my estate has not otherwise vested indefeasibly in one or more of my issue pursuant to the foregoing provisions, then on the date when it is determined that the portion of my estate will fail to vest (the "Vesting Date") I direct my Trustees to divide that portion into as many equal parts as are necessary to carry out the following provisions and to deal with the parts as follows:

  i. to pay or transfer one (1) equal part to CHARLOTTE if she is alive on the Vesting Date; and

  ii. to pay or transfer one (1) equal part to DAVID if he is alive on the Vesting Date.

Payments For Minors

4.   a. If any person becomes entitled to receive a share of my estate while under the age of majority, my Trustees shall keep that share invested and, until that person attains the age of majority, my Trustees shall pay or apply for the benefit of that person as much of the income and capital as my Trustees in the exercise of an absolute discretion consider advisable.

   b. I authorize my Trustees to make any payments for a person under the age of majority to a parent or guardian or other person standing *in loco parentis* to that person, or to make any payment directly to the person that my Trustees in their absolute discretion consider appropriate. Any evidence that my Trustees have made a payment shall be a sufficient discharge to my Trustees.

Investments

5.   My Trustees when making investments for my estate shall not be limited to investments authorized by law for trustees but may make any investments they in their absolute discretion consider prudent and in the bests interests of my estate.

Powers of Trustees

6.   In order to carry out the trusts of my Will, I give my Trustees the following powers to be used in the exercise of an absolute discretion at any time:

Distribution in Specie

   a. My Trustees may divide, distribute or allocate any asset of my estate in kind and at the valuation to be determined by my Trustees in their absolute discretion. In determining the valuation, my Trustees may consider future expectation for the asset as my Trustees in their absolute discretion consider appropriate, including any tax liability or credit. Any decision made by my Trustees in this regard shall be binding on all persons concerned.

Real Property

   b. If any real or leasehold property forms part of my estate, my Trustees may, in their absolute discretion:

   i. exchange, partition, or otherwise dispose of the whole or any part of the property either for cash or credit or for part cash and part credit as my Trustees consider appropriate;

ii. lease property for any term or terms and subject to any conditions and covenants;

iii. accept surrenders of leases and tenancies;

iv. pay money out of the income and capital of my general estate for repairs or improvements and generally manage and maintain the property;

v. give options; and

vi. give or renew any mortgage or borrow any money upon any mortgage or pay off any mortgage at any time after my death.

Elections

c. My Trustees may make, or choose not to make, any allocations, elections, determinations, designations, and applications as my Trustees in their absolute discretion consider to be in the best interests of my Estate, and specifically any allocations and elections necessary under the *Income Tax Act* (Canada) or any similar legislation of any province or other jurisdiction in force from time to time.

Borrowing

d. My Trustees may borrow on behalf of my estate such amount or amounts and on such terms and conditions as they in their absolute discretion deem advisable, and, for the repayment of any amount borrowed, may mortgage, charge, pledge, hypothecate or otherwise encumber any of the assets of my estate.

Employment Agents

e. I authorize my Trustees at any time to engage the services of any trust company, lawyer, accountant, bookkeeper, investment advisor or other professional advisor or organization to assist them in the management and administration of my estate, and my Trustees shall pay for any of these services out of the income or the capital of my estate as they in their absolute discretion determine.

Power of Trustee To Purchase Assets

f. In my Trustees' personal capacity, my Trustees may purchase any assets from my estate if the purchase price and other terms are unanimously approved by my Trustees and by the adult beneficiaries of my estate. My Trustees shall not be required to obtain approval of any Court for the purchase.

Exclusions From Net Family Property

7. I declare that the income, including capital gains, arising from any interest passing to a beneficiary under my Will shall be excluded from such beneficiary's net family property or from the value of the beneficiary's assets on the death, divorce or separation of such beneficiary pursuant to the *Family Law Act.*

"Issue Per Stirpes"

8. Whenever in my Will I have directed a division "per stirpes" among the issue or any person, I intend to designate the children of that person and not his or her remoter issue unless a child of that person is then deceased, in which case I intend that the share to which such deceased child would have been entitled, if living shall in turn be divided equally among his or her children and so on with each representation by a deceased individual at each level by his or her children.

IN TESTIMONY WHEREOF I have to my Will, which is written upon this and * preceding pages of paper, subscribed my name this * day of *, 2003.

SIGNED by the will-maker, ANNE AMAZING, also known as ANNE CLIENT, as her last Will, in the presence of us, both present at the same time, who at her request, in her presence and in the presence of each other have hereunto subscribed our names as witnesses:))))))))))	_____ Anne Amazing

Witness #1: _____

Name:

Address:

Occupation:

Witness #2: _____

Name:

Address:

Occupation:

Trust Will

This is the Last Will of me, ANNE AMAZING, also known as ANNE CLIENT, of the City of Kingston in the County of Frontenac, Province of Ontario.

Revocation

1. I revoke all former wills and codicils made by me.

Executor and Trustee

2. a. I appoint my husband, CLAUDE CLIENT ("CLAUDE"), to be the Estate Trustee, Executor, and Trustee of my Will, but if CLAUDE dies before me or is or becomes unwilling or unable to act as my Estate Trustee, Executor and Trustee before the trusts set out in my Will have been fully performed, then I appoint my sister, CHARLOTTE SIMPKINS ("CHARLOTTE"), and my friend, DAVID DINO ("DAVID"), to be the Estate Trustees, Executors, and Trustees of my Will in the place of CLAUDE.

   b. I refer to my Estate Trustee, Executor and Trustee or Estate Trustees, Executors, and Trustees, original, substituted or surviving, as "my Trustees".

Insurance Declaration

3. a. I hereby designate my husband, CLAUDE CLIENT ("CLAUDE"), if he survives me, as beneficiary of the proceeds of all policies of insurance on my life, including my policy with Perpetual Life Insurance Co. Policy No. 12345, (collectively referred to as the "Proceeds").

   b. If CLAUDE dies before me, the Proceeds shall be paid to the Insurance Trustees (as defined below) and held in a separate trust fund (the "Insurance Trust Fund"). For greater certainty, I designate the Insurance Trustees for the purposes of the *Insurance Act* as the recipients of the Proceeds.

   c. The Insurance Trustees shall invest and reinvest the Insurance Trust Fund for the benefit of my children and their issue, upon the same trusts, terms and conditions as to the payment of income and capital of the Insurance Trust Fund as I have provided for the residue of my estate, and I hereby incorporate by reference the trust and dispositive provisions of clause 4(*h*) of my Will into this paragraph of my Will with the necessary modification as terms of the Insurance Trust Fund.

d. I authorize the Insurance Trustees in their absolute discretion to advance the Proceeds, or any part of them, by way of loan to my general estate and if the Insurance Trustees consider it desirable to do so, to buy from my general estate whatever assets the Insurance Trustees consider advisable. The Insurance Trustees shall have the same powers and discretions in administering the Proceeds as the Trustees of my estate have for the administration of my residuary estate.

e. The Insurance Trustees shall be my sister, CHARLOTTE SIMPKINS, and my friend, DAVID DINO.

f. This is a designation within the meaning of the *Insurance Act* and I revoke any previous designation.

g. For greater certainty, the Proceeds shall not form part of my estate and shall be administered as a separate trust notwithstanding that the Insurance Trustees may be the same persons as the Trustees of my estate.

h. The receipt of the Insurance Trustees fully discharges the institution paying the Proceeds which shall not be required to see to the carrying out of the terms of the Trust.

Transfers To Trustees

4. I give my all my property to my Trustees upon the following trusts:

Personal Property

a. My Trustees shall deliver all articles of personal, domestic and household use or ornament belonging to me at my death, including consumable stores, and all automobiles, vehicles, boats, motors and accessories then owned by me to CLAUDE, if he survives me for a period of thirty (30) days, for his own use absolutely. If CLAUDE dies before me or survives me but dies within a period of thirty (30) days after my death, then on the death of the survivor of CLAUDE and me ("the Date of Distribution") my Trustees shall divide these articles among my children alive on the Date of Distribution as my Trustees in their absolute discretion consider appropriate. If my Trustees are of the opinion that any one or more of my children are not old enough to make use of these articles or any of them, they may sell the article and add the proceeds of sale to the residue of my estate or hold the articles until the child for whom it is set aside is old enough to make use of it.

Debts and Death Taxes

b. My Trustees shall pay out of and charge to the capital of my general estate my just debts and funeral and testamentary expenses and I hereby authorize my Trustees to defer, commute or prepay any of these debts, funeral or testamentary expenses.

Conversion of My Assets

c. My Trustees shall use their discretion in the realization of my estate with power to sell any part of my estate at any time and on any terms, and either for cash or credit or for part cash and part credit as they, in their absolute discretion decide. I further authorize my Trustees to postpone the conversion of any part or parts of my estate for whatever length of time they in their absolute discretion determine. My Trustees shall have a separate power to retain any of my investments or assets in the form existing at my death at their absolute discretion without responsibility for loss and whether or not it is an investment or asset in which a trustee may by law invest.

Legacies

d. My Trustees shall pay to ABC Charity, ten thousand dollars ($10,000) in cash or the equivalent value in marketable securities or cash and marketable securities in such proportion as my Trustees in their absolute discretion decide.

e. If CLAUDE dies before me or survives me but dies within thirty (30) days after my death, my Trustees shall pay to CHARLOTTE if she is living at the Date of Distribution, the sum of $150,000 in recognition of the many years she has stood by me, and to compensate her for the hardship she has endured at the hands of her husband; but if CLAUDE and I die within thirty (30) days of each other and as a consequence CHARLOTTE is also entitled to receive the sum of $150,000 in CLAUDE's Will, I direct that the legacy here provided for be reduced to $75,000, it being my intention and expectation that in those circumstances the legacy will be paid equally from CLAUDE's estate and my estate, but if the gift from CLAUDE's estate is more or less than $75,000, the amount payable from my estate shall be adjusted so that the total sum of $150,000 is paid to CHARLOTTE from the estate of CLAUDE and me.

f. I declare that any benefits received by CHARLOTTE under the provisions of my Will shall be in addition to any remuneration to which CHARLOTTE may be entitled for services rendered as a Trustee for my estate.

Residue

g. My Trustees shall pay or transfer the residue of my estate to CLAUDE, if he survives me for a period of thirty (30) days.

h. If CLAUDE dies before me or survives me but dies within a period of thirty (30) days after my death, then on the Date of Distribution my Trustees shall divide the residue of my estate into as many equal shares as are necessary to carry out the following provisions, and shall deal with those shares as follows:

   (i)   one (1) equal share shall be paid or transferred to each child of mine alive on the date of Distribution who has attained the age of thirty-five (35) years;

   (ii) one (1) equal share shall be set aside for each child of mine alive on the Date of Distribution who has not attained the age of thirty-five (35) years; and

   (iii) one (1) equal share shall be set aside for each child of mine who has died before the Date of Distribution leaving issue then alive.

i. My Trustees shall deal with the shares set aside as follows:

   (1) Each share set aside for a child alive on the Date of Distribution shall be kept invested. Until the child for whom the share is held attains the age of thirty-five (35) years, my Trustees shall pay to or apply for the general benefit of that child so much of the net income and capital of the share as my Trustees in their absolute discretion consider appropriate from time to time. Any surplus income shall be accumulated and added to the capital of the share, but after twenty-one (21) years from my death, all the net income shall be paid to the child for whom the share is held.

   (2) If at the Date of Distribution a child of mine has attained the age of twenty-five (25) years or when a child of mine attains the age of twenty-five (25) years, my Trustees shall pay one-third of the capital and accumulated income of that child's share then remaining to that child for his or her own use absolutely.

   (3) If at the Date of Distribution a child of mine has attained the age of thirty (30) years or when a child of mine attains the age of thirty (30) years, my Trustees shall pay and transfer one-half of

the capital and accumulated income then remaining to that child for his or her own use absolutely.

(4) When that child attains the age of thirty-five (35) years, my Trustees shall pay or transfer the balance of that child's share then remaining to that child for his or her own use absolutely.

(5) If a child of mine dies before attaining the age of thirty-five (35) years leaving issue then alive, my Trustees shall divide that child's share or the amount of it then remaining among the issue of that child in equal parts per stirpes. If that child leaves no issue then alive and I have issue then alive, the share shall be divided among my issue in equal shares per stirpes.

(6) If, however, an interest passes to a child of mine for whom a share of my estate is already being held in trust under my Will, that interest shall be added to that child's trust and administered in the same manner.

(7) One share for each issue of a child of mine who has died before the Date of Distribution leaving issue then alive shall be divided among the issue of that deceased child in equal parts per stirpes, and my Trustees shall hold those parts in trust for any issue under the age of thirty-five (35) years on the same terms with the necessary modifications as are provided for the shares held for children of mine.

Failure of Gifts

If at any time after my death any portion of my estate shall not otherwise vest indefeasibly in possession of my spouse or one or more of my issue pursuant to the foregoing provisions, then on the date when it is determined that the portion of my estate will fail to vest (herein called the "Vesting Date"), I DIRECT my Trustees to divide that portion into as many equal parts as are necessary to carry out the following provisions and to deal with the parts as follows:

(i) My Trustees shall divide one equal part between the following individuals who are alive on the Vesting Date, namely my husband's sister, SAMANTHA DAVIDSON, and my husband's brother, JEFFREY CLIENT, in equal shares per capita; and

(ii) My Trustees shall divide one equal part between the following individuals who are alive on the Vesting Date, namely my sister, CHARLOTTE, and my friend, DAVID, in equal shares per capita.

Payments For Minors

5.   a. If any person becomes entitled to receive a share of my estate while under the age of majority, my Trustees shall keep that share invested and, until that person attains the age of majority, my Trustees shall pay or apply for the benefit of that person as much of the income and capital as my Trustees in the exercise of an absolute discretion consider advisable.

   b. I authorize my Trustees to make any payments for a person under the age of majority to a parent or guardian or other person standing *in loco parentis* to that person, or to make any payment directly to the person that my Trustees in their absolute discretion consider appropriate. Any evidence that my Trustees have made a payment shall discharge my Trustees with regard to that payment.

Investments

6.   My Trustees when making investments for my estate shall not be limited to investments authorized by law for trustees but may make any investments they in their absolute discretion consider prudent and to be in the best interests of my estate.

Powers of Trustees

7.   In order to carry out the trusts of my Will, I give my Trustees the following powers to be used in the exercise of an absolute discretion at any time:

Distribution in Specie

   a. My Trustees may divide, distribute or allocate any asset of my estate in kind and at the valuation to be determined by my Trustees in their absolute discretion. In determining the valuation, my Trustees may consider future expectations for the asset as my Trustees in their absolute discretion consider appropriate, including any tax liability or credit. Any decision made by my Trustees in this regard shall be binding on all persons concerned.

Real Property

   b. If any real or leasehold property forms part of my estate, my Trustees may, in their absolute discretion:

      (i) exchange, partition, or otherwise dispose of the whole or any part of the property either for cash or credit or for part cash and part credit as my Trustees consider appropriate;

(ii) lease property for any term or terms and subject to any conditions and covenants;

(iii) accept surrenders of leases and tenancies;

(iv) pay money out of the income and capital of my general estate for repairs or improvements and generally manage and maintain the property;

(v) give options; and

(vi) give or renew any mortgage or borrow any money upon any mortgage or pay off any mortgage at any time after my death.

Elections

c. My Trustees may make, or choose not to make, any allocations, elections, determinations, designations, and applications as my Trustees in their absolute discretion consider to be in the best interests of my Estate, and specifically any allocations and elections necessary under the *Income Tax Act* (Canada) or any similar legislation of any province or other jurisdiction in force from time to time.

Borrowing

d. My Trustees may borrow on behalf of my estate such amount or amounts and on such terms and conditions as they in their absolute discretion deem advisable, and, for the repayment of any amount borrowed, may mortgage, charge, pledge, hypothecate or otherwise encumber any of the assets of my estate.

Employment Agents

e. I authorize my Trustees at any time to engage the services of any trust company, lawyer, accountant, bookkeeper, investment advisor or other professional advisor or organization to assist them in the management and administration of my estate, and my Trustees shall pay for any of these services out of the income or the capital of my estate as they in their absolute discretion determine.

Power of Trustee To Purchase Assets

f. In my Trustees' personal capacity, my Trustees may purchase any assets from my estate if the purchase price and other terms are unanimously approved by my Trustees and by the adult beneficiaries of my estate. My Trustees shall not be required to obtain approval of any Court for the purchase.

Early Vesting

g. Notwithstanding anything else in my Will and any Codicil, if my Trustees are holding any share of my estate in trust for any beneficiary and my Trustees in their absolute discretion determine that the cost of administering the fund is disproportionate to the value of the share, I authorize my Trustees to pay the remainder of that share to the beneficiary or to the parent or legal guardian of the beneficiary as they in their absolute discretion determine.

Lending

h. My Trustees may from time to time lend money from my estate on such terms and conditions and for such length of time as my Trustees in their absolute discretion determine. I also declare that my Trustees may lend money for the express purpose of earning income for my estate or for such other purposes connected with my estate as my Trustees in their discretion from time to time may deem advisable. My Trustees may lend out of my estate to any person or corporation notwithstanding that the person or corporation may be a member of my family or a beneficiary. My Trustees shall not be liable for any loss that may happen to my estate in connection with any loan made by them in good faith.

Co-Mingling of Trusts

i. My Trustees may in their absolute discretion co-mingle assets of my estate, or insurance proceeds held in a separate testamentary trust, with other moneys or assets held by my Trustees either in trust for any one or more of the beneficiaries of my estate or under trusteeship of my Trustees outside of my estate.

Charitable Gifts

j. For the purposes of this Will:

(i)   The receipt of any person purporting to be the proper officer of the charitable institution named as a beneficiary shall be a sufficient discharge to my Trustees.

(ii) If, at the time of distribution, any institutional beneficiary never existed or has amalgamated with another institutional beneficiary or has changed its name or objects, any provision for it in this Will shall not fail and I declare that notwithstanding the particular form of the bequest, my paramount intention is to benefit a general charitable purpose and my Trustees are hereby authorized in their absolute discretion to pay the bequest to the institutional beneficiary that my Trustees consider most closely fulfils the objects I intend to benefit.

Guardian

8. If CLAUDE dies before me and if at my death any child of mine is under the age of majority, I appoint my friend, DAVID, to be the guardian to have care of any of my minor children during their minorities and, to the extent that I am capable so of doing, to be the guardian of the property of each minor child but if DAVID is or becomes unable or unwilling to act, I appoint my sister, CHARLOTTE, to be the guardian of care and property in his place. If the guardian here appointed consents to have custody of a minor child of mine, it is my wish that within ninety (90) days from my death, he or she apply to court to have custody of my child and to act as the guardian of the property of my child pursuant to the *Children's Law Reform Act*. The costs of the application, if any, shall be paid from the residue of my estate.

Exclusions From Net Family Property

9. a. I declare that the income, including capital gains, arising from any interest passing to a beneficiary under this Will shall be excluded from such beneficiary's net family property or from the value of the beneficiary's assets on the death, divorce or separation of such beneficiary pursuant to the *Family Law Act*.

b. All gifts made to a beneficiary shall be the separate property of my beneficiaries and shall not fall into any Community of Property or be subject to any other matrimonial rights of the spouses of my beneficiaries and shall not be liable for the obligations of any such spouses or Community. All such gifts shall not be subject to seizure for the payment of any debts of beneficiaries or their representatives while in the possession and control of my Trustees.

"Issue Per Stirpes"

10. Whenever in my Will I have directed a division "per stirpes" among the issue or any person, I intend to designate the children of that person and not his or her remoter issue unless a child of that person is then deceased, in which case I intend that the share to which such deceased child would have been entitled if living shall in turn be divided equally among his or her children and so on with each representation by a deceased individual at each level by his or her children.

Governing Law

11.   This Will shall be governed by the laws of the Province of Ontario.

IN TESTIMONY WHEREOF I have to my Will, which is written upon this and * preceding pages of paper, subscribed my name this * day of *, 2003.

SIGNED by the will-maker, ANNE)	
AMAZING, also known as ANNE)	
CLIENT, as her last Will, in the)	
presence of us, both present at the)	
same time, who at her request, in)	_____
her presence and in the presence)	Anne Amazing
of each other have hereunto)	
subscribed our names as witnesses:)	
)	

Witness #1:   _____

Name:

Address:

Occupation:

Witness #2:   _____

Name:

Address:

Occupation:

Primary Will

THIS IS THE LAST WILL of me, CLIFFORD CLIENT, of the City of Ottawa in the County of Carleton, Province of Ontario with respect to all of my property except my Secondary Estate (as defined), made this 1st day of March, 2003. I refer to this Will as my "Primary Will".

Revocation

1. I revoke all former wills and codicils made by me. I DECLARE that subsequent to the execution of this Will, I will execute a Secondary Will dealing with certain of my assets defined therein as my Secondary Estate.

Executor and Trustee

2. a. I appoint my spouse, ARABELLA CLIENT ("ARABELLA"), to be the Estate Trustee, Executor, and Trustee of this my Primary Will, but if my spouse, ARABELLA, dies before me or is or becomes unwilling or unable to act as my Estate Trustee, Executor, and Trustee before the trusts set out in my Primary Will have been fully performed, then I appoint my brother, SAM THOMAS ("SAM"), and my sister, PATRICIA QUINTE ("PATRICIA"), to be the Estate Trustees, Executors, and Trustees of this my Primary Will in the place of ARABELLA.

    b. I refer to my Estate Trustee, Executor and Trustee or Estate Trustees, Executors, and Trustees, original, substituted or surviving, as "my Trustees".

Definition of Estates

3. a. The term "my Primary Estate" means all my worldwide and personal property other than my Secondary Estate, including any real property disclaimed by the Trustees of my Secondary Estate.

    b. The term "my Secondary Estate" means all my worldwide real and personal property that is in fact disposed of by my Secondary Will. My Secondary Estate shall include the following:

    i. any shares or indebtedness of ABC Limited, or any successor corporation to it, or any shares or securities received in exchange or substitution of those shares or indebtedness ("ABC");

    ii. all articles of personal, household, and gardening use or ornament including all automobiles (including any car collection I may own), snowmobiles and accessories, boats, motors and accessories, garden implements and vehicles, domestic animals, sports equipment and machinery, guns and accessories, brass, silver plate and plated articles, linen, china and glass, books (except books of account), pictures, paintings and prints, furniture, jewellery, wearing apparel, musical instruments, antiques and curios, manuscripts (but not any copyright that I may own), wines and liquors, consumable stores and provisions in storage or in or about or belonging to, or generally used in connection with, any and every dwelling house, apartment and recreational residence that I own or in which I reside at my death, (collectively, my "Personal Effects"); and

iii.   whatever interest I may have in the lands and buildings municipally known as 123 River Street, Smith Falls, Ontario, at my death.

Transfers to Trustees

4.   I give my Primary Estate to my Trustees upon the following Trusts:

Debts and Death Taxes

a.   My Trustees shall pay out of the capital of my general Primary Estate my debts and funeral and testamentary expenses and I hereby authorize my Trustees to prepay any taxes. I have made a similar provision for the payment of debts, expenses and taxes in my Secondary Will and I direct my Trustees along with the Executors and Trustees of my Secondary Will to determine a reasonable allocation of the debts, expenses and taxes between my Primary Estate and my Secondary Estate.

Conversion of My Assets

b.   My Trustees shall use their discretion in the realization of my Primary Estate with power to sell any part of my Primary Estate at any time and on any terms, and either for cash or credit or for part cash and part credit as they in their absolute discretion decide. I further authorize my Trustees to postpone the conversion of any part or parts of my Primary Estate for whatever length of time they in their absolute discretion determine. My Trustees shall have a separate power to retain any of my investments or assets in the form existing at my death at their absolute discretion without responsibility for loss and whether or not it is an investment or asset in which a trustee may by law invest.

Legacies

 c. If my spouse, ARABELLA, dies before me or survives me but dies within a period of 30 days after my death, my Trustees shall pay to my friend, JOSIAH SAMUELS, if he is living at the death of the survivor of ARABELLA and me, the sum of $100,000; but if ARABELLA and I die within 30 days of each other and as a consequence JOSIAH SAMUELS is also entitled to receive the sum of $100,000 in ARABELLA's Will, I direct that the legacy here provided for be reduced to $50,000, it being my intention and expectation that in those circumstances the legacy will be paid equally from the ARABELLA's Primary Estate and my Primary Estate, but if the gift from ARABELLA's Primary Estate is more or less than $50,000, the amount payable from my Primary Estate shall be adjusted accordingly so that the total sum of $100,000 is paid to JOSIAH SAMUELS from ARABELLA's Primary Estate and my Primary Estate.

Residue

 d. My Trustees shall pay or transfer the residue of my Primary Estate to ARABELLA if she survives me for a period of 30 days. If ARABELLA dies before me or survives me but dies within a period of 30 days after my death, then on the death of the survivor of ARABELLA and me ("Date of Distribution") my Trustees shall divide the residue of my Primary Estate equally among my children alive on the Date of Distribution; but if any child of mine dies before the Date of Distribution leaving issue alive on the Date of Distribution, my Trustees shall divide the part to which that deceased child would have been entitled if alive on the Date of Distribution among that deceased child's issue in equal shares per stirpes.

Payments For Minors

5. a. If any person becomes entitled to receive a share of my Primary Estate while under the age of majority, my Trustees shall keep that share invested and, until that person attains the age of majority, my Trustees shall pay or apply for the benefit of that person as much of the income and capital as my Trustees in the exercise of an absolute discretion consider advisable.

 b. I authorize my Trustees to make any payments for a person under the age of majority to a parent or guardian or other person standing in the place of a parent to that person, or to make any payment directly to the person that my Trustees in their absolute discretion consider appropriate. Any evidence that my Trustees have made a payment shall discharge my Trustees with regard to the payment.

INVESTMENTS

6.   My Trustees when making investments for my Primary Estate shall not be limited to investments authorized by law for trustees but may make any investments they in their absolute discretion consider prudent and to be in the best interests of my Primary Estate.

Powers of Trustees

7.   In order to carry out the trusts of this Primary Will, I give my Trustees the following powers to be used in the exercise of an absolute discretion at any time:

Distribution in Specie

a.   My Trustees may divide, distribute or allocate any asset of my Primary Estate in kind and at the valuation to be determined by my Trustees in their absolute discretion. In determining the valuation, my Trustees may consider future expectation for the asset as my Trustees in their absolute discretion consider appropriate, including any tax liability or credit. Any decision made by my Trustees in this regard shall be binding on all persons concerned.

Real Property

b.   If any real or leasehold property forms part of my Primary Estate, my Trustees may, in their absolute discretion:

   i.   exchange, partition, or otherwise dispose of the whole or any part of the property either for cash or credit or for part cash and part credit as my Trustees consider appropriate;

   ii.   lease property for any term or terms and subject to any conditions and covenants;

   iii.   accept surrenders of leases and tenancies;

   iv.   pay money out of the income and capital of my general Primary Estate for repairs or improvements and generally manage and maintain the property;

   v.   give options; and

   vi.   give or renew any mortgage or borrow any money upon any mortgage or pay off any mortgage at any time after my death.

Elections

c. My Trustees may make, or choose not to make, any allocations, elections, determinations, designations, and applications as my Trustees in their absolute discretion consider to be in the best interests of my Primary Estate, and specifically any allocations and elections necessary under the *Income Tax Act*(Canada) or any similar legislation of any province or other jurisdiction in force from time to time.

Borrowing

d. My Trustees may borrow on behalf of my Primary Estate such amount or amounts and on such terms and conditions as they in their absolute discretion deem advisable, and, for the repayment of any amount borrowed, may mortgage, charge, pledge, hypothecate or otherwise encumber any of the assets of my Primary Estate.

Employment Agents

e. My Trustees may make, or choose not to make, any allocations, elections, determinations, designations, and applications as my Trustees in their absolute discretion consider to be in the best interests of my Primary Estate, and specifically any allocations and elections necessary under the *Income Tax Act*(Canada) or any similar legislation of any province or other jurisdiction in force from time to time.

Power of Trustee To Purchase Assets

f. In my Trustees' personal capacity, my Trustees may purchase any assets from my Primary Estate if the purchase price and other terms are unanimously approved by my Trustees and by the adult beneficiaries of my Primary Estate. My Trustees shall not be required to obtain approval of any Court for that purchase.

Settlement of Claims

g. Without the consent of any person interested under my Will, my Trustees may compromise, settle, contest or waive any claim at any time made due to or made by my Primary Estate and may make any agreement with any person, government or corporation which shall be binding upon all persons interested in my Primary Estate.

Power To Carry On Business

h. I authorize my Trustees without being liable for any loss occasioned thereby to retain as an investment of my Primary Estate any business or company which I may own or in which I may have a controlling or proprietary interest at the time of my death ("the Business"), to continue and carry on or to participate in the carrying on of the Business, to reorganize, incorporate, wind up, or dispose of the Business, to advance capital out of my general Primary Estate, and generally to do all things in connection with the Business that I myself could do if living.

Securities

i. My Trustees shall have the power to deal with any shares or other interests which I may have in a company at my death to the same extent as if I were alive. My Trustees shall have the power to take up new or further shares, join in any reorganization, exchange shares or interests, and give, accept or exercise options. My Trustees may pay any money out of the income or capital of my Primary Estate as determined by my Trustees which may be necessary for any of these purposes.

Expansion of Powers

j. (i)   Until the final distribution of my estate and until the trusts set out in this Will have been fully performed, my Trustees have the power to perform, without court authorization, every act which a prudent person would perform for the purposes of these trusts under this Will.

(ii) My Trustees may do all supplementary or ancilliary acts or things and execute all instruments to enable them to carry out the intent and purpose of the powers set out here.

Exclusions From Net Family Property

8. a. I declare that the income, including capital gains, arising from any interest passing to a beneficiary under my Primary Will shall be excluded from such beneficiary's net family property or from the value of the beneficiary's assets on the death, divorce or separation of such beneficiary pursuant to the *Family Law Act.*

b. All gifts made to a beneficiary shall be the separate property of my beneficiaries and shall not fall into any Community of Property or be subject to any other matrimonial rights of the spouses of my beneficiaries and shall not be liable for the obligations of any such spouses or Community. All such gifts shall not be subject to seizure for the payment of any debts of beneficiaries or their representatives while in the possession and control of my Trustees.

"Issue Per Stirpes"

9. Whenever in my Primary Will I have directed a division "per stirpes" among the issue or any person, I intend to designate the children of that person and not his or her remoter issue unless a child of that person is then deceased, in which case I intend that the share to which such deceased child would have been entitled, if living shall in turn be divided equally among his or her children and so on with each representation by a deceased individual at each level by his or her children.

Governing Law

10. My Primary Will shall be governed by the laws of the Province of Ontario.

I have signed this Primary Will, which is written upon this and * pages of paper, in the presence of both witnesses whose names appear below.

SIGNED BY CLIFFORD CLIENT,   )
as his Will with respect to his   )
Primary Estate, in the presence of   )
both, present at the same time,   )
who at his request, in his presence,   )   _____
and in the presence of each other   )   Clifford Client
have subscribed our names as   )
witnesses:

Witness #1:   _____
Name:
Address:
Occupation:

Witness #2:   _____
Name:
Address:
Occupation:

Secondary Will

THIS IS THE LAST WILL of me, CLIFFORD CLIENT, of the City of Ottawa in the County of Carleton, Province of Ontario with respect to my Secondary Estate (as defined), made this 1st day of March, 2003. I refer to this Will as my "Secondary Will".

1.   I declare that I have an existing Will executed on the 1st day of March, 2003, dealing with certain of my assets defined therein as my Primary Estate, and which Will I do not intend to revoke by the provisions of this Will.

Executor and Trustee

2.   a.   I appoint my spouse, ARABELLA CLIENT ("ARABELLA"), to be the Estate Trustee, Executor, and Trustee of this Secondary Will, but if ARABELLA dies before me or is or becomes unwilling or unable to act as my Estate Trustee, Executor, and Trustee before the trusts set out in my Secondary Will have been fully performed, then I appoint my brother, SAM THOMAS ("SAM"), and my sister, PATRICIA QUINTE ("PATRICIA"), to be the Estate Trustees, Executors, and Trustees of this Secondary Will in the place of ARABELLA.

b.   I refer to my Estate Trustee, Executor and Trustee or Estate Trustees, Executors, and Trustees, original, substituted or surviving, as "my Trustees".

Definition of Estates

3.   a.   The term "my Primary Estate" means all my worldwide and personal property other than my Secondary Estate, and any real property disclaimed by the Trustees of my Secondary Estate.

b.   The term "my Secondary Estate" means all my worldwide real and personal property that is in fact disposed of by my Secondary Will. My Secondary Estate shall include the following:

i.   any shares or indebtedness of ABC Limited, or any successor corporation to it, or any shares or securities received in exchange or substitution of those shares or indebtedness ("ABC");

ii.   all articles of personal, household, and gardening use or ornament including all automobiles (including any car collection I may own), snowmobiles and accessories, boats, motors and accessories, garden implements and vehicles, domestic animals, sports equipment and machinery, guns and accessories, brass, silver plate and plated articles, linen, china and glass, books (except books of account), pictures, paintings and prints, furniture, jewellery, wearing apparel, musical instruments, antiques and curios, manuscripts (but not any copyright that I may own), wines and liquors, consumable stores and provisions in storage or in or about or belonging to, or generally used in connection with, any and every dwelling house, apartment and recreational residence that I own or in which I reside at my death, (collectively, my "Personal Effects"); and

iii. whatever interest I may have in the lands and buildings municipally known as 123 River Street, Smith Falls, Ontario, at my death.

I authorize my Trustees to disclaim entitlement to receive any property listed in the definition of my Secondary Estate, and any property so disclaimed by my Trustees within 60 days following the date of my death shall not form part of my Secondary Estate, but shall be part of my Primary Estate to be dealt with under my Primary Will. My Trustees may disclaim property for any reason that they in their absolute discretion consider appropriate, including, without derogating from the scope of that discretion, securing the result that my Secondary Will does not have to be submitted to the Court for the granting of Letters Probate or a Certificate of Appointment of Estate Trustee.

Transfers To Trustees

4. I give my Secondary Estate to my Trustees upon the following trusts:

PERSONAL PROPERTY

a. My Trustees shall deliver my Personal Effects to ARABELLA if she survives me, for her own use absolutely, but if she dies before me, my Trustees shall divide my Personal Effects among those of my children who survive me as my Trustees in their absolute discretion consider appropriate.

Debts and Death Taxes

b. My Trustees shall pay out of the capital of my general Secondary Estate my debts and funeral and testamentary expenses and I hereby authorize my Trustees to prepay any taxes. I have made a similar provision for the payment of debts, expenses and taxes in my Primary Will and I direct my Trustees along with the Executors and Trustees of my Primary Will to determine a reasonable allocation of the debts, expenses and taxes between my Primary Estate and my Secondary Estate.

Bequest of ABC

c. i. My Trustees shall transfer to ARABELLA all of my interest in ABC if she survives me, or if ARABELLA dies before me, shall divide my shares of ABC owned by me at my death equally between those of my children, BRIAN CLIENT ("BRIAN") and CARMEN CLIENT ("CARMEN") who survive me.

ii. If for any reason, including the terms of a shareholders' agreement, my interest in ABC may not be transferred to ARABELLA, I direct my Trustees to take whatever steps are required to see that there vests in ARABELLA an interest in ABC equivalent as to value and control to what I enjoyed at the time of my death, or the equivalent value from the residue of my Secondary Estate.

Conversion of My Assets

d. My Trustees shall use their discretion in the realization of my Secondary Estate with power to sell any part of my Secondary Estate at any time and on any terms, and either for cash or credit or for part cash and part credit as they in their absolute discretion decide. I further authorize my Trustees to postpone the conversion of any part or parts of my Secondary Estate for whatever length of time they in their absolute discretion determine. My Trustees shall have a separate power to retain any of my investments or assets in the form existing at my death at their absolute discretion without responsibility for loss and whether or not it is an investment or asset in which a trustee may by law invest.

Incorporation

e. To the extent that those assets of my Primary Estate, governed by the provisions of my Primary Will, executed on the 1st day of March, 2003, which Primary Will was executed prior to this Secondary Will, are insufficient to satisfy the debts, expenses, duties and taxes as provided for in Paragraph 5(1) of my Primary Will and/or the legacies set out in Paragraph 4(c) of my Primary Will, I direct the Trustees of my Secondary Estate to satisfy any such deficiencies with the assets held by my Trustees under my Secondary Will and to that extent I incorporate by reference the provisions of Paragraphs 4(a) and 4(c) of my Primary Will into my Secondary Will with the necessary modifications.

Residue

    f. My Trustees shall pay or transfer the residue of my Secondary Estate to ARABELLA if she survives me. If ARABELLA dies before me, my Trustees shall divide the residue of my Secondary Estate equally among my children alive at my death; but if any child of mine dies before me leaving issue alive at my death, my Trustees shall divide the part to which that deceased child would have been entitled if alive at my death among that deceased child's issue in equal shares per stirpes.

Payments For Minors

5. a. If any person becomes entitled to receive a share of my Secondary Estate while under the age of majority, my Trustees shall keep that share invested and, until that person attains the age of majority, my Trustees shall pay or apply for the benefit of that person as much of the income and capital as my Trustees in the exercise of an absolute discretion consider advisable.

    b. I authorize my Trustees to make any payments for a person under the age of majority to a parent or guardian or other person standing *in loco parentis* to that person, or to make any payment directly to the person that my Trustees in their absolute discretion consider appropriate. Any evidence that my Trustees have made a payment shall be a sufficient discharge to my Trustees.

Investments

6. My Trustees when making investments for my Secondary Estate shall not be limited to investments authorized by law for trustees but may make any investments they in their absolute discretion consider prudent and to be in the best interests of my Secondary Estate.

    7. Because of the special nature of my private corporation forming part or all of the assets of my Secondary Estate, my Trustees shall incur no liability for any loss which may be sustained by reason of their retention of such shares or because of anything which may be done or omitted to be done by my Trustees in good faith in connection with the retention of such shares or the exercise of any other power conferred upon them with respect to those shares.

Powers of Trustees

8.   In order to carry out the trusts of this Secondary Will, I give my Trustees the following powers to be used in the exercise of an absolute discretion at any time:

Distribution in Specie

a.   My Trustees may divide, distribute or allocate any asset of my Secondary Estate in kind and at the valuation to be determined by my Trustees in their absolute discretion. In determining the valuation, my Trustees may consider future expectations for the asset as my Trustees in their absolute discretion consider appropriate, including any tax liability or credit. Any decision made by my Trustees in this regard shall be binding on all persons concerned.

Real Property

b.   If any real or leasehold property forms part of my Secondary Estate, my Trustees may, in their absolute discretion:

i.   exchange, partition, or otherwise dispose of the whole or any part of the property either for cash or credit or for part cash and part credit as my Trustees consider appropriate;

ii.   ease property for any term or terms and subject to any conditions and covenants;

iii.   accept surrenders of leases and tenancies;

iv.   pay money out of the income and capital of my general Secondary Estate for repairs or improvements and generally manage and maintain the property;

v.   give options; and

vi.   give or renew any mortgage or borrow any money upon any mortgage or pay off any mortgage at any time after my death.

Elections

c.   My Trustees may make, or choose not to make, any allocations, elections, determinations, designations, and applications as my Trustees in their absolute discretion consider to be in the best interests of my Secondary Estate, and specifically any allocations and elections necessary under the *Income Tax Act*(Canada) or any similar legislation of any province or other jurisdiction in force from time to time.

Borrowing

d. My Trustees may borrow on behalf of my Secondary Estate such amount or amounts and on such terms and conditions as they in their absolute discretion deem advisable, and, for the repayment of any amount borrowed, may mortgage, charge, pledge, hypothecate or otherwise encumber any of the assets of my Secondary Estate.

Employment Agents

e. My Trustees may make, or choose not to make, any allocations, elections, determinations, designations, and applications as my Trustees in their absolute discretion consider to be in the best interests of my Secondary Estate, and specifically any allocations and elections necessary under the *Income Tax Act* (Canada) or any similar legislation of any province or other jurisdiction in force from time to time.

Power of Trustee To Purchase Assets

f. In my Trustees' personal capacity, my Trustees may purchase any assets from my Secondary Estate if the purchase price and other terms are unanimously approved by my Trustees and by the adult beneficiaries of my Secondary Estate. My Trustees shall not be required to obtain approval of any Court for that purchase.

Settlement of Claims

g. Without the consent of any person interested under this Will, my Trustees may compromise, settle, contest or waive any claim at any time made due to or made by my Secondary Estate and may make any agreement with any person, government or corporation which shall be binding upon all persons interested in my Secondary Estate.

Power To Carry on Business

h. I authorize my Trustees without being liable for any loss occasioned thereby to retain as an investment of my Secondary Estate any business or company which I may own or in which I may have a controlling or proprietary interest at the time of my death ("the Business"), to continue and carry on or to participate in the carrying on of the Business, to reorganize, incorporate, wind up, or dispose of the Business, to advance capital out of my general Secondary Estate, and generally to do all things in connection with the Business that I myself could do if living.

Securities

i. My Trustees shall have the power to deal with any shares or other interests which I may have in a company at my death to the same extent as if I were alive. My Trustees shall have the power to take up new or further shares, join in any reorganization, exchange shares or interests, and give, accept or exercise options. My Trustees may pay any money out of the income or capital of my Secondary Estate as determined by my Trustees which may be necessary for any of these purposes.

Expansion of Powers

j. i. Until the final distribution of my Secondary Estate and until the trusts set out in this Secondary Will have been fully performed, my Trustees have the power to perform, without court authorization, every act which a prudent person would perform for the purposes of these trusts under my Secondary Will.

ii. My Trustees may do all supplementary or ancilliary acts or things and execute all instruments to enable them to carry out the intent and purpose of the powers set out here.

Exclusions From Net Family Property

9. a. I declare that the income, including capital gains, arising from any interest passing to a beneficiary under my Secondary Will shall be excluded from such beneficiary's net family property or from the value of the beneficiary's assets on the death, divorce or separation of such beneficiary pursuant to the *Family Law Act.*

b. All gifts made to a beneficiary shall be the separate property of my beneficiaries and shall not fall into any Community of Property or be subject to any other matrimonial rights of the spouses of my beneficiaries and shall not be liable for the obligations of any such spouses or Community. All such gifts shall not be subject to seizure for the payment of any debts of beneficiaries or their representatives while in the possession and control of my Trustees.

"Issue Per Stirpes"

10. Whenever in my Secondary Will I have directed a division "per stirpes" among the issue or any person, I intend to designate the children of that person and not his or her remoter issue unless a child of that person is then deceased, in which case I intend that the share to which such deceased child would have been entitled if living shall in turn be divided equally

among his or her children and so on with each representation by a deceased individual at each level by his or her children.

Governing Law

11. My Secondary Will shall be governed by the laws of the Province of Ontario.

I have signed this Secondary Will, which is written upon this and * pages of paper, in the presence of both witnesses whose names appear below.

SIGNED BY CLIFFORD CLIENT,) as his Will with respect to his) Secondary Estate, in the presence) of us both, present at the same) time, who at his request, in his) presence, and in the presence of) each other have subscribed our) names as witnesses:	_____ Clifford Client

Witness #1:   _____

Name:

Address:

Occupation:

Witness #2:   _____

Name:

Address:

Occupation:

APPENDIX B

Glossary

A

Abatement

Abatement is the reduction of a gift under a will when the estate is insufficient to satisfy all the gifts in full. The order of abatement depends upon the nature of the bequests under the will. A testator's estate must be used first to pay the testator's debts, then to effect devises and pay demonstrative and specific legacies, then to pay general legacies, and finally to pay residual gifts. Gifts of a like kind abate rateably. *Lindsay v. Waldbrook* (1897), 24 O.A.R. 604 (C.A.).

> "In the payment of debts, the residuary estate must first be exhausted and residuary personalty and realty are liable rateably for the debts. After the residuary estate has been exhausted, general legacies abate *pro rata*, then demonstrative and specific legacies rateably and after that, finally devises. Devises abate last because of the general rule that personalty is primarily liable for the payment of debts."

Mickler v. Larson-Shorten (2000), 35 E.T.R. (2d) 258, 198 Sask. R. 146 (Q.B.).

Absentee

"1. An absentee within the meaning of this Act means a person who, having had his or her usual place of residence or domicile in Ontario, has disappeared, whose whereabouts is unknown and as to whom there is no knowledge as to whether he or she is alive or dead."

Absentees Act, R.S.O. 1990, c. A.3, s. 1.

Absolute

"While there may be no magic in the addition of the word 'absolute' it does serve to emphasize the wish to the testator that the trustee is to have an unfettered right to make the decisions relating to any encroachment of capital." *Fox v. Fox Estate* (1994), 5 E.T.R. (2d) 174 (Gen. Div.); reversed on other grounds (1996), 10 E.T.R. (2d) 229, 28 O.R. (3d) 496, (sub nom. *Fox v. Fox*) 88 O.A.C. 201 (C.A.).

Absolutely

"First, there is the use of the word 'absolutely'. No doubt it might, especially if used by someone acquainted with legal language, be construed as describing the extent of the interest in the property given — namely, the fee-simple in freehold property and the absolute interest in personal property. But I think in this extremely untechnical will the testator must have used it to mean 'out and out', and that it therefore carried not merely the full legal interest but the beneficial interest as well." Sargant, J. in *In re Ford*, [1922] 2 Ch. 519, 92 LJ Ch 46.

"The fact that the testator used the word 'absolutely' in giving all his estate to his widow for her natural life does not mean more than that he gave his widow the entire life interest, that is, an interest embracing all of the attributes which by law are included in, and comprise, a life interest." *Re King*, [1940] O.W.N. 57 (H.C.).

"First, this will, far from being an untechnical document, is manifestly a lawyer's document. Secondly, I think that in this will the word 'absolutely' should be construed, not as conferring a beneficial interest, but as defining the extent of the interest in the property given, so as to confer on the trustees the property given to them — and I borrow the language used by Cohen, L.J. during the argument — free of any fetter which would prevent their carrying out his express wishes." Sir Raymond Evershed, M.R. in *In re Rees' Will Trusts; Williams v. Hopkins*, [1950] Ch. 204, 66 T.L.R. (Pt. 1) 23, [1949] 2 All E.R. 1003.

Accumulation

Accumulation is the re-investing of the interest generated by a fund so as to increase the capital of the fund. See the *Accumulations Act* for the prohibition of accumulation of interest after a period of a maximum of 21 years.

Ademption

The rule of ademption holds that if the property that is the subject of a specific legacy is not owned by the will-maker at the time of death or cannot be located, the gift fails and the beneficiary receives nothing. The gift has adeemed. *Re Hunter* (1975), 8 O.R. (2d) 399 (H.C.J.).

Adequate Provision

"The words 'adequate, just and equitable' (in s. 2 of the *Wills Variation Act*, R.S.B.C. 1979, c. 435) may be interpreted in different ways. At one end of the spectrum, they may be confined to what is 'necessary' to keep the dependants off the welfare roles. At the other extreme, they may be interpreted as requiring the court to make an award consistent with the lifestyle and aspirations of the dependants. Again, they may be interpreted as confined to maintenance or they may be interpreted as capable of extending to fair property division. Complicating these questions are the issues of the weight to be placed on the 'right' of the testator to dispose of his estate as he chooses — i.e., testamentary autonomy — and the equities as between the beneficiaries: spouses and children. Different courts, applying a variety of approaches to these questions have, over time, arrived at different interpretations of the meaning of 'adequate, just and equitable'. Whatever the answers to the specific questions, this much seems clear. The language of the Act confers a broad discretion on the court. The generosity of the language suggests that the legislature was attempting to craft a formula which would permit the courts to make orders which are just in the specific circumstances and in light of contemporary standards. ... If the phrase 'adequate, just and equitable' is viewed in light of current societal norms, much of the uncertainty disappears. Furthermore, two sorts of norms are available and both must be addressed. The first are the obligations which the law would impose on a person during his or her life were the question of provision for the claimant to arise. These might be described as legal obligations. The second type of norms are found in society's reasonable expectations of what a judicious person would do in the circumstances, by reference to contemporary community standards. These might be called moral obligations, following the language traditionally used by the courts. Together, these two norms provide a guide to what is 'adequate, just and equitable' in the circumstances of the case." *Tataryn v. Tataryn Estate* (1994), 93 B.C.L.R. (2d) 145, [1994] 7 W.W.R. 609, 169 N.R. 60, 3 E.T.R. (2d) 229, [1994] 2 S.C.R. 807, 46 B.C.A.C. 255, 75 W.A.C. 255, 116 D.L.R. (4th) 193 (S.C.C.).

Adjusted Cost Base

The adjusted cost base (ACB) is the cost of capital property determined under the *Income Tax Act*, and used for calculating the amount of a capital gain or loss. The ACB is calculated by adjusting the actual cost of the property according to the adjustments under s. 53 of the *Income Tax Act.*

Administration, Letters of Administration

Letters of administration were granted to the personal representative of a person who had died intestate, or to the person appointed by the court to administer a will under which no executor was appointed or all executors were unable or unwilling to act. Letters of administration have now been replaced by a Certificate of Appointment of Estate Trustee, with or without a will.

Administratrix De Son Tort

[A]n *administratrix de son tort* is one who intermeddles with the personal, not the real, estate of the deceased: *R. v. Tschetter,* [1918] 1 W.W.R. 934, 11 Sask. L.R. 116, 29 C.C.C. 179, 39 D.L.R. 688, 29 C.C.C. 178 (C.A.).

Adoption

Sec. 158   "Status of adopted child" —

(1) In this section,

adopted child means a person who was adopted in Ontario.

(2) *Same* — For all purposes of law, as of the date of the making of an adoption order,

   (a)   the adopted child becomes the child of the adoptive parent and the adoptive parent becomes the parent of the adopted child; and

   (b)   the adopted child ceases to be the child of the person who was his or her parent before the adoption order was made and that person ceases to be the parent of the adopted child, except where the person is the spouse of the adoptive parent, as if the adopted child had been born to the adoptive parent.

(3) *How relationships determined* — The relationship to one another of all persons, including the adopted child, the adoptive parent, the kindred of the adoptive parent, the parent before the adoption order was made and the kindred of that former parent shall for all purposes be determined in accordance with subsection (2).

(4) *Reference in will or other document* — In any will or other document made at any time before or after the 1st day of November, 1985, and whether the maker of the will or document is alive on that day or not, a reference to a person or group or class of persons described in terms of relationship by blood or marriage to another person shall be deemed to

refer to or include, as the case may be, a person who comes within the description as a result of an adoption, unless the contrary is expressed.

(5) *Application of section* — This section applies and shall be deemed always to have applied with respect to any adoption made under any Act heretofore in force, but not so as to affect,

(*a*) any interest in property or right of the adopted child that has indefeasibly vested before the date of the making of an adoption order; and

(*b*) any interest in property or right that has indefeasibly vested before the 1st day of November, 1985.

(6) *Exception* — Subsections (2) and (3) do not apply for the purposes of the laws relating to incest and the prohibited degrees of marriage to remove a person from a relationship that would have existed but for those subsections.

Sec. 159 Effect of foreign adoption — An adoption effected according to the law of another jurisdiction, before or after the 1st day of November, 1985, has the same effect in Ontario as an adoption under this Part. *Child and Family Services Act*, R.S.O. 1990, c. C.11, s. 159.

Advancement

Under the doctrine of advancement, the recipient of an *inter vivos* gift does not receive the gift a second time under a testamentary instrument. The equitable doctrine of advancement is sometimes expressed as "the presumption against double portions". A portion is the giving of some money to a child by way of advancement.

Advancement in Life

Some occasion out of the everyday course, when the beneficiary has in mind some new act or undertaking, which calls for pecuniary outlay, and which, if properly conducted, holds out a prospect of something beyond a mere transient benefit or employment. Thus if the beneficiary were going to enter upon a business or profession, or to get married or to build a dwelling house, or to make some unusual repairs or renovation, it would be a proper occasion for the trustee to use his discretion.

Age of Majority

Every person attains the age of majority and ceases to be a minor on attaining the age of eighteen years. *Age of Majority and Accountability Act*, R.S.O. 1990, c. A.7, s. 1.

Alienation

Alienation means conveyance of an indefeasible fee simple in real property or title to personal property. An interest that prohibits alienation is not absolute.

All of the Income

"The words 'all of the income' in a direction to executors of a will 'to pay to my beloved wife all of the income from my estate during her lifetime' mean the net income after annual outgoings for the preservation of the property." *Re Jackson*, (1977), 17 O.R. (2d) 318, 80 D.L.R. (3d) 275 (S.C.).

Alter Ego Trust

This is a trust set up *inter vivos* for the benefit of the settlor during his or her lifetime, and to which assets may be transferred without a disposition under the *Income Tax Act.*

Alternative Minimum Tax

Under the *Income Tax Act,* the alternative minimum tax is a calculation of tax payable that may result in a higher tax payable by certain high income taxpayers. The AMT may be recovered in certain instances.

Ancilliary Grant

This is the authority given by the court in Ontario to a personal representative who has been duly appointed by a court outside the Commonwealth, in order to allow him or her to administer assets in Ontario, given under a Certificate of Ancilliary Appointment of Estate Trustee with a Will.

Annuity

An annuity represents a right to receive fixed, periodic payments. An annuity is a contract for the payment of periodic amounts during the lifetime of a particular person, or for a fixed or guaranteed period.

Ascendant

This is an ancestor, who is related to a person in an ascending direct line, such as the parent, grandparents, and so on of the person.

Assets

The assets of a deceased consist of such property as before his or her death would have been made available for the payment of his or her debts.

Attestation

Attestation is the act of witnessing the execution of a will and sub-scribing as a witness. The clause at the end of a will, where witnesses state that the will has been singed before them and they sign their own names is referred to as the "attestation clause".

B

Bare Trust

A bare trust exists where a trustee holds property at the absolute disposal and for the absolute benefit of the beneficiaries. Bare trustees have also been compared to agents. The existence of a bare trust will be disre-garded for income tax purposes where the bare trustee holds property as a mere agent or for the beneficial owner.

Beneficiary

A beneficiary is one who benefits from the act of another, including under the terms of a will or trust. A beneficiary may be entitled to income only (income beneficiary), or to capital (capital beneficiary). The person named to receive the proceeds in a declaration or designation under a contract for life insurance or a registered plan is also referred to as the beneficiary. A beneficiary is a party who will benefit from a transfer of property or other arrangement. "[Regarding] whether 'beneficiary' includes one who merely has a contingent or residual interest under the will or trust ... it does." *Ontario (Attorney General) v. Ballard Estate* (1994), 33 C.P.C. (3d) 373, 6 E.T.R. (2d) 34, 119 D.L.R. (4th) 750, 20 O.R. (3d) 350 (Gen. Div. [Commercial List]).

Bequest

A bequest is a gift of personal property by will.

Buy-Sell Agreement

This is a clause in a shareholder agreement, whereby the parties agree on how to dispose of the interests in the corporation of a deceased (or otherwise departing) shareholder.

C

Capacity

See testamentary capacity.

Certainty — The Three Certainties

"In order to constitute a trust under general principles of law, the 'trust' must possess three essential attributes: certainty of intention, certainty of subject matter, and certainty of objects. If any of these attributes are missing the Court will not find a trust. Certainty of intention will exist where the transferor of the property intended to create a trust. For certainty of subject matter to exist, the property which is subject to the trust must be clearly identifiable. Certainty of objects exists where the intended beneficiaries of the trust are ascertainable." See D.W.M. Waters, Law of Trusts in Canada, 2d ed. (Toronto: Carswell, 1984) at 108-27).

Certificate of Appointment of Estate Trustee

Under the latest revisions to the Rules of Civil Procedure, a Certificate of Appointment of Estate Trustee is the court's certificate, either that a will has been proved or that the named person has been appointed by the court to administer the estate of a deceased person.

Charitable

"A trust must always be shown to promote a public benefit of a nature recognized by the Courts as being such if it is to qualify as being charitable. A trust for the attainment of political objects is invalid, not because it is illegal but because the Court has no means of judging whether a proposed change in the law will or will not be for the public benefit. Each Court in deciding on the validity of a gift must decide on the principle that the law is right as it stands. Anomalous and undesirable consequences might ensue if Courts began to encroach on the function of the Legislature by ascribing charitable status to trusts of which a main object is to procure a change in the law." *Ontario (Public Trustee) v. Toronto Humane Society* (1987), 27 E.T.R. 40, 60 O.R. (2d) 236, 40 D.L.R. (4th) 111, 60 O.R. (2d) 236 (H.C.).

Child

"Child" includes a person toward whom a parent has demonstrated a settled intention to treat as a child of his or her family, except under an arrangement where the child is placed for valuable consideration in a foster home by a person having lawful custody. *Family Law Act*, R.S.O. 1990, c. F.3, s. 1 (1); 1997, c. 20, s. 1; 1999, c. 6, s. 25 (1).

"Child" includes a child conceived before and born alive after the parent's death.

"Grandchild" means the child of a child.

"Issue" includes a descendant conceived before and born alive after the person's death. *Succession Law Reform Act*, R.S.O. 1990, c. S.26, s. 1.

"Child" means a child as defined in subsection 1(1) and includes a grandchild and a person toward whom the deceased has demonstrated a settled intention to treat as a child of his or her family, except under an arrangement where the child is placed for valuable consideration in a foster home by a person having lawful custody. *Succession Law Reform Act*, R.S.O. 1990, c. S.26, s. 57; 1999, c. 6, s. 61 (1, 2).

Class

This is a group defined by relationship to the will-maker, rather than by name, such as "my nieces and nephews".

Class Gift

This is a gift to a body of persons defined by relationship to the will-maker and uncertain in number at the time of gift, to be ascertained at a future time. The share of each beneficiary who is a member of the class will depend for its amount upon the ultimate number.

Codicil

A codicil is an amendment to a will, which may add or delete portions, or change one clause for another, but does not revoke the will, and cannot be admitted for probate as a free-standing document.

Cohabitation

The factual *indicia* of cohabitation are outlined in *Molodowich v. Penttinen* (1980), 17 R.F.L. (2d) 376 (Ont. Dist. Ct.) at pages 381 to 382, as follows:

(i) Shelter

    (a) Did the parties live under the same roof?

    (b) What were the sleeping arrangements?

    (c) Did anyone else occupy or share the available accommodation?

(ii) Sexual and Personal Behaviour

    (a) Did the parties have sexual relations?

    (b) Did they maintain an attitude of fidelity to each other?

    (c) What were their feelings towards each other?

    (d) Did they communicate on a personal level?

(e) Did they eat their meals together?

(f) What, if anything, did they do to assist each other with problems or during illness?

(g) Did they buy gifts for each other on special occasions?

(iii) What was the conduct and habit of the parties in relation to:

(a) preparation of meals?

(b) washing and mending clothes?

(c) shopping?

(d) household maintenance?

(e) any other domestic services?

(iv) Social

(a) Did they participate together or separately in neighbourhood and community activities?

(b) What was the relationship and conduct of each of them toward members of their respective families and how did such families behave towards the parties?

(v) Societal

(a) What was the attitude and conduct of the community toward each of them and as a couple?

(vi) Economic Support

(a) What were the financial arrangements between the parties regarding the provision of or contribution toward the necessities of life?

(b) What were the arrangements concerning the acquisition and ownership of property?

(c) Was there any special financial arrangement between them which both agreed would be detrimental to their overall relationship?

(vii) Children

(a) What was the attitude and conduct of the parties concerning children?

Commorientes

Commorientes are two or more persons who die at or about the same time such that it is not possible to determine the order of their deaths.

Compensation

Compensation is the remuneration to which a personal representative is entitled, as determined by the instrument, by statute or by the court.

Consanguinity

This is relationship by blood, either by descent, in a line, such as parents and children, or by descent from common ancestors, such as siblings or cousins.

Contingent

Contingent means determined or to be determined by some event or condition which has yet to occur, and thus is uncertain, as opposed to vested.

Coparcener

Coparceners are persons to whom an estate of inheritance descends jointly, and by whom it is held as an entire estate.

Custodian

This is a person appointed by will to have custody of the person of a minor child, but not his or her property.

Cy-près Rule

This is a doctrine used by the courts to approve a scheme where the specified intent of a charitable donor is impossible as far as performance, but a clear charitable intent can be discerned. The court may use the doctrine to apply the gift to an object as near as possible to that specified in the original gift.

According to Waters, *Law of Trusts in Canada*, (2nd ed.), the cy pres jurisdiction is only exercised where the charitable objects set out by the settlor are either impossible to carry out, or are impracticable (p. 514). English courts have taken the view, however, that as long as the original objects can still be carried out, even if with more limited value than they once would have had, they cannot be interfered with. That is to say, impossibility and impracticability have been kept within narrow limits, a restriction which has had particular significance in the handling of cy pres application on the basis of supervening impossibility or impracticability (see Waters at p. 622-3).

Even when it is applied, the cy-près jurisdiction is narrow. Under it, trust property is applied cy-près — that is, to some other object or objects as near as possible to the charitable objects set out by the settlor. *Cumberland Trust v. Maritime Electric Co.* (2000), 29 R.P.R. (3d) 104, 184 Nfld. & P.E.I.R. 217, 559 A.P.R. 217, 31 E.T.R. (2d) 177 (S.C.T.D.).

Granfield Estate v. Jackson (1999), 27 E.T.R. (2d) 50, 1999 Carswell BC 644 (S.C. [In Chambers]).

D

Dependant

"Dependant" means,

(a) the spouse or same-sex partner of the deceased,

(b) a parent of the deceased,

(c) a child of the deceased, or

(d) a brother or sister of the deceased, to whom the deceased was providing support or was under a legal obligation to provide support immediately before his or her death. *Succession Law Reform Act*, Part V, R.S.O. 1990, c. S.26, s. 57; 1999, c. 6, s. 61 (1, 2).

Depreciable Capital Property

Capital property is depreciable if, under the *Income Tax Act*, a deduction may be taken for a percentage of the capital cost as a capital cost allowance. The allowance is designed to reflect the decline in the value of the property over time due to consumption and wear and tear.

Descendants

This means issue, or those who are related to a person in a descending direct line, such as the children, grandchildren, and so on of the person.

Devise

This is a gift by will of real property.

Devolution of Executorship

This is the transmission on the death of a sole or last surviving executor to his or her own personal representatives of the duties of executorship.

Dispositive Clauses

This refers to those parts of a will that direct to whom and in what proportion the assets of the estate are to be given, as opposed to the administrative parts of a will.

Distributive Share

This is the share of an estate passing to the heirs at law of a person who has died intestate, after the spouse preferential share has been paid.

Distribute

"Standing alone, the verb 'to distribute' means 'to deal or divide out in proportion or shares'. However, in the context of a direction in a will trust that the executor 'distribute [a fund] equally among' several charities, the verb 'distribute' has the sense of 'dividing into parts', i.e. dividing one endowment into several smaller endowments, to be allocated to the respective charities." *Arthritis Society v. Vancouver Foundation*, [1993] 1 W.W.R. 748, 47 E.T.R. 1, 72 B.C.L.R. (2d) 245, 1992 Carswell BC 299 (S.C. [In Chambers]).

Dividend

A dividend is a payment from the profits of a corporation to the shareholders. Dividends declared but unpaid at the time of death may be included as Rights or Things on a separate tax return.

Donatio Mortis Causa

This is a death-bed gift of property, which may be revoked if the donor recovers.

Dower

At common law, a dower is the right of a widow to a one-third interest in all real property beneficially owned by the deceased at any time during his life. Dower has been abolished in Ontario.

E

Encroachment

This is the power of a trustee to pay sums of capital to an income beneficiary.

Estate

Estate Pur Autre Vie

This is a life estate held by someone other than the person on whose death it will terminate, or an estate terminable on the death of another person.

This is the new term, under the revised Rule of Civil Procedure, for both an executor and an administrator.

F

Fiduciary

This means a relationship between two persons, obligating one person to act in the best interests of the other, to a greater or lesser extent.

G

General Legacy

"The commonest form of a general legacy is a gift of a sum of money: 'I give A 100l'. This is sometimes called a pecuniary legacy. The essence of a general legacy is that it is payable out of the general estate. Consequently, a pecuniary legacy payable exclusively out of real estate is not a general legacy." Jarman on Wills, vol. 2, 7th ed. (London: Sweet & Maxwell Ltd.,1930) at p. 1025.

Gift

The Concise Oxford Dictionary (Fourth Edition) and Black's Dictionary (Fourth Edition) both define gift in part as the voluntary transference of property without consideration. Here the codicil directs the transfer of the home, but requires the recipients ... to pay the full market value of the home. This is not a gift within the normal meaning of the word, and is a significant financial burden to the recipients. *Grund Estate, Re,* 1998 Carswell BC 242 (S.C.).

Gift over

A gift over is a provision for a gift to an alternate beneficiary in the event that the first named beneficiary is unable to receive the gift.

H

Holograph Will

This is a will written entirely in the hand of the will-maker, and signed by him or her without witnesses.

"To be valid, a holograph will must be wholly in the handwriting of the testator or testatrix and must be signed by him or her. There is no necessity for the presence, attestation or signature of a witness." *Facey v. Smith* (1997), 17 E.T.R. (2d) 72, 35 O.T.C. 372, 35 O.T.C. 372 (Gen. Div).

Human Remains

"Human remains" means a dead human body and includes a cremated human body. *Cemeteries Act*, R.S.O. 1990, c. C.4, s. 1; 1999, c. 12, Sched. G, s. 15 (1); 2001, c. 9, Sched. D, s. 13; 2002, c. 17, Sched. F, Table.

I

Illegitimacy (of Children)

See "Legitimacy".

In Specie

This means in kind or in the original form. A gift is made in specie if the property is passed to the beneficiary without conversion, in the form in which it existed at the time of death.

Insurance

This is a contract for the payment of a sum to a third party on the death of the insured life. Although the contract is usually with the person whose life is insured, this is not always the case.

Inter Vivos Gift

An *inter vivos* gift is a gratuitous transfer of property from its owner (the donor) to another person (the donee) with the intention that the transfer have present effect and the title to the property pass to the donee.

Issue

"The law is clear that the primary meaning of the word 'issue' in a will is descendants to the remotest degree." *Re Gardner Estate* (1991), 85 Alta. L.R. (2d) 119 (Surr. Ct).

J

Joint Partner Trust

This is a trust settled during the lifetime of the donor or donors, for the benefit of the settlor or settlors and his or her spouse, during their joint lives.

Joint Will

A joint will is a single document, whereby two will-makers together make a disposition of property belonging to the two of them.

Jointly

"The ordinary meaning of the adverb 'jointly' was stated in *Kidson (Inspector of Taxes) v. Macdonald* and another, [1974] 1 All E.R. 849 (Ch.D.), as 'concurrently or in common'. *Re White* (1987), 59 O.R. (2d) 488, 38 D.L.R. (4th) 631 (H.C.)."

"At common law this would probably effect a joint tenancy. Under the *Conveyancing and Law of Property Act*, R.S.O. 1937, c. 152, s. 12, unless an intention sufficiently appears on the face of the will, it must be held that the daughters take as tenants in common. While the word 'jointly' has been held to effect a joint tenancy, here the testator made an additional provision in which he used the expression 'equal share'. This resembles 'jointly and equally' which is treated in the cases as effecting a tenancy in common, along with such expressions as 'equally' and 'to be divided'. Finally, there is a tendency of the courts to favour a tenancy in common. *McEwen v. Ewers*, [1946] O.W.N. 573, [1946] 3 D.L.R. 494 (H.C.)."

(4) By the following clause a testator provided: "I hereby bequeath unto my nephew, J., and my sister, M., jointly, a piece of land situate west side of the south part of Lot No. 5 in the ninth concession of East Hawkesbury . . . and they are to pay my nephew George Campbell, the sum of two hundred dollars within three years after my decease". Apart from special circumstances, the use of the word "jointly" in a will creates a joint tenancy. The four unities which are the requisites of a joint tenancy all exist here: Campbell, Re (1912), 23 O.W.R. 233, 4 O.W.N. 221, 6 D.L.R. 452, 7 D.L.R. 452, 1912 Carswell Ont 558 (Ontario Ottawa Weekly Court).

(5) The right of survivorship is the essence of joint occupancy. Hence a clause in a will bequeathing and devising all the property of testatrix "to my executors in trust to allow my husband and T to jointly enjoy the same as long as my husband remains unmarried, but if he remarry than to T for life", should, where the husband dies without remarrying, be construed as giving the survivor, T, a life interest in the property. Estate of Elizabeth Ann Perrie, Re (1910), 16 O.W.R. 90, 21 O.L.R. 100, 1910 Carswell Ont 206 (Ex. Ct.).

L

Land

"'Land' includes messuages, and all other hereditaments, whether corporeal or incorporeal, chattels and other personal property transmissible to heirs, money to be laid out in the purchase of land, and any share of the same hereditaments and properties, or any of them, and any estate of inheritance, or estate for any life or lives, or other estate transmissible to heirs, and any possibility, right or title of entry or action, and any other interest capable of being inherited, whether the same estates, possibilities, rights, titles and interests, or any of them, are in possession, reversion, remainder or contingency. *Trustee Act*, R.S.O. 1990, c. T.23, s. 1."

Lapse

This is the failure of a gift by reason of the death or disclaimer of the named beneficiary, or the failure of some condition in a contingent gift. If the gift is other than residual, the subject of the gift will form part of the residue to be disposed of according to the terms governing residue. A gift or residue will not lapse, but will create a partial intestacy.

Legacy

A legacy is a gift by will of personal property, also known as a bequest. Specific legacies are gifts or items of personal property in kind. Demonstrative legacies are cash gifts, to be paid from a particular fund or source, general legacies are also cash gifts, but paid from the general estate. Residuary legacies are those consisting of some part of the residue of the estate.

Legitimacy (of Children)

Sec. 1   Rule of parentage —

(1) Subject to subsection (2), for all purposes of the law of Ontario a person is the child of his or her natural parents and his or her status as their child is independent of whether the child is born within or outside marriage.

Sec. 2   Exception for adopted children —

(2) Where an adoption order has been made, section 158 or 159 of the *Child and Family Services Act* applies and the child is the child of the adopting parents as if they were the natural parents.

(3) *Kindred relationships* — The parent and child relationships as determined under subsections (1) and (2) shall be followed in the determination of other kindred relationships flowing therefrom.

(4) *Common law distinction of legitimacy abolished* — Any distinction at common law between the status of children born in wedlock and born out of wedlock is abolished and the relationship of parent and child and kindred relationships flowing therefrom shall be determined for the purposes of the common law in accordance with this section.

Sec. 2.   Rule of construction —

(1) For the purposes of construing any instrument, Act or regulation, unless the contrary intention appears, a reference to a person or group or class of persons described in terms of relationship by blood or marriage to another person shall be construed to refer to or include a person who comes within the description by reason of the relationship of parent and child as determined under section 1.

(2) *Application* — Subsection (1) applies to

(a) any Act of the Legislature or any regulation, order or by-law made under an Act of the Legislature enacted or made before, on or after the 31st day of March, 1978; and

(b) any instrument made on or after the 31st day of March, 1978. *Children's Law Reform Act*, R.S.O. 1990, c. C.12, s. 2(2).

Sec. 18   Matrimonial Home —

(1) Every property in which a person has an interest and that is or, if the spouses have separated, was at the time of separation ordinarily occupied by the person and his or her spouse as their family residence is their matrimonial home. *Family Law Act*, R.S.O. 1990, c. F.3, s. 18(1).

M

Memorandum

This is a document used to expand on the provisions of the testator's will, which may be incorporated by reference or operate as a guide to the executor's discretion.

Movables

Movables are those items of property that can be carried out of the jurisdiction by the owner, as opposed to those that, by their very nature, cannot be so transported, such as real property.

Money

See *Perrin v. Morgan*, (1943) A.C. 399, (1943) 1 All E.R. 187 (H.L.).

Mirror Wills

Mirror wills dispose of property belonging to two will-makers, who are usually spouses of one another, by conferring reciprocal benefits on each other and after the death of the survivor, to other persons. Persons who make mirror wills have not bound themselves to keep their will unchanged.

Mutual Wills

Mutual wills dispose of property belonging to two will-makers, who are usually spouses of one another, who have agreed to provide by their wills for an agreed scheme of disposition. The scheme provides for conferring reciprocal benefits on each other for the survivor and after the death of the survivor, for disposal of the property to other persons, as the parties have agreed. Persons who make mutual wills usually agree not to alter or revoke them without the other's consent and it is out of this agreement not to revoke that a constructive trust may arise.

O

Owned

"[P]olicy of insurance owned by deceased" [as used in s. 72(1)(f) of the *Succession Law Reform Act*, R.S.O. 1990, c. S.26] does not include a group life insurance policy available through employment, with no personal benefits and which insured had no right to amend or alter. *Skilton v. Petley Estate* (2000), 35 E.T.R. (2d) 132 (S.C.J.).

P

Partner

"Same-sex partner" means either of two persons of the same sex who have cohabited,

(a) continuously for a period of not less than three years, or

(b) in a relationship of some permanence, if they are the natural or adoptive parents of a child. *Succession Law Reform Act*, R.S.O. 1990, c. S.26, s. 57; 1999, c. 6, s. 61 (1, 2).

Passing of Accounts

This is the formal presentation to the court of the accounts of an estate of trust for scrutiny and approval.

Per capita

This means by the head, thus, a method of distribution whereby each person will take an equal share, as opposed to per stirpes whereby persons will take by stocks, and only if their immediate ascendant has predeceased.

Per Stirpes

This means by stocks of descent, so that on the death of one beneficiary, he or she will be represented in the division of the gift by his or her descendants of the next degree.

Perpetuity

Perpetuity means without any end, and generally repugnant to the law, which has developed a number of rules to prohibit gifts from vesting at a date very far in the future or gifts being held without a determined end, except in the case of charities.

Personal Representative

"Personal representative" means an executor, an administrator, or an administrator with the will annexed. *Estates Administration Act*, R.S.O. 1990, c. E.22, s. 1; *Succession Law Reform Act*, R.S.O. 1990, c. S.26, s. 1.

Plene Administravit

"If an executor or administrator has no assets to satisfy the debt upon which an action is brought, in the absence of a plea of no assets or *plene administravit*, he will be taken to have conclusively admitted that he has assets to satisfy the judgment and will be personally liable for the debt and costs if they cannot be levied on the assets of the deceased. If the executor has some, but insufficient, assets to satisfy the judgment and costs, a plene administravit praeter will render him liable only to the amount of assets proved to be in his hands as executor." *Edwards v. Law Society of Upper Canada* (2000), 48 O.R. (3d) 321, 133 O.A.C. 305, 50 C.P.C. (4th) 231, 36 E.T.R. (2d) 192 (C.A.).

Polygamous Marriages

In the definition of "spouse", a reference to marriage includes a marriage that is actually or potentially polygamous, if it was celebrated in a jurisdiction whose system of law recognizes it as valid. *Succession Law Reform Act*, R.S.O. 1990, c. S.26, s. 1.

Power of Appointment

This is a power to choose the persons (who may include the donee of the power) to whom a gift will be made. A general power of appointment allows the donee to designate anyone, including himself or herself. A limit of special power restricts the person to whom the gift may be designated.

Precatory Trust

"A precatory trust is not a true trust, but rather an expression of the desire of the donor to have the funds used for a specific purpose without the creation of a true trust for the purpose. That desire is not binding on the corporation and such funds are beneficially owned by the corporation and not shielded from execution." *Re Christian Brothers of Ireland in Canada*, (2000), 47 O.R. (3d) 674, 184 D.L.R. (4th) 445, 33 E.T.R. (2d) 32, 17 C.B.R. (4th) 168, 6 B.L.R. (3d) 151, 132 O.A.C. 271 (C.A.).

Preferential Share

This is the share of the estate of an intestate that will be paid to his or her spouse before the division of the estate among the heirs.

Probate

This is the process by which a will was submitted to court for certification that it was the valid last will of the deceased and that the person or persons named in it were entitled to administer the estate.

Property

Property is what one owns, a possession or possessions collectively, one's wealth or goods and the right to the possession, use or disposal of any of those things.

"Property" means any interest, present or future, vested or contingent, in real or personal property and includes:

(a) property over which a spouse has, alone or in conjunction with another person, a power of appointment exercisable in favour of himself or herself,

(b) property disposed of by a spouse but over which the spouse has, alone or in conjunction with another person, a power to revoke the disposition or a power to consume or dispose of the property, and

(c) in the case of a spouse's rights under a pension plan that has vested, the spouse's interest in the plan including contributions made by other persons. *Family Law Act*, R.S.O. 1990, c. F.3, s. 4 (1).

R

Remainderman

This is the person entitled to what remains of an estate after a prior interest.

Resealing

Resealing is the authority given by the court in Ontario to a personal representative who has been duly appointed by a court in the Commonwealth, in order to allow him or her to administer assets in Ontario, given under a Confirmation by Resealing of Appointment of Estate Trustee.

Residue

This refers to that part of an estate remaining after the payment of debts, legacies and devises.

Rights and Things

These are payments to which a deceased person was entitled at the time of death, but which had not yet been paid, such as dividends or work in progress. Rights and things may be declared on a separate tax return in the year of death.

S

Secret Trust

A secret trust arises when a person gives property to another, communicating to that person an intention that the property be dealt with in a specific way, and the donee accepts the obligation. The essential elements are the intention of the donor, a communication of the intention to the donee and acceptance of the obligation by the donee. If the gift on the face appears to be a gift outright to the putative trustee, then the trust is fully secret. If the gift itself indicates an intention that the property is to be held in trust, but with any indication of from whom or on what terms, the trust is semi-secret.

"A fully secret trust is a trust which a court of equity imposes on a person who has obtained title to property obliging him to hold it for the benefit of the persons for whom or purposes for which he knew that it was given or allowed to pass to him. It arises where a testatrix gives property to a person apparently beneficially, but has communicated to that person during his lifetime certain trusts on which the property is to be held. The trust arises outside the will. Any trust obligation which the legatee has undertaken is hidden from view, revealed only by extrinsic evidence. In such circumstances, where the testator has communicated the intention that the legacy should be held in trust for others, where the objects of the trust are known to the legatee, and where the legatee agrees to act as trustee or acquiesces in that arrangement, the trust will be enforced and extrinsic evidence is admissible to prove the essential facts." *Jankowski v. Pelek Estate*, [1996] 2 W.W.R. 457, 10 E.T.R. (2d) 117, 131 D.L.R. (4th) 717, 107 Man. R. (2d) 167, 109 W.A.C. 167, 131 D.L.R. (4th) 717 (C.A.).

Securities

"Security" includes,

(a) any document, instrument or writing commonly known as a security,

(b) any document constituting evidence of title to or interest in the capital, assets, property, profits, earnings or royalties of any person or company,

(c) any document constituting evidence of an interest in an association of legatees or heirs,

(d) any document constituting evidence of an option, subscription or other interest in or to a security,

(e) any bond, debenture, note or other evidence of indebtedness, share, stock, unit, unit certificate, participation certificate, certificate of share or interest, preorganization certificate or subscription other than a contract of insurance issued by an insurance company licensed under the *Insurance Act* and an evidence of deposit issued by a bank listed in Schedule I or II to the *Bank Act* (Canada), by a credit union or league to which the *Credit Unions and Caisses Populaires Act, 1994* applies or by a loan corporation or trust corporation registered under the *Loan and Trust Corporations Act*,

(f) any agreement under which the interest of the purchaser is valued for purposes of conversion or surrender by reference to the value of a proportionate interest in a specified portfolio of assets, except a contract issued by an insurance company licensed under the *Insurance Act* which provides for payment at maturity of an amount not less than three-quarters of the premiums paid by the purchaser for a benefit payable at maturity,

(g) any agreement providing that money received will be repaid or treated as a subscription to shares, stock, units or interests at the option of the recipient or of any person or company,

(h) any certificate of share or interest in a trust, estate or association,

(i) any profit-sharing agreement or certificate,

(j) any certificate of interest in an oil, natural gas or mining lease, claim or royalty voting trust certificate,

(k) any oil or natural gas royalties or leases or fractional or other interest therein,

(l) any collateral trust certificate,

(m) any income or annuity contract not issued by an insurance company,

(n) any investment contract,

(o) any document constituting evidence of an interest in a scholarship or educational plan or trust, and

(p) any commodity futures contract or any commodity futures option that is not traded on a commodity futures exchange registered with or recognized by the Commission under the *Commodity Futures Act* or the form of which is not accepted by the Director under that Act, whether any of the foregoing relate to an issuer or proposed issuer. *Securities Act*, R.S.O. 1990, c. S.5, s. 1 (1); 1994, c. 11, s. 350; 1994, c. 33, s. 1 (1, 2); 1997, c. 19, s. 23 (1); 1999, c. 6, s. 60 (1); 1999, c. 9, s. 193; 2001, c. 23, s. 209; 2002, c. 22, s. 177 (1, 2).

Settlor

A settlor is the person who, by transferring property to a trustee, brings a trust into being.

Stock

"Stock" includes fully paid-up shares, and any fund, annuity, or security transferable in books kept by any incorporated bank, company or society, or by instrument of transfer, either alone or accompanied by other formalities, and any share or interest therein. *Trustee Act.*

Spousal Trust

This is a trust, the principal beneficiary of which is the settlor's or will-maker's spouse. To be a Qualifying Spousal Trust, under the *Income Tax Act*, the trust must comply with the rule in s. 70(6) of the Act.

Spouse

"Spouse" means either a man and woman who,

(a)   are married to each other, or

(b)   have together entered into a marriage that is voidable or void, in good faith on the part of a person relying on this clause to assert any right. *Succession Law Reform Act*, R.S.O. 1990, c. S.26, s. 1.

"Spouse" means a spouse as defined in subsection 1 (1) and in addition includes either of a man and woman who,

(a)   were married to each other by a marriage that was terminated or declared a nullity, or

(b)   are not married to each other and have cohabited,

   (i)   continuously for a period of not less than three years, or

   (ii)   in a relationship of some permanence, if they are the natural or adoptive parents of a child. *Succession Law Reform Act*, R.S.O. 1990, c. S.26, s. 57; 1999, c. 6, s. 61 (1, 2).

Sui juris

This means having full legal capacity, being both mentally competent and of the age of majority.

Survivorship

Survivorship is the right by which a joint tenant takes the whole of a property on the death of the other joint tenant.

T

Tangible

Tangible property, whether real or personal, is that which is corporeal and can be touched. Intangible property consists of rights or interest which may be represented by a tangible object (such as a share certificate), but is itself incorporeal.

Testament

Testamentary Capacity is the ability to know the nature of the will-making act, the nature and extent of one's property and those persons who might naturally be expected to benefit under one's will.

"A 'disposing mind and memory' is one able to comprehend, of its own initiative and volition, the essential elements of will-making, property, objects, just claims to consideration, revocation of existing dispositions, and the like." *Leger v. Poirier,* [1944] S.C.R. 152.

"It is essential to the exercise of such a power that a testator shall understand the nature of the act and its effects; shall understand the extent of the property of which he is disposing; shall be able to comprehend and appreciate the claims to which he ought to give effect; and, with a view to the latter object, that no disorder of the mind shall poison his affections, pervert his sense of right, or prevent the exercise of his natural faculties — that no insane delusion shall influence his will in disposing of his property and bring about a disposal of it which, if the mind had been sound, would not have been made... It may be here not unimportant to advert to the law relating to unsoundness of mind arising from another cause — namely, from want of intelligence occasioned by defective organization, or by supervening phys-ical infirmity or the decay of advancing age, as distinguished from mental derangement, such defect of intelligence being equally a cause of incapacity. In these cases it is admitted on all hands that though the mental power may be reduced below the ordinary standard, yet if there be sufficient intelli-gence to understand and appreciate the testamentary act in its different bearings, the power to make a will remains." *Banks v. Goodfellow* (1870), L.R. 5 Q.B. 549, 39 L.J.Q.B. 237.

"The capacity required of a testator is that he should be able rationally to consider the claims of all those who are related to him and who according to the ordinary feelings of mankind are supposed to have some claim to his consideration when dealing with his property as it is to be disposed of after his death. It is not sufficient that the will upon the face of it should be what might be considered a rational will. You must go below the surface and consider whether the testator was in such a state of mind that he could rationally take into consideration not merely the amount and nature of his property but the interest of those who by personal relationship or otherwise had claims upon him... It is essential to the exercise of such a power (testamentary disposition) that a testator shall understand the nature of the act and its effects, shall understand the extent of the property of which he is disposing, shall be able to comprehend and appreciate the claims to which he ought to give effect, and with a view to the latter object that no disorder of the mind shall poison his affections, pervert his sense of right or prevent the exercise of his natural faculties, that no insane delusion shall influence his will in disposing of his property and bringing about a disposal of it which, if the mind had been sound, would not have been made... [T]he standard of capacity in case of impaired mental power is, to use the words of the judgment, the capacity on the part of the testator to comprehend the extent of the property to be disposed of and the nature of the claims of those he is excluding. Why should not this standard be also applicable to mental unsoundness produced by mental disease? It may be said the analogy between the two cases is imperfect; that there is an essential difference between unsoundness of mind arising from congenital defect or supervening infirmity, and the perversion of thought and feeling produced by mental disease, the latter being far more likely to give rise to an inofficious will than the mere deficiency of mental power. This is no doubt true but it becomes immaterial in the hypothesis that the disorder of the mind has left the faculties on which the proper exercise of the testamentary power demands unaffected and that a rational will uninfluenced by the mental disorder has been the result." *Skinner v. Farquharson* (1902), 32 S.C.R. 58 (S.C.C.).

Testimonium

This is the clause reciting the date on which the will is executed and by whom.

Testator

A testator is a male will-maker.

Testatrix

A testatrix is a female will-maker.

Tissue

This means a part of a living or dead human body and includes an organ but, unless otherwise prescribed by the Lieutenant Governor in Council, does not include bone marrow, spermatozoa, an ovum, an embryo, a foetus, blood or blood constituents; ("tissue"), *Trillium Gift of Life Net-*

work Act, R.S.O. 1990, c. H.20, s. 1; 1998, c. 18, Sched. G, s. 58; 2000, c. 39, s. 2.

Transplant

"Transplant" as a noun means the removal of tissue from a human body, whether living or dead, and its implantation in a living human body, and in its other forms it has corresponding meanings; ("transplantation"), *Trillium Gift of Life Network Act*, R.S.O. 1990, c. H.20, s. 1; 1998, c. 18, Sched. G, s. 58; 2000, c. 39, s. 2.

Trust

A trust is an equitable obligation, binding a person (who is called a trustee) to deal with property over which he has control (which is called the trust property) for the benefit of persons (who are called the beneficiaries or *cestuis qui trustent*), of whom he may himself be one and any one of whom may enforce the obligation.

Trustee

A trustee is a person who holds property legally, but is bound in conscience to use it for the benefit of another or others.

U

Undue Influence

"I adopt the definition of undue influence found in the judgment of Henry J. in *Brooks v. Alker* (1975), 22 R.F.L. 260, 9 O.R. (2d) 409, 60 D.L.R. (3d) 577 (H.C.), at p. 416 [O.R., p. 266 R.F.L.]. There undue influence was defined as the 'unconscientious use by one person of power possessed by him over another in order to induce the other to' do something." *Berdette v. Berdette* (1991), 33 R.F.L. (3d) 113, 41 E.T.R. 126, 3 O.R. (3d) 513, 81 D.L.R. (4th) 194, 47 O.A.C. 345, (C.A.).

V

Vested

Vested means fixed, settled, accrued and absolute. A vested gift has all the attributes of ownership, and is not contingent on any condition which might defeat the gift.

W

Whole Estate

"In *Royal Trust Co. v. Downton* (1980), 109 D.L.R. (3d) 221 (Nfld. C.A.), the Court took a common sense approach to what was meant by the words, 'the whole estate', as found in the provisions of s. 10 of their *Family Relief Act*, R.S.N. 1970, c. 124. The Court held: 'The "whole estate" must mean the net estate available for distribution to the beneficiaries, and, in our view to interpret the phrase in any other way would lead to a totally illogical, and often inequitable, result'. The Court, in that instance, held that the whole estate meant the value of the estate distributable under the Will after the deduction of liabilities of the estate, including expenses properly incurred in its winding-up. Thus, the common sense approach in the case at bar is to acknowledge that a testator may plan her or his estate as she or he sees fit. There is no prohibition in our legislation which prevents a testator from having both a Primary and a Secondary Will." *Granovsky Estate v. Ontario* (1998), 156 D.L.R. (4th) 557, 21 E.T.R. (2d) 25 (Gen. Div.).

Will

A will is a disposition or declaration, which conforms with certain formal requirements, by which the will-maker provides for the distribution or administration of property to take effect upon his or her death. A will has no effect until the will-maker's death and until then is a mere declaration of intention at all times subject to revocation or variation.

A "will" includes,

(a) a testament,

(b) a codicil,

(c) an appointment by will or by writing in the nature of a will in exercise of a power, and

(d) any other testamentary disposition. *Succession Law Reform Act,* R.S.O. 1990, c. S.26, s. 1.

A P P E N D I X C

SELECTED BIBLIOGRAPHY

WEB SITES

Federal

- *http://www.parl.gc.ca/LEGISINFO/* Library of Parliament: Provides information on legislation currently before Parliament.

- *http://canada.justice.gc.ca* Department of Justice: Useful for those requiring access to legal policy on federal and provincial/territorial levels. Also has excellent links to other resources.

- *http://www.fin.gc.ca* Finance Canada: Offers extensive coverage of budgets, documents, news releases, departmental policies and legislation.

- *http://www.archives.ca* National Archives of Canada: Provides links to collections of resources on a variety of topics such as access to information for persons with disabilities.

- *http://www.nlc-bnc.ca* National Library of Canada: The most extensive library resource in Canada, including links to more than 500 Canadian libraries.

- *http://www.statcan.ca* Statistics Canada: Statistical research and discussion papers on a vast array of subjects is available here. Also includes links to other statistical centres.

- *http://www.jl-jd.gc.ca/jlcPubLevel3.jsp?lang+eng&categoryID=234* Government of Canada's Justice and the Law: This web site contains information for the public on various legal topics under "Legal Life Events". For example, the sub-heading on "Dealing with Wills and Estates" gives links to helpful resources that provide information for the public on this subject area.

- *http://www.scc-csc.gc.ca* Supreme Court of Canada: This is the home page of the SCC. The decisions, however, are more easily accessed through other web sites, such as: *http://www.lexum.umontreal.ca/csc-scc* or *http://www.canlii.*

Provincial

- http://www.canlii.net The Federation of Law Societies of Canada's legal information web site offers access to case law, at various levels and jurisdictions, for all provinces and territories. Statutes and regulations are also included.

- *http://www.gov.on.ca* Government of Ontario: You can link directly to all ministries from this home page. Also includes links to government agencies and all other provincial governments.

- *http://www.attorneygeneral.jus.gov.on.ca* Ontario Attorney General's web site. Perhaps the most efficient way to check the status of legislation, as it links directly to the Legislative Assembly's web site.

- *http://www.e-laws.gov.on.ca* Government of Ontario: This is the Queen's Printer for Ontario, containing the text of both statutes and regulations. An alternate site is *http://www.gov.on.ca/mbs/english/publications/statregs/index.htm.*

Law Society of Upper Canada

- *http://www.lsuc.on.ca* Law Society of Upper Canada: As well as providing information for members and the complete text of submissions to Convocation on various topics, it provides a direct link to the Great Library. The on-line catalogue is extensive, and the Great Library web site contains valuable links such as the practice areas sub-headings. For example, the "What's New in Law: Wills, Estates and Trusts" gives summaries and digests on new developments in estates practice. *http://library.lsuc.on.ca/GL/whats_wills.htm.*

- *http://www.BARflyer.com* Legal Search Engine: BAR-eX provides the electronic exchange of law-related information, including indexes of web pages.

Practice of Law

- *http://www.donorsguide.ca/* The Canadian Donor's Guide: Provides a link to an online Donors guide with information on making charitable donations through current gifts or bequests.

- *http://www.jurist.law.utoronto.ca* Jurist Canada: A non-commercial forum in which law professors, students, lawyers, judges, journalists and citizens can share a wide range of Canadian legal information and ideas.

- *http://plainlanguagenetwork.org/Legal/index.html* Plain Language and the Law: The web site of the Plain Language Association International provides a number of useful resources and links for lawyers and law drafters including articles, publishing guidelines and a legal bibliography.

- http://www.disinherited.com/attacking-will. A web site maintained by R. Trevor Todd, a B.C. lawyer, who provides a list of errors by solicitors that have been brought before the courts.

- *http://www.marketing.lp.findlaw.com* Findlaw: One of the many branches of Findlaw. This site has detailed tips for marketing your practice.

U.S. Case Law and Statutes

- *http://www.findlaw.com/casecode* Findlaw: This Case Law and Legal Codes Finder locates U.S. federal and state laws as well as Supreme Court and Federal Court decisions.

SECONDARY SOURCES: MONOGRAPHS

Allen, William P. and John P. Allen. *Estate Planning Handbook*, 3rd ed. (Toronto: Carswell, 1999).

Baker, F. S. ed. *Widdifield on Executor's Accounts*, 5th ed. (Toronto: Carswell, 1967).

Canadian Bar Association — Ontario, Continuing Legal Education. *Estates News: Of Plans, Schemes, Strategies, Plots and Conspiracies.* (Toronto, Ont.: Canadian Bar Association — Ontario, Institute of Continuing Legal Education, 2001).

———. *The Pitfalls of Being an Executor and Trustee.* (Toronto, Ont.: Canadian Bar Association — Ontario, Continuing Legal Education, 1999).

_____ . *Precedent Bound: Tips and Traps of Specialty Drafting for Generalists.* (Toronto, Ont.: Canadian Bar Association Ontario, Continuing Legal Education, 2000).

_____ . *Trusts and Estates Update: Tips, Traps and Tactics.* (Toronto, Ont.: Canadian Bar Association — Ontario, Continuing Legal Education, 1997). *Will Planning — Problems and Prevention: Solicitors' Negligence, Impact of Domestic Contracts and Multi-jurisdictional Issues.* (Toronto, Ont.: Canadian Bar Association — Ontario, Continuing Legal Education, 1992).

Canadian Bar Association — Ontario, Trusts and Estates Section. *The Essential Guide for Drafting Wills.* (Toronto, Ont.: Canadian Bar Association — Ontario, Trusts and Estates Section, 1997).

Canadian Bar Association — Ontario, et al. *New Developments in Will* and Estate Planning [electronic resource]. (Richmond Hill, Ont.: Content Management Corp., 1999).

Community Foundation of Ottawa-Carleton. *Adventures in Charitable Giving.* (Ottawa: Community Foundation of Ottawa-Carleton, 1999).

Dick, Robert C. *Legal Drafting.* (Toronto: Carswell, 1972).

Dickerson, Reed. *The Fundamentals of Legal Drafting.* (Boston: Little, Brown, 1965).

Dickson, Mary Louise, Rod Walsh and Orville Endicott. *The Wills Book: Benefits, Wills, Trusts and Personal Decisions Involving People with Disabilities in Ontario,* rev. ed. (North York, Ont.: Ontario Association for Community Living, 1999).

Eagleson, Robert D. *The Case for Plain Language.* (Toronto: Canadian Law Information Council, Plain Language Centre, 1989).

Estates and Trusts Forum, Law Society of Upper Canada. *Estates and Trusts Forum: Estate Administration, Substitute Decision-making, Estate Disputes and Litigation.* (Toronto, Ont.: Continuing Legal Education, Law Society of Upper Canada, 1998).

_____ . *Estates and Trusts Forum: Estate Planning, Wills Drafting and Trusts.* (Toronto, Ont.: Continuing Legal Education, Law Society of Upper Canada, 1998).

_____ . *Fifth Annual Estates and Trusts Forum.* (Toronto, Ont.: Continuing Legal Education, Law Society of Upper Canada, 2002).

_____ . *Fourth Annual Estates and Trusts Forum.* (Toronto, Ont.: Continuing Legal Education, Law Society of Upper Canada, 2001).

_____ . *Second Annual Estates and Trusts Forum*. (Toronto, Ont.: Continuing Legal Education, Law Society of Upper Canada, 1999).

Feeney, Thomas G. *The Canadian Law of Wills*, 3rd ed. (Toronto: Butterworths, 1987).

Frost, Martyn. *With the Best Will in the World: Negligence in Will Preparation*. (London: Legalease, 2000).

Hull, Ian M. *Challenging the Validity of Wills*. (Scarborough, Ont: Carswell, 1996).

Insight Information Inc. *Creative Uses of Trusts in Estate Planning*. (Toronto, Ont.: Insight Press, 1997).

Kerridge, Roger. *Parry and Clark: The Law of Succession*, 11th ed. (London: Sweet and Maxwell, 2002).

Kessler, James. *Drafting Trusts and Will Trusts: a Modern Approach*, 6th ed. (London: Sweet & Maxwell, 2002). Law Society of Upper Canada. Estates and Trusts for the General Practitioner: New Developments. (Toronto, Ont.: Law Society of Upper Canada, 1992).
_____ . *Estates: Planning, Administration and Litigation: Special Lectures of the Law Society of Upper Canada*. (Scarborough, Ont.: Carswell, 1996).
_____ . *Recent Developments in Estate Planning and Administration: Special Lectures of the Law Society of Upper Canada*. (Toronto: Richard de Boo, 1980).

Law Society of Upper Canada, Continuing Legal Education. *The Annotated Will*. (Toronto, Ont.: Continuing Legal Education, Law Society of Upper Canada, 2003).
_____ . *Drafting Wills to Avoid Litigation*. (Toronto, Ont.: Continuing Legal Education, Law Society of Upper Canada, 2000).
_____ . *A Practitioner's Guide to Using Trusts Effectively*. (Toronto, Ont.: Continuing Legal Education, Law Society of Upper Canada, 1999).
_____ . *Will Power: Will Planning and Drafting*. (Toronto, Ont.: Continuing Legal Education, Law Society of Upper Canada, 1994).
_____ . *Wills Drafting Workshop*. (Toronto, Ont.: Continuing Legal Education, Law Society of Upper Canada, 1998).

Law Society of Upper Canada, Dept. of Education. *Advising People with Disabilities and Their Families*. (Toronto, Ont.: Dept. of Education, Law Society of Upper Canada, 2001).

_____ . Estate Planning and Administration: Reference Materials for Bar Admission Course. (Toronto: Dept. of Education, Law Society of Upper Canada, 2001–).

_____ . *Family Law Issues for Estates Practitioners.* (Toronto, Ont.: Dept. of Education, Law Society of Upper Canada, 2001.)

_____ . *Wills Drafting.* (Toronto, Ont.: Dept. of Education, Law Society of Upper Canada, 1987).

Law Society of Upper Canada, Professional Standards Sub-Committee. *Wills and Estates Checklist.* (Toronto, Ont.: Law Society of Upper Canada, Professional Standards Committee, 1995).

MacGregor, Mary L. *Preparation of Wills and Powers of Attorney: First Interview to Final Report.* (Aurora, Ont.: Canada Law Book, 1996).

MacKenzie, James. *Feeney's Canadian Law of Wills,* 4th ed. (Markham, Ont.: Butterworths, 2000–).

Maitland, Frederic William. *Equity: a Course of Lectures, by F.W. Maitland, ed. by A. H. Chaytor and W. J. Whittaker, 2nd ed.* rev. (Cambridge: University Press, 1936; reprinted 1969).

McIntyre, W. A. *Practical Wills Drafting.* (Toronto: Butterworths, 1992).

Ontario Bar Association, Annual Institute. *Estate, Trusts and Capacity Law: A Decade in Review.* (Toronto, Ont.: Ontario Bar Association, 2002).

_____ . *Estates News: Of Plans, Schemes, Strategies, Plots and Conspiracies.* (Toronto, Ont., Ontario Bar Association, 2001).

Ontario Bar Association, Continuing Legal Education. *Beneficiary Planning 2002: Gifts from Beyond the Grave.* (Toronto, Ont.: Ontario Bar Association, Continuing Legal Education, 2002).

_____ . *Dotting the I's and Crossing the T's: Fundamentals of Estate Administration.* (Toronto, Ont.: Ontario Bar Association, 2001).

_____ . *The Fundamentals of Estate Planning and Administration.* (Toronto, Ont.: Ontario Bar Association, Continuing Legal Education, 2002).

_____ . *Insurance to Die For: What Every Advisor Should Know About Insurance Planning for High Net Worth Clients.* (Toronto, Ont.: Ontario Bar Association, Continuing Legal Education, 2001).

Ontario Bar Association, Trusts and Estates Section. *Solicitor's Liability [sound recording]: Liability as Executor and Liability as Will Drafter.* (Richmond Hill, Ont.: Audio Archives of Canada, 2002).

Ontario Law Reform Commission. *Report on Administration of Estates of Deceased Persons.* (Toronto, Ont.: The Commission, 1991).

_____. *Report on the Law of Trusts.* (Toronto, Ont.: The Commission, 1984).

Oosterhoff, A. H. *Oosterhoff on Wills and Succession: Text, Commentary and Materials*, 5th ed. (Scarborough, Ont.: Carswell, 2001).

Oosterhoff, A. H. and E. E. Gillese. *Oosterhoff & Gillese: Text, Commentary and Cases on Trusts*, 5th ed. (Scarborough, Ont.: Carswell, 1998).

Pettit, Philip H. *Equity and the Law of Trusts*, 9th ed. (London: Reed Elsevier (UK) Ltd., 2001).

Piesse, E. L. *The Elements of Drafting*, 6th ed. (Sydney: Law Book Co., 1981).

Sokol, Stan J. *Mistakes in Wills in Canada.* (Scarborough, Ont.: Carswell, 1995).

Sweatman, M. Jasmine. *Guide to Powers of Attorney.* (Aurora, Ont.: Canada Law Book, 2002).

Theriault, Carmen S. *Widdifield on Executors and Trustees*, 6th ed. (Scarborough, Ont.: Carswell, 2002–).

Waters, D.W.M. *The Law of Trusts in Canada*, 2nd ed. (Toronto: Carswell, 1984).

Zwicker, Milton W. *Successful Client Newsletters: The Complete Guide to Creating Powerful Newsletters.* (American Bar Association: ABA Law Practice Management Section, 2003).

ARTICLES

Beyer, Gerry W., Rob G. Dickinson, and Kenneth L. Wake. "The Fine Art of Intimidating Disgruntled Beneficiaries with *In Terrorem* Clauses" (1998), 51 SMU L. Rev. 225.

Brady, James C. "Solicitor's Duty of Care in the Drafting of Wills" (1995), 46 N. Ir. Legal Q. 434.

Corbin, Barry S. "Amending Multiple Wills" (2002) 21 E.T. & P.J. 156.

Ellinghaus, Ted, Lorne Greville and Ian Morrison. "Common Problems in Will Drafting" (1994) 68 Law Inst. J. 34.

Ferguson, Michael C. "Wills and Trusts: Meeting the Drafting Challenges" (1997) 43 Practical Lawyer 31.

Garvey, John L. "Drafting Wills and Trusts: Anticipating the Birth and Death of Possible Beneficiaries" (1992) 71 Oregon Law Review 47.

Grozinger, K. Thomas. "The Ontario Law of Advancement on an Intestacy" (1993) 12 E. & T.J. 396.

Halbach, Edward C. "Drafting and Overdrafting: a Voyeur's View of Recurring Problems" (1985) 19 Annual Institute on Estate Planning 13.

Harris, Robert M. "Drafting Tips for Simple Wills" (1995) 41 Practical Lawyer 25.

Hawley, William D. "Current Issues in Charitable Tax Planning" (2002) 16 Philanthropist 272.

Hayes, Michael. "Will Preparation and Drafting: Avoiding Negligence Claims" (2000) 144 Solicitors' Journal 1068.

Henry, J. Gordon. "How Not to Draft Wills and Trusts — Common Drafting Errors to Avoid" (1980) 5 Notre Dame Estate Planning Institute, Annual Proceedings 841.

Jackman, Richard. "Solicitor Liability for Negligence in Drafting and Execution of a Will" (1971) 5 Ottawa L. Rev. 242.

Joslyn, Robert B. "Use of Plain English in Drafting Wills and Trusts" (1984) 63 Michigan Bar Journal 612.

Leimberg, Stephen R., Morey S. Rosenbloom and Daniel J. Kaliner. "Will Drafting: It's Simple, Right? The Top 10 (or more) Will Drafting Mistakes" (2000) 15 Practical Tax Lawyer 35.

Lunney, Mark. "In Support of the Chancellor's Foot" (1998) 9 King's Coll. L.J. 116.

Milne, Paul. "Solicitors' Obligations — Suggestions for an Estates Practice" (2001) 20 E.T. & P.J. 230.

Rawlins, Bonnie Leigh. "Liability of a Lawyer for Negligence in the Drafting and Execution of a Will" (1983) 6 E. & T.Q. 117.

Rich, Barbara. "Errors in Will-Drafting: the Limits of a Remedy in Negligence" (1999) 15 Professional Negligence 211.

Roberts, Helen. "Liability of Solicitors to Disappointed Beneficiaries" (1997) 71 Aust. Law J. 674.

Rogers, Bill. "Estates and Trusts Law: Videotaping Will Signings" (2002) 26 Can. Law. 21(5).

Scheetz, Douglas D. "Estate Tax Issues Under the 1995 Protocol to the U.S.-Canada Tax Convention" (1996) 27 Tax Adviser 407.

Schnurr, Brian A. "Some Special Will Drafting Problems" (1983) 6 E. & T.Q. 70.

Simmonds, David C. "Accomplishing Estate Planning Objectives by Marriage Contracts" in Roche, E. M. and D. C. Simmonds, *Marriage Contracts*. (Toronto: Carswell, 1988).

Simmonds, David C. "Wills Drafting and the *Family Law Act*" (1987/88) 2 C.F.L.Q. 209.

Soskin, William H. "What do you say? Will Drafting for Dying Clients" (2001) 87 ABA Journal 95.

Stillabower, Linda and William J. Strain. "U.S. Estate Planning for Canadians with U.S. Real Property: Life After the Protocol" (1995) 43 Can. Tax J. 239.

Wallworth, Christopher. "Will Drafting: a Job for the Specialist" (1994) 138 Solicitors' Journal 1040.

Weir, Tony. "*A Damnosa Heriditas?*" (1995) 111 Law Q. Rev. 357.

Whitaker, Marni M. K. "Hotchpot Clauses" (1992) 12 E. & T.J. 7.

Zwicker, Milton W. and M. Jasmine Sweatman. "Who Has the Right to Choose the Deceased's Final Resting Place?" (2002) 22 E.T. & P.J. 43.

TOPICAL INDEX

322   DRAFTING WILLS IN ONTARIO: A LAWYER'S PRACTICAL GUIDE